MAIN LINES
ACROSS
THE BORDER

1 Tebay in the days of
transition September 1963: Class '40' diesels
on passenger trains; steam on freight and the
bankers. No. D331 on Crewe-Perth express,
IS53, approaching; No. D299 on Glasgow-
Manchester express in foreground.

2 Heavy pulling in heavy weather on the lower part of the Shap incline April 1965: a 'Black Five' No. 45093, with an oil tanker train, banked in rear. Note the steam sanders in use under the driving wheels.

MAIN LINES ACROSS THE BORDER

O.S.Nock
BSc, CEng, FICE, FIMech E.

Derek Cross
BA, MSc

LONDON

IAN ALLAN LTD

Front cover: 'Jubilee' class 4-6-0 No. 45627 *Sierra Leone* passes Crosti-boilered 9F 2-10-0 No. 92024 at Greskine in July 1964.

Back cover, top: Class 40 No. D290 seen at Beattock Summit with the down 'Royal Scot' in April 1961.

Back cover, bottom: Class 87 No. 87.026 *Redgauntlet* seen near Abington with a Glasgow-London train in May 1978.

First published 1960
This revised edition 1982

ISBN 0 7110 1118 4

Published by Ian Allan Ltd, Shepperton, Surrey; and printed by Ian Allan Printing Ltd at their works at Coombelands in Runnymede, England

CONTENTS

PREFACE TO NEW EDITION

THIS new edition of a book of more than 20 years ago that has always been one of my greatest favourites was intended to be a memorial to my great friend and collaborator the late Bishop Eric Treacy, in which the majestic scene of the main lines crossing the Border that we jointly illustrated and described was to be brought up to date with additional chapters and photographs. Although since his death commercial conditions have been imposed upon the use of all his photographs of such a nature that this is not now practicable, he was very much the trail-blazer and I am very fortunate to have now, in Derek Cross, another great friend and a collaborator who has carried on the traditions of artistry and technical excellence set by Eric Treacy at a period some 10 years later; so he has enabled the scene to be brought pictorially, nearer to the present time. For me it has been another very happy 'words and music' partnership with results showing that in the magnificent scenery of the Border country the poetry and magic appeal of the 'train in motion', as it used to be called in my boyhood, is not confined to steam traction.

Much has happened on these lines since the first edition of this book was published in 1960. The West Coast main line has been electrified, and one can travel up the Shap incline at 95 mph as well as down it. On the East Coast route the reign of the 'Deltics' which was then just beginning, has now ended, and the HSTs have not only brought increased speed, but also increased uniformity to the scene. The Waverley Route is, alas no more, and so far as temporary closures were concerned the disaster at Penmanshiel Tunnel brought the HSTs across to Carlisle and the Caledonian route to reach Edinburgh, and places farther north on the East Coast route. The construction of the M6 motorway has banished for ever the lone grandeur of the line through the Lune valley south of Tebay, but perhaps the saddest prospect for 'Main Lines Across the Border', is the possibility that the Settle and Carlisle line will have to close. Romantic though it is, and full to overflowing with personal memories for both Eric Treacy and me, extending back in my case to school days, a ruthless breakdown of the revenue it earned for the Midland Railway and its successors, set against its operating and maintenance costs would probably show that it has never paid, and that now, faced with the cost of the renovation of Ribblehead viaduct and other major structures the future is bleak. And so, the publication of this book may well nearly coincide with the obituaries of one of the most beloved 'Main Lines Across the Border', beloved equally by Eric, who died beside it, and me, who saw it first as a schoolboy not yet entered into his teens.

I have resisted the temptation to revise the text of the fourteen chapters of the original book, because as they stand they constitute a period piece of some importance, symptomatic of the positively shattering metamorphosis sustained, not only by the railways of the Border country, but by the network of Great Britain as a whole. It has not been solely in motive power, but in the whole concept of operation. Who would have imagined, for example, that the great new marshalling yards then building, in which I was deeply involved professionally, would now be lying almost idle and virtually redundant. So the first fourteen chapters of this new edition remain as an account of what was, when Eric Treacy and I did our field work some twenty-five years ago.

Now it is only when there are steam specials, over the prescribed routes, that the laborious grandeur of working heavy trains over the steep gradients of the Border country recaptures something of the romance of railway operation in high regions that gripped our fathers. But who can say that romance is dead when one reflects upon the marvellous engineering built into the modern trains, and sees the APT sweeping round curves that restricted conventional trains to 75 mph at 100 mph, or even more. I am sure that Joseph Locke, that supreme architect of 'Main Lines Across the Border', would approve.

O. S. Nock
28 High Bannerdown
Batheaston
Bath
June 1982

All photographs by Derek Cross

7

ABOUT THE PICTURES

WHEN the first edition of *Main Lines Across the Border* came into my ken I was astonished by the sheer evocative brilliance not only of the text but of the photographs. To all who knew these lines well from having seen and tried to photograph them in all weathers and all seasons this *was* the Main Lines Across the Border. You could smell the heather in its autumnal glory; you could get wet feet tramping across their bogs. Above all you had the sound, sight, and scent of steam tackling hard grades in an even harsher landscape, a form of railway working never envisaged when railways were first surveyed in Belloc's Midlands, 'sodden and unkind'. The railways of the Borders were often sodden and frequently unkind; this was their fascination and to a photographer, their frustration. As O. S. Nock has shown in the text they were no lines for ineffectual locomotives.

The Settle and Carlisle, and equally the Nith Valley line were not easy to photograph. With the former the grandeur and sheer scale of the scenery tended to make a train look like a tormented worm meandering in an endless oblivion. The scale of the Nith Valley was less, but by the law of natural perversity, the line in its most attractive length through the Drumlanrig gorge was built on the 'wrong' side of the valley, and all the best vantage points were suitable for photography only early in the morning when there were few trains about. By contrast the Lancaster and Carlisle, and the Caledonian were splendidly photogenic. The Waverley route, unfortunately, I neglected until steam had all but gone. The snag was not only its relatively sparse traffic, but its inaccessibility from my home in Ayrshire, and to make matters worse, much of the heavier traffic ran at night. This was a dream for Peter Handford and his tape recorder, but not much use to a photographer!

What then is the genesis of the photographs in this book — I can answer in one word, Luck. Now I know the great experts will say this is wrong, but is it? In the end the weather and the wind holds all the aces. If I set forth between Appleby and Settle, as a rule the heavens opened, but by contrast I was lucky with sunshine on Shap. The few ventures to the Waverley route tended to be kind, whereas those to the East Coast Main Line were not, which I often found wrapped in a sea fog known locally as a 'North Sea Haar', when a few miles inland the sun shone brightly. An old saying could be well adapted to railway photography, thus: 'You can't win any of them, any of the time', though occasionally luck does play you an ace, such as a day on Shap without a cloud in the sky.

Now as to equipment, and methods, my earliest efforts on the Border railways were taken with a folding Zeiss 116 camera of venerable years and considerable dignity; but as the maximum shutter speed was supposed to be 1/200th sec, and was probably much less I was limited to trains that were not travelling fast. Yet for all that the old Zeiss, like the Ancient Mariner, 'stoppeth one of three', and some of its better efforts are still among my favourite negatives. I seriously believe that with ultra sophisticated equipment you tend to get bogged down in technique to a degree when you can't suddenly see a freak light, a sudden change in composition, or eddy of smoke or steam. With simpler equipment you could shoot from the hip at the last second, and it was surprising how often this came off. For the same reason I have never used an exposure meter as the human eye is better making a snap judgment of the lighting conditions at the exact spot you want. My greatest lesson in photography was in 1951, in New York, when I dropped my exposure meter, and lacking dollars to have it repaired left it where it lay.

My next photographic foray into the Borders found me with an excellent and little known folding 120 camera, the Agfa Record 3, which I still have as a standby. By modern standards this is a primitive camera with a 4.5 lens and a maximum shutter speed of 1/400 sec, but it could use panchromatic film, was throughly reliable and the shutter more or less produced the speed it claimed. But what really forced my hand into buying a camera with both interchangeable backs and interchangeable lenses was my work as a geologist in the Pacific, and the need to take detailed technical photographs of rock formations and the aftermath of earthquakes. At the time, around 1958, it meant a 'Press' type camera, and I chose a Linhof Technika. It was a superb camera, sophisticated yet simple, and rugged to a degree. What that camera withstood was beyond belief: a 'back' was dropped into a lava flow; it was badly shaken up

9

(together with its owner), in a major earthquake, and it fell into a bog on Shap. Its only snag for railway photography was its maximum shutter speed of 1/500 sec, which was not really fast enough to stop modern electrics, or HSTs in full flight.

With the end of steam in 1968 I parted with it for the Rolliflex 66 with which most of the pictures of modern motive power in this book have been taken; it has a maximum shutter speed of 1/1000th sec, and a focal plane shutter. Modern power, even diesels, did need 1/500th sec, and electrics 1/1000th by my reckoning, and even at that they sometimes tended to be muzzy — why? Not because of their forward speed, but because of vibration. Where the trouble starts is when the moving object is lurching laterally or vibrating like a collapsing *blancmange*, a tendency alas of latter day motive power. No matter how steady you hold the camera the locomotives tend to shake.

In writing this, and indeed in providing illustrations for this book, I cannot but feel presumptuous, as I am *not* Eric Treacy; though having had the good fortune to know Eric well I am sure he will forgive my misdemeanours and be the first to laugh at my misfortunes. We both knew the Main Lines Across the Border, their triumphs and their tribulations, the agony and the occasional ecstasies; but I would like to say that had it not been for Eric Treacy's example and his considerable encouragement I would not have had the material to try. I may have proved a bad pupil, but he was a remarkable inspiration.

Derek Cross
Maybole
Ayrshire

CHAPTER 1

Lines across the Border

WHEREVER railways have to cut through mountainous country their fascination seems to be increased tenfold. From the earliest days at which one could read *The Wonder Book of Railways*—and that was very early indeed !—the stories of the Canadian Pacific through the Rockies, Swiss railways through the Alps, and even our own Highland main line gripped the imagination. There seemed so tremendous a sense of endeavour in the ordinary day-to-day business of railroading in such conditions. The very names were enough to stir the blood, and youthful imagination began to conjure up pictures of what is was like in the Pass of Druimuachdar (Drumochter), high up at the St Gotthard tunnel, or on the C.P.R., deep in the Kicking Horse Canyon. But with all these extreme examples of mountain railroading, even on the Swiss electrified lines, the terrain is such as to enforce fairly slow running. In our own Border country, with the one exception of the Waverley route no such restrictions apply, and one of the most fascinating and exciting features of a journey to Edinburgh or Glasgow is that one often travels through the mountains at breath-taking speed. Eighty-five miles per hour down Beattock, or over the Lune viaduct at Tebay, or, as I have done, nearly 90 mph within sight of Pennyghent can be a great deal more exciting than 100 mph down Dauntsey bank with the *Bristolian*.

I was never more conscious of the spirit of the mountain sections of the Anglo-Scottish main lines than on a journey with the down Waverley express in the late autumn of 1957. From the very outset the day had been gloomy, with lowering skies; but as we raced through the green farming shires interest was held by much first-rate locomotive work, giving an average of 60 mph start to stop from St Pancras to Nottingham. Northwards however, to the lay mind, our progress must have been dispiriting to the last degree. The passing scene between Nottingham and Leeds is never exactly thrilling, and without even a semblance of sustained high speed the combination of gloom, grime, and oncoming rain on that October

11

day could have made it depressing beyond measure. Depressing, yes; but only for those with eyes that cannot see beyond the image recorded on a photographic plate. For on all hands there was evidence of industry, some struggling, much of it thriving, and it was among this murk, carrying the staple products of the Erewash Valley, of Clay Cross, of Chesterfield, of the Rother Vale, and of mighty Sheffield itself that the Midland Railway grew and prospered. Its revenue did not come from carrying a relatively few passengers to see the beauties of the Peak District, in running trains down the Lickey to connect with the Great Western holiday expresses at Bristol, or even in the famous four-coach dining specials between St Pancras and Manchester. The old Yorkshire saying, 'Where there's muck there's money,' was as true of the Midland Railway as of any other institution in the shire of the White Rose.

While all this was in my mind we had passed within sight of Wakefield, and were threading the curves through Normanton. It was time to be stirring. I was riding on the footplate north of Leeds, and there were overalls to be donned. In drizzling rain the last miles of the old North Midland line looked drab in the extreme, but my mood had changed from reflection to one of eager anticipation, and I grew impatient at signal checks that prolonged our passage over those last miles. Then, as we rounded the curve from Whitehall Junction, I saw to my intense disappointment that two engines were waiting to take us forward. Our load was 309 tons it is true, but Leeds had nothing bigger than a Stanier Class 5 4–6–0 for us, and coupled on ahead of her was an old Midland 7 ft. Class 2 4–4–0, No. 40552. Both engines looked dingy, and on so miserable a day I must confess to fleeting thoughts of giving up and going back to the comfort of the train. The thought was gone as soon as it came, however; for no matter what the conditions, opportunities for riding on the footplate from Leeds to Carlisle do not come every day. I climbed up into the cab of the Black Stanier, and there was time for no more than the usual friendly greeting from the crew before we were away.

At first all was much the same as any other footplate journey on a dark and wet autumn afternoon. Steam beat down from the leading engine; our own engine rattled and banged along in the manner born of common-user, general-utility machines, and although hills were close at hand, at times rising steeply on both sides of the line, the prospect for the first fifteen miles out of Leeds is still largely industrial. Yet already there was a ' something ' about this journey that tended to lift it out of the commonplace: for one thing, the pace was much hotter than south of Leeds, and between the mills there were glimpses of wild glens, and fine country no more than vaguely seen through the mist and rain. Then again in our leading engine there was a very strong and effective link with the Midland Railway of old. Watching her ahead through the cab glasses it did not need a great deal of imagination to picture her in spotless ' Derby red,' as many a time she must have piloted ' 999 ' class 4-4-0s, or compounds, over this same route. Once through Keighley, and out into the broader stretches of Airedale we were really going—and now, just as we were coming into fine open country, with range upon range of hills rising up ahead, the clouds were lifting and some colour was at last tinging the landscape.

A brief stop at Skipton, and then we were away again, into the strong air and windy pasture lands of Craven. The sky was not clearing to a fine afternoon, for the clouds were still scudding across from the east bringing showers of rain with them, but indeed the magic of the north country was beginning to weave its spell: the massive stone-built farms, with dry-point stone walls extending in all directions over the hillsides; little streams—becks, as they are known hereabouts—swollen with the rains, and spouting down many a gully; and along the line so many evidences of the character and solidity of the Midland Railway, in the neat stone-built stations, the distinctive signal boxes, and many survivals of the Midland's own pattern of lower-quadrant semaphore that used to have a white disc instead of a stripe on the face. It is of course true that such lineside survivals can also be seen in the Home Counties, and south of the Lickey Incline; but here, with the engines thrusting vigorously uphill, and the track ahead swinging this way and that, rounding successive waves in a rolling upland country there was an urge to press on, to see what lay round the next curve, with the prospect of higher fells bidding us go ever harder.

And then, for a brief spell, the call of the high country, the impending approach to great watersheds is nearly lost. The line dips down prosaically into the broad valley of the Ribble; there

13

is a stop at that most unattractive and unromantic of stations, Hellifield, and a downhill start of such swiftness as to suggest a quick return to more populous regions, instead of deeper thrusting into the wilds. But then, sweeping past Settle Junction at nearly 70 mph, all those emotions, vaguely sensed between Gargrave and Bell Busk, return in a flood. To be sure, although I have special associations with the Settle and Carlisle line, the same kind of emotions come surging up as a West Coast express streaks over the level between Hest Bank and Carnforth with the mountains of the Lake District ahead, and as one first sees the Berwickshire heights from the footplate of the *Flying Scotsman* near Belford, or when a Caledonian express clears Lockerbie and the majestic hills of Annandale begin to block in the entire picture ahead of the train.

The ' Settle and Carlisle ' is an epitome of all that is grandest in the lines leading to, and crossing the Scottish Border. Lofty mountains ahead; the pull of the gradient, the loudening exhaust beats of the engines, lone picturesque farmsteads, clouds still touching down on the higher crags; the hill streams in foaming spate—these are just a few of the ingredients contributing to that fascinating aura of romance clinging to railways leading through northern fastnesses to the Border. For the romance to be true to the Continental style the frontier should be up among the great fells, now crowding into the picture, as at the Brenner Pass, or in the Simplon Tunnel. England and Scotland certainly have a geographical equivalent at Carter Bar, but no railway takes this direct cut from the valley of the North Tyne into Teviotdale, and when the Midland Railway reaches the wastes of Blea Moor and plunges into that dank, fearsome tunnel that might in other circumstances have been a modest counterpart of the Mont Cenis, or the St Gotthard, it is nothing more than the county boundary between Yorkshire and Westmorland that is being approached.

However slight may be the administrative significance of the Pennine watershed, from the railway point of view it provides one of the most fascinating and exciting pieces of line in all Britain. A superb road is carried over lofty viaducts, in cuttings where the snow fences are ranged one behind the other up the hills, through more tunnels; and through this swiftly changing landscape our two engines were doing 65 to 70 mph all the way. I watched old

14

40552 in front, swaying and rolling as she took curve after curve; it was not the dangerous lurch, or continued hunting, but the easy buoyant ride of a swing. With screaming whistle she led us diving into Rise Hill Tunnel; out again, on to that dizzy ledge above Garsdale to the highest water troughs in England. The fireman of 40552 lowered his scoop; the tender was evidently fuller than he thought for in seconds the tank overflowed, and we on the train engine were smothered. Involuntarily I ducked, for the water came over in a solid cascade and hit our cab glasses with a roar rather than a splash. Our stormy progress matched the rising wind and elemental ferment in that wild country and as we finally topped Aisgill summit and went thunder and turf down to Appleby, there was just a moment to realise that my calm contemplative mood of the morning had changed to one of well-nigh mad exhilaration.

The cynics might dismiss it all as mere romantic hysteria, engendered by sentiment over a couple of obsolete and very inefficient forms of motive power. Yet if one such could be tempted away from his armchair into hanging on to a wild swaying compound or an old 'Class 2' tearing through Hawes Junction, over the summit and down to Kirkby Stephen in the teeth of a mountain storm he would probably agree that there is more in railroading across the Border than mere statistics of ton-miles, drawbar horsepower hours, or the aggregate assistant engine mileage. But I wonder if any of us, cynics and enthusiasts alike, will find the same kind of exhilaration in future years in the cabs of the new diesels ?

CHAPTER 2

THE LANCASTER AND CARLISLE

I CAN never think of this great, historic line of railway without associating it in some way with my own school days, and the transfer of my father's place of business from Reading to Barrow-in-Furness in 1916. Even then I was something of a North Western fan. Despite my living within sight and sound of the Great Western, my boyish imagination had been fired by engines of more distant railways; the Great Northern 'Atlantics' were among the favourite 'pin-ups' for the nursery walls, but then a new edition of *The Wonder Book of Railways* brought news of the *Sir Gilbert Claughton,* and my earlier allegiances began to totter. Nevertheless it was one thing to read about Shap, but quite another to imagine what it was really like up in that wild country of the Westmorland fells. Even after we moved to Barrow my contacts with the Lancaster and Carlisle were at first rather slight; but they were enough to complete my conquest. At the beginning and end of each school term I travelled through Carnforth on my way to and from Giggleswick. The long waits for connections were to me a pure joy, and it only needed one or two sights of the down 'Corridor' tearing through at what always seemed a fantastic speed to fire my imagination almost to bursting point!

In those wartime years the engine was nearly always a 'Claughton,' sometimes piloted by a 'Jumbo,' and as the train went charging through Carnforth with the station bell ringing, and the whistles screaming, the whole party seemed a veritable epitome of the spirit of Shap. As our Midland trains made their way up the Furness Joint line, towards Borwick, for several miles the North Western main line was still in sight, cutting straight as a die into the hill country lying to the north. But before journeying over the line to Carlisle we must retrace our steps southward to Lancaster itself, for that first seven miles is a pleasant curtain-raiser to the run through the fells. The Lancaster and Carlisle Railway, in its brief independent days, began at the signal box formerly known as Lancaster Old Junction, the point of diversion, one mile south of the Castle station, from the old Lancaster and Preston Junction Railway. I often wondered why the London and North Western never realigned the curve at this point, so as to permit of full speed with expresses not stopping at Lancaster. The main line remained a ' turnout,' and I shall remember to my dying day what happened on the one occasion in my own experience when a train did take the junction at full speed: it was the down Ulster Express with two Midland compounds treating a 550-ton train as if it were a featherweight. Featherweight or not, the whole ' contents,' animal, vegetable, and mineral alike became airborne as we went over the junction at 72 mph!

Just north of the Castle station the line crosses the river Lune, but the girders are so deep that the view, both upstream and down is cut off, and it is not until Morecambe South Junction has been passed and the seashore is approached at Hest Bank that the prospect broadens, and there is a wide panorama of the Lakeland mountains seen across Morecambe Bay. At low tide the mud flats stretch as far as the eye can see, but on a fair day the vast arc of blue sky is reflected on the shining sands recently washed by the sea, and even this waste is beautiful. The railway historian inevitably lets his mind wander back to the various projects for crossing the sands, and making a level, coastal trunk line from Lancaster to Carlisle. How the mountains were dreaded in those early days of railways! John Hague proposed to take an almost dead straight line from Lancaster to Dalton in Furness, with an embankment 10 miles long over the sands; George Stephenson was not so daring, and made Humphrey Head, near Kents Bank his landfall on the Furness side. And even prior to 1840 there were two other schemes for railways between Lancaster and Carlisle. Both of these are worth recalling.

The first would have been a very fast and direct route, passing through Kendal, going up Long Sleddale, tunnelling to Haweswater and thence to Penrith; while the second went up the Lune Valley, through Kirkby Lonsdale, Tebay, Crosby Ravensworth and Newby to Penrith. The accompanying map shows these two proposals together with the line actually built. Both the earlier proposals secured relatively good gradients at the expense of tunnels, but a Royal Commission that examined the rival proposals felt that the

Long Sleddale tunnel was impracticable since at one point, beneath the Gatescarth pass, the line of railway would have been no less than 1,140 ft. below the level of the ground. But this was long before the time of such tunnelling masterpieces as the St Gotthard, the Lötschberg and the Simplon, and the cost of the Gatescarth project was thought prohibitive. Neither the Kendal nor the Lune Valley route had a gradient steeper than 1 in 140, and they would have been considerably easier to operate than the present line. The Grand Junction Railway, one of the largest and most important in the whole country at that time, was deeply interested in the building of a western route to Scotland, and it was through this interest that their great engineer, Joseph Locke, came to examine the rival projects. He finally decided upon a route that was in some ways a compromise between the two, but having no tunnels at all, and relatively little in the way of heavy earthworks was far cheaper to construct. The gradients were much more severe, including the long pull up to Grayrigg, and the world-famous Shap Incline. It will be seen from the map that it was a more roundabout route, too. Locke cut down the constructional costs, but left a permanent legacy of increased mileage, and the necessity of much bank engine working.

George Stephenson, who had become estranged from Locke following disputes in the building of the Grand Junction Railway, criticised the route of the Lancaster and Carlisle very severely. He thought the gradients much too heavy for a trunk line; but for good or ill Locke had his way, and the bugbear of Shap has been with us ever since. But forgetting what might have been, if the line had gone up Long Sleddale, and after the Gatescarth tunnel had given us a ride of great beauty past Mardale and Haweswater, one could hardly wish for a finer run through the Westmorland fell country than the present route, as between Oxenholme and Penrith. I should mention that the Lancaster and Carlisle was, in 1859, leased to the L & NWR for a term of 999 years. One truly comical clause in the agreement was that 'the plant, rolling stock, and movable property to be used by the lessees during, and to be restored at the end of, the lease.' One wonders in what kind of condition the old Lancaster and Carlisle engines would have been after 99 years, let alone 999! But the North Western took early steps to evade any obligations they might have had in this respect,

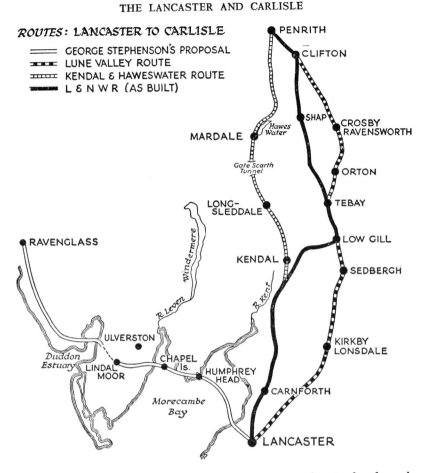

ROUTES: LANCASTER TO CARLISLE

══════ GEORGE STEPHENSON'S PROPOSAL
▭▭▭ LUNE VALLEY ROUTE
⊞⊞⊞ KENDAL & HAWESWATER ROUTE
▰▰▰ L & N W R (AS BUILT)

as full amalgamation between the two companies took place in 1879.

The Grayrigg bank begins at the crossing of the Beela river, half a mile south of Milnthorpe station; at once the gradient becomes 1 in 173 and in the next 13 miles the line rises 485 ft., an average ascent of 1 in 142. Milnthorpe itself lies on 'A6,' more than a mile to the west of the railway, and a motorist heading for Carlisle does not begin to notice the gradient until he is at least 10 miles farther on. But Joseph Locke was able to engineer a more gradual rise into the fells, by carrying his line higher and higher up the hills lying east of the river Kent, and rounding the

19

shoulder of Hay Fell near to the 500-ft. contour. This was not at all to the liking of the townsfolk of Kendal, for here was an inversion of the more familiar tale of proud old towns and early railways. Kendal wanted the railway—not high up on the fells to the east but through its boundaries, and all it got was the inconvenience of the long gradual pull up to Oxenholme, a change of trains there, and an abrupt drop back into the valley!

To a railway enthusiast however, Oxenholme and the Grayrigg bank are fascinating places. They will always be dear to me as the scene of my earliest explorations without parental control! Many a time I have cycled the 30 miles or so from Barrow to be up at Hay Fell in time to see the midday group of expresses go by. In 1921 and 1922 there were seven of them between 1.15 and 3.15 p.m., and what a feast of good things and a host of memories they provided. The road from Kendal to Tebay runs alongside the line for about a mile on that short stretch where the direction is almost west–east, and even at that time of the day one could still photograph from the up side of the line. Away to the north-west the land dropped away sheer to the Mint beck, and gave a tremendous prospect of the Lakeland mountains to the west, including a brief glimpse of the Langdale Pikes. Many a summer day I have spent there. The party opened with the 10 a.m. Edinburgh to Euston, which then conveyed its own Liverpool and Manchester portions as far south as Preston; then came the 10 a.m. Glasgow to Euston, with a through GWR coach for Plymouth, followed by the Glasgow to Liverpool and Manchester express. The up procession was completed by the Aberdeen, then due in Euston at 7.30 p.m. On the down road the Liverpool and Manchester Scotsman (1.32 p.m. from Preston) came first, while the day—so far as I was concerned—ended with the two sections of the 10 a.m. from Euston, both running non-stop from Crewe to Carlisle.

I must not allow personal memories to obtrude too much into the story, but I cannot resist three high-lights of those early observations of mine. One came in the Easter holidays of 1921 when train services were much reduced due to a coal strike. I was at Oxenholme station, waiting for the 10 a.m. from Euston to pass; she was then running as one huge train, and calling additionally at Preston to pick up Scotch traffic from Liverpool and Manchester.

I fully expected her to be double-headed, particularly as the corresponding up train had but recently passed—15 on, behind a 'Jumbo' and a 'Prince.' But then, not unduly late, she came—and how! With 14 on she stormed through, unassisted, and at her head was the pride of the line, the war memorial engine No. 1914 *Patriot*. The second reminiscence is of this same train, but when the Glasgow portion was running separately. I was at Hay Fell this time, and one really needed a sound-track as well as a camera to record her passing. Long before she emerged from the rock-cutting I heard the roar of her exhaust, and she blasted her way along the high embankment and past me doing at least 40 mph and probably nearer 45 on the 1 in 133 gradient. The engine that time was one of the very first batch of 'Claughtons' built in 1913, No. 163 *Holland Hibbert*.

Looking critically at my old photographs that record these two brief incidents, occasions when those grand engines were being flogged for all they were worth, I notice that both *Patriot* and *Holland Hibbert* were showing the white feather at the safety valves, and neither showing the slightest sign of leakage of steam at the front end. The third occasion was one on which I was farther north—at Dillicar water troughs in fact; but it was typical of the spirit of the North Western. Shap never ceased to be a challenge to the skill of the enginemen. It was never treated lightly; it was charged pell-mell, and the five miles of almost level road through the gorge of the river Lune were taken as an opportunity to pile on speed after the long ascent to Grayrigg. Imagine therefore the reactions on the footplate when, on this occasion, the 10 a.m. from Euston was practically stopped by signal at Dillicar box, two miles to the south of Tebay! From my vantage point near the troughs I could see she was double-headed, but I was hardly prepared for the sight and sound she made coming round the hill and passing me, after she had the road. The two drivers were just flailing their engines into speed—a superheated 'Precursor' No. 643 *Sirocco,* and an unnamed 'Prince,' No. 198; they passed with exhausts shooting sky-high, roaring as only products of Old Crewe could. Sirocco indeed! 'Hot wind from the south'; never, it seemed at that moment, was a North Western engine more truly named. *Sirocco* was the very last survivor of the Crewe 4-4-0s, and one can only regret that the present solicitude for historic old engines was not under way before the time came for her to be scrapped. If ever locomotives deserved a place of honour in a transport museum those engines were the ' Precursors ' and ' George the Fifths ' of the North Western.

From the moment the gorge of the Lune is entered, at Low Gill, the passing scene assumes a new and more immediate grandeur. No longer are we looking to mountain ranges ten or fifteen miles away; the fells are towering above the line on both sides. But impressive as it all is seen from the carriage window, and still more so from the footplate, one must cycle or motor over the road from Kendal to Tebay to see the railway in its true proportions in this mighty landscape. On a brilliant June day my wife and I picnicked by the roadside, 800 ft. up the slopes of Whinfield Beacon, and while we were there the up *Royal Scot* passed by; the big ' Duchess ' class engine and her thirteen coaches looked tinier than any ' 00 ' gauge model, and one could only guess at what the trains looked like from that height, and from that road, a hundred years ago, when Alexander Allan's 2–2–2s and 2–4–0s were the standard engines on the Lancaster and Carlisle. At the northern end of the Lune Gorge railway, road and river are all at much the same level, and we come to that bleak little outpost of civilisation, Tebay. Had the fashion of our own times grown up earlier Tebay might have been an engine-spotter's paradise; for here came not only the North-Westerns in their hundreds, but glittering, spotless North Eastern 2–4–0s from Darlington. The big 0–8–0 ' T ' class were also used on the mineral trains to and from the Furness line, which also reminds me that the haematite-red Furness engines used to bring these trains into Tebay from the south.

Even today Tebay has lost little of its old character. It is still a banking station, and the prevailing engine livery is still that of the old L & NWR. But in contrast to Grayrigg and the Lune Gorge, Shap itself is the least impressive of all our great inclines. The line ascends at 1 in 75 over a bleak open moorland. Even on the fairest day there is little to be seen except wave upon wave of heather, and only when nearing Summit are there glimpses away to the west of the high mountains grouped around the head of Haweswater. What Shap means, even to the big engines of today will be apparent in the next chapter, and the arrangements for providing assistance are in many ways the same as they were on the

L & NWR. Freight trains are banked in rear both from Oxenholme, and from Tebay; but with passenger trains practice varies
according to circumstances. With the ' Pacifics ' assistance is rarely
needed at all. The 4–6–0s of the various classes sometimes stop
only at Tebay for rear end help to Summit, but in cases of heavy
loading a pilot is coupled on ahead at Oxenholme, and works
through to Shap Summit. In North Western days there was, for
some time, a reciprocal arrangement for pilot-engine working between Oxenholme and Carlisle, and a number of 2–4–0 ' Jumbos '
were set aside for this duty; up expresses carried their pilots as far
south as Oxenholm, where they were ready to assist north-bound
trains. There is nowadays no regular scheme of balanced workings
of bank engines, and up trains that need assistance put off their
pilots at Shap Summit.

Having reached this altitude, 915 ft. above ordnance datum, it
will be as well to pause briefly; to put aside for one moment thoughts
of the magnificent natural setting, and the aura of romance that is
inevitably associated with the haulage of heavy trains through such
a country, and get down to the ' brass tacks ' of what is actually
involved in the way of locomotive effort. I always regard the old
2 p.m. ' Corridor ' as providing the yardstick of performance in
London and North Western days; she was allowed 42 min. in which
to climb the 31·4 miles from Carnforth to Summit, and 32 min. for
the downhill run of 31·4 miles from Summit to Carlisle. It is most
interesting to compare the sectional times then booked, with a
scientifically compiled schedule based on a constant rate of steaming
as set forth in the bulletin issued by the British Transport Commission on the performance of the BR Class 8 express locomotive
No. 71000:

Section	Miles	L & NWR 2 p m Euston	BTC Bulletin
Carnforth–Oxenholme	12·8	14	14·4
Oxenholme–Tebay	13·1	18	19·3
Tebay–Summit	5·5	10	10·8
Summit–Penrith	13·5	14	13·3
Penrith–Carlisle	17·9	18	16·2
Total (pass to stop)	62·8	74	74

The schedule of the old 2 p.m. from Euston was maintained
regularly by ' George the Fifth ' class 4–4–0s hauling up to 360 tons

23

tare. This, it will be seen, was $2\frac{1}{2}$ min. faster than the ' scientific ' schedule between Carnforth and the Summit, and $2\frac{1}{2}$ min. slower in consequence on the north side.

It is interesting to compare the steam rates involved, on a theoretical basis, taking data from the bulletin published concerning the BR engine No. 71000.

STEAM RATE : CARNFORTH–SUMMIT

Load tons tare	Schedule	Coal per mile lb.	Evaporation lb./hr. steam to cyl.
360	LNWR 2 p.m.	40½	18,500
460	BTC Bulletin	48½	21,000
550	BTC Bulletin	53½	23,000

The above figures are those computed in each case for the *Duke of Gloucester,* but they show, in no uncertain measure what was expected daily from the ' George the Fifth ' more than 40 years ago. Again, however, it is interesting to compare the effort needed up Shap with work on the level. With the 460-ton train, a sustained evaporation of 21,000 lb. per hr. would give a speed of 75 mph on level track, whereas in North Western days the ' Corridor ' used to run at speeds of 65 to 70 mph between Preston and Lancaster, on the level. Then, it would seem, the hardest efforts were those made uphill, whereas nowadays it is rare to see engines really ' hammered ' to the same extent as of old north of Carnforth.

To the railway enthusiast bound for Scotland there is inevitably some feeling of anti-climax after Shap Summit has been passed; a formidable task has been completed, and one looks forward eagerly to the crossing of the Border. On the footplate there is a feeling of relaxation: if the engine is coming off at Carlisle the fire will be worked down, the cab swept up, and the fireman will probably find time for a wash; if they are continuing to Glasgow, or to Perth this is the time for a snack. A Canadian friend of mine, who has done a good deal of footplating, remarked once that he sensed the feeling of relaxation so keenly that he felt like throwing his pencil, notebook and stop-watch overboard, as impedimenta no longer required! But while we may be bowling downhill beside the Leith beck, riding the curves amid the beautiful woods of Sherriffs Park, and coming out finally on the broad expanse of Clifton Moor, with the Pennines ranged along the eastern skyline, it only needs the

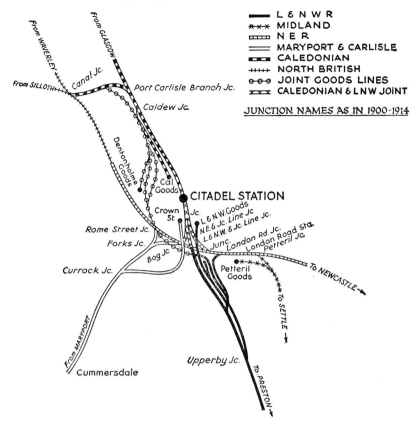

approach of an up train, pounding up the long ascent of 1 in 125 to remind us that ' Shap ' is a two-way job! In many ways the south-bound ascent is the more trying, or was so in North Western days, for the engine had to start ' cold ' from Carlisle, and there was no chance to charge at it. This difference was in some ways reflected in the old schedule times; the up day Scotch expresses were allowed 50 min. for the 31·4 miles from Carlisle up to Shap Summit, despite the fact that there is no gradient steeper than 1 in 125 on the north side.

With down expresses speed must be moderated over the series of curves approaching and through Penrith; but once through that junction engines can be given their head for a while, and in present conditions one expects the highest speed of the whole descent in

25

the neighbourhood of Calthwaite or Southwaite. There is a marked reverse curve past the now closed station of Wreay where speed is usually eased off a good deal, and after that we are getting too near to Carlisle for much use to be made of the final descent, where the gradient is at 1 in 132. So we come to the complicated railway geography of Carlisle. Much has been written in the past about the fascination of engine and train working in pre-grouping days; but the ownership of the various lines was not generally appreciated, and I have, therefore, prepared the map on page 15 to show 'who owned what.' So far as passenger working was concerned the North Western and the Caledonian were joint owners of the Citadel station, but the North Eastern and the Maryport and Carlisle approached very closely on their own metals. The Midland came in over the North Eastern, and the North British over the Caledonian, while the Glasgow and South Western approached over nearly 9 miles of the Caledonian, and reached its engine sheds at Currock Road by running powers over the Maryport and Carlisle. But having reached Carlisle it is now time to retrace steps to Lancaster and Carnforth to see something of the locomotive work involved in lifting the West Coast expresses over Shap.

3   Oxenholme, in July 1961: still a bank engine station. Dundee-Manchester express standing, hauled by Class '5XP' 4-6-0 No. 45688, *Polyphemus*.

4   In the Lune Gorge, between Low Gill and Tebay: a Keswick Convention Special in July 1963, hauled by rebuilt 'Scot' No. 46118 *Royal Welch Fusilier*.

5   The bleak prospect of Shap Summit July 1960: a southbound goods hauled by one of the Stanier Moguls, No. 42988.

6 Tebay shed August 1960: an impressive line up of engines — left to right, Fowler 2-6-4T No. 42396, Ivatt 2-6-0 No. 46422, Fowler 2-6-4T No. 42404, Ivatt 2-6-0 No. 43011, Fowler 2-6-4T, No. 42403.

7 Shap Summit July 1965: the banker 2-6-4T, No. 42080, just dropping clear, having assisted a train of empty motorcar wagons.

CHAPTER 3

LOCOMOTIVE PERFORMANCE OVER SHAP

IN studying locomotive performance over the Lancaster and Carlisle line one is immediately struck by the great changes in service requirements since the hey-day of the Crewe superheater 4–4–0 locomotives. The Glasgow portion of the 10 a.m. from Euston was then a 6-coach train at normal times: four 'eights' and a 12-wheeled diner from Euston, and a brake composite from Birmingham attached next to the engine at Crewe. The Edinburgh portion was a little heavier, as it carried the Aberdeen through coach in addition. The basic formation of the 2 p.m. 'corridor' was seven of the special 12-wheelers built particularly for that service, but more often than not there were 'extras' on that very popular train. Today, Birmingham has a day Scotch express of its own, and a very heavy train it is. In addition to separate portions for Glasgow and Edinburgh it attaches the Perth portion of the Royal Scot at Crewe. This latter includes a dining car of its own. The effect of this is, that instead of the two pre-grouping trains totalling 14 coaches in the aggregate we have now at least 25 coaches, and usually more, even though there is no through portion nowadays from Euston to Edinburgh on the Royal Scot. In the winter service of 1959 there were changes in train make-up, dictated by the incidence of heavy engineering works south of Crewe. The present train formations are probably in a transitional stage.

When it comes to estimating what a certain locomotive ought to be able to do with a specified load one cannot base any such estimates on theoretical conditions alone when it comes to a road like the Lancaster and Carlisle. Once under way up the bank from Milnthorpe if nature is harsh or unfriendly it is indeed a case of railroading 'in the raw.' High wind, drizzle or sleet can make nonsense of basic performance data obtained in the seclusion of a stationary testing plant, and even the experienced recorder travelling as a passenger in the train may find himself taking down details of times and speeds that just do not make sense if an attempt is made afterwards to reduce them to a logical analysis. I was travelling one day on the morning Liverpool and Manchester Scotsman, in 1932, behind one of the large boilered ' Claughtons '; the load was 375 tons all told, and the engine in the superb condition then typical of the Preston ' Claughtons.' Despite poor weather we started well, but on Grayrigg bank in thick driving rain we finally got down to $24\frac{1}{2}$ mph and lost $3\frac{1}{2}$ min. between Oxenholme and Tebay. As we laboured up to Grayrigg summit I felt certain we should have to stop at Tebay for rear-end assistance to Shap; but once we turned into the Lune gorge driver and engine appeared to regain complete mastery, and we not only took Shap unaided, but even regained a little of the lost time!

Before coming to exceptional cases however it will be as well to take a normal trip over the line, and see at first hand what is needed in the working of a heavy modern express. I have no better example than a run I was privileged to make on the foot-plate of the down ' Birmingham Scotch,' running non-stop from Crewe to Carlisle. The engine for that train comes on fresh at Crewe, and works through to Glasgow; on this occasion we had No. 46234 *Duchess of Abercorn,* with Polmadie men on the job—Driver Black and Fireman Falconer. We had the pleasure, too, of Inspector Craik, of Carlisle (Upperby), also on the footplate. The load was a heavy one, fifteen coaches, 514 tons tare; except for the Edinburgh portion, which was packed with Rugger enthusiasts travelling to see the Calcutta Cup match on the following day the train was not unduly full, and the gross load would be about 540 tons behind the tender. From the outset the locomotive per-formance had been excellent, and how splendid it was, too, to find the road between Crewe and Preston back into its old good shape, and to cover that initial 51 miles in $56\frac{3}{4}$ min. But we were badly checked at Morecambe South Junction and slackened again for permanent-way repairs at Bolton-le-sands. Thus it took $90\frac{3}{4}$ min. to cover the 78·2 miles from Crewe to Carnforth, and we began the mountain section at much reduced speed.

I had already noted that our driver was quite an artist in his adjustments of the reverser. For the most part he had run with cut-offs of 15 to 18 per cent with the regulator open only about two-fifths, and there was a pleasing touch at Brock troughs, where to counteract the slight decelerating effect of the scoop ploughing through the water he had increased cut-off by 5 per cent while the scoop was down. But although all was going well on the footplate—good coal, the engine steaming freely, and a fine spring day—the ascent to Shap is no light task, even for a very large modern engine, with a tare load of 514 tons behind the tender. But, again, by comparison with the old days, a Stanier 'Duchess' has slightly more than twice the tractive effort of a 'George the Fifth,' and half 514 tons—257—would have been considered a light load when those incomparable 4–4–0s were the regular engines on the 2 p.m. 'Corridor.'

Beyond Carnforth we reached 49 mph; but there is a short foretaste of the stuff to come before reaching Burton-and-Holme— $2\frac{1}{4}$ miles at 1 in 134; here speed fell to 39 mph, but before topping this intermediate summit Driver Black had, for the first time in the whole journey, opened out to full regulator. Cut-off had been advanced to 27 per cent, but on the $3\frac{1}{2}$ slightly falling and level road to crossing of the Beela river the driver linked up once more to 20; then to 18, and finally to 15 per cent. When we struck the initial gradient of the Grayrigg bank, 1 in 173, our speed was 62 mph. We made a beautiful ascent—beautiful not only in the quiet competence with which this heavy train was taken up, but in the good judgment of the driver in maintaining a very even demand upon the boiler. Thus as the speed gradually fell the cut-off was increased: from 15 per cent at 62 mph to 22 per cent at 52; 25 at 46 mph; 27 at 42 mph, and the final adjustment to 30 per cent at 40 mph. This last named change took place about 2 miles above Oxenholme, and we took the last 5 miles of the climb, including the final 2 miles, where the grade stiffens from 1 in 131 to 1 in 106, entirely on 30 per cent. Speed came down finally to 32 mph.

Mere figures cannot, however, give any impression of the supreme fascination of the footplate on this stretch of line. The 'Duchesses' are grand engines to ride. My earliest trips on them were made immediately after the War, when the track was well below the old West Coast standards, and I rather got the impression that they were very prone to rolling; but on all my recent trips, through from Euston to Carlisle and back, and on the Liverpool line, the going has been exceptionally steady and smooth. On this trip I was riding on the tender, standing just behind the driver where I could watch all his adjustments of the controls, and as we climbed I had perforce to divide my attention between technicalities and the wonderful views over this wild country as we mounted higher and higher : Kendal lying far in the valley below; the old highway to Grayrigg, up the last miles of which I had pushed my bicycle so often; the panorama of the Lakeland mountains seen from the Hay Fell embankment, and here, too, symbols of the changing order, in that remotely controlled colour light signals replaced the 60-ft. high semaphores originally worked from that tiny little signal box.

Over the Docker viaduct we pounded on, with the fells closing in ahead of us now. The speed was just about the ' standard ' pace for the old 2 p.m. Looking back over the old records one sees a wonderful consistency about the work of the ' George the Fifths '; on six runs, with tare loads varying between 325 and 370 tons the speed at Grayrigg summit did not vary between a highest minimum of $33\frac{1}{4}$ mph and a lowest of $31\frac{1}{4}$. One would dearly wish to have been on the footplate of No. 1188 *Penmaenmawr* as she roared up the last mile to Grayrigg at 33 mph with 372 tons tare behind her tender ! But on my recent trip the *Duchess of Abercorn* was doing her work with economy and comparative ease; how much inside her maximum capacity this was may be judged by comparison with the great test run made in the early spring of 1939, when this same engine took a special train of 604 tons tare, and topped Grayrigg summit at 41 mph after a very fast climb from Carnforth. On my run we had covered the 13·6 miles from Milnthorpe to Grayrigg in exactly 18 min., an excellent average of 45·3 mph.

Once over Grayrigg summit and entering the Lune gorge there was no need to press the engine to an all-out assault on Shap. We could take full advantage of the respite afforded by the $5\frac{1}{2}$ miles of level and slightly favourable road. Driver Black eased the regulator back to the first port, and linked up to 20 per cent cut-off, and we had not exceeded 58 mph when we passed over Dillicar water troughs, and entered upon the approach grade to the Shap incline proper—$1\frac{3}{4}$ miles at 1 in 146. But here the regulator was pushed hard over once again, and cut-off advanced to 25 per cent; thereafter cut-off changes were made in carefully judged relation to the fall in speed:

Speed mph	53	44½	36	30	28
Cut-off %	27	35	40	42	48

This working took us up the 5½ miles from Tebay to Shap Summit in 9¼ min., but even on a run so free from trouble we suffered some loss of pressure during the climb, and above Scout Green, on the wildest and most exposed part of the moorland, we were down to 200 lb. per sq. in. in the boiler, and our fireman was using the long poker. The complete climb from Carnforth to Summit, 31·4 miles, had taken 43½ min.—a little longer than the old ' Corridor ' timing, but handicapped a little at the start by the check at Bolton-le-Sands.

Once over the summit we ran much of the way to Carlisle without steam. At Shap station 2 miles north of Summit, the regulator was closed altogether and the reverser put into 50 per cent cut-off; speed rose gradually to 78 mph before Penrith, and after a short spell of steaming after the slack through Penrith coasting was resumed north of Plumpton, with a maximum speed of 75 mph before Wreay. We were in good time for an arrival at Carlisle in the level half-hour from Summit, 31·4 miles; but we were a little before time and were stopped dead for 2 min. outside the Citadel station. Our actual time over the 62·8 miles from Carnforth was 77¼ min. and our net time, pass to stop, not more than 72 min. The engine had been worked considerably harder on Shap than Grayrigg; but the former incline is much shorter, and there is the immediate and total respite to follow in the half-hour of little more than coasting to follow Shap Summit.

In company with this run I have tabulated details of two others recorded on occasions when I was travelling as a passenger, and when the loads were similar. They illustrate the variations in style of working that can be noted over this route. The *City of Bristol* was on the Midday Scot, while the *Duchess of Devonshire* was on the second of the two night Highland Expresses, running non-stop from Wigan to Carlisle. Both engines made good overall times, but there was a considerable difference between the intermediate times and speeds. The driver of No. 46227 charged each of the big banks at high speed, and by lengthening his cut-off before the pace had time to fall off maintained higher speed up the earlier

33

part of each incline. The contrast between 46227 and 46237 was most marked on Shap itself. The initial speeds were $69\frac{1}{2}$ and 53 mph respectively, and although No. 46237 was opened out so as to pass Summit with no lower speed than $24\frac{1}{2}$ mph against the $21\frac{1}{2}$ mph of No. 46227 the latter engine, by reason of the far higher initial speed made much the faster time.

It is rare to see the fullest advantage taken of the falling gradients between Shap Summit and Carlisle. The road is now in superb condition, and with careful observation of the prescribed slowings at Eamont Bridge Junction and through Penrith there is still ample opportunity to make really fast time if an engine crew so desire. The *City of Bristol* came down unusually fast for these days; but I hardly need add that the travelling in the train was most comfortable—in fact in running at a speed more nearly equal to that for which the super-elevation of the track on the curves is designed the riding was really *more* comfortable than at slower speeds. On this trip, the curving length from Shap station and past Thrimby Grange box was taken at 70 to 75 mph, after which speed was allowed to rise to $80\frac{1}{2}$ mph over Clifton Moor, before the marked slack through Penrith. After that the driver took us really fast down to Carlisle, with a maximum of $86\frac{1}{2}$ mph near Southwaite, and making the very brisk total time of only 27 min. 20 sec. pass to stop for the 31·4 miles from Shap Summit into Carlisle.

On another very interesting trip with the same engine I was on the footplate from Crewe. The train this time was the Royal Scot, with a winter load of 385 tons tare and about 415 tons gross. The run was of particular interest to me, as not so very long previously I had ridden in the Swindon dynamometer car behind this same engine, and witnessed a very fine performance on the Cornish Riviera Express. In the four months that had elapsed the engine had not been to shops, but when I rode on her from Crewe to Carlisle she was still in superb 'nick.' Carlisle men were in charge, working through from Euston—Driver Hodgson and Fireman Irving, with Inspector King, of Preston, also on the footplate. I was interested to learn that Driver Hodgson was a former Midland man, who had done most of his footplate work from Durran Hill shed. We left 9 min. late, and despite two heavy permanent-way checks, at Warrington and Garstang, and a signal check at Farington, we had regained 3 min. clear on passing Lancaster: 72 miles in 81 min., or 73 min. net. With a load of only 415 tons gross this had not involved any exceptional effort from the engine; but having passed Lancaster the really interesting part of the journey began. We passed Hest Bank at 74 mph, and then sighted an adverse colour light signal in the distance; it cleared before we had needed to reduce speed seriously, and Carnforth was passed at 69½ mph, 6¼ min. late. Then, with the speed rising to 72 mph on the brief downgrade north of the Midland bridge, our driver put the reverser into 25 per cent cut-off, with the regulator opened well out on to the second valve.

This was charging the bank, with a vengeance! The short, but sharp rise to Yealand was cleared at 62 mph, Milnthorpe was passed at 75½, and we were well above Oxenholme before the speed had dropped below 60 mph. Never personally had I travelled up Grayrigg bank at such a pace. Still the regulator and reversing gear positions were unchanged; we came through the rock cutting and out on to the high embankment by Hay Fell Box at 57 mph, the Docker viaduct was crossed at 55, and so we came finally on to the last 2 miles of the bank, inclined at 1 in 106. The engine was in grand form. It all looked so easy! With no more than a gentle purr from the exhaust, with the water only an inch from the top of the glass, and the fire in first-class shape we topped the Grayrigg bank at exactly 50 mph. The 19·9 miles from Carnforth to the summit point had taken only 18 min. 23 sec. Naturally the engine was very much eased for the stretch through the gorge of the Lune, and with only the first port of the regulator speed did not rise above 65 mph at Tebay trough. But then once again Driver Hodgson opened out, and with 30 per cent cut-off straight away, and regulator opened well on to the main valve we were making another remarkable climb. Just as in the ascent of Grayrigg we had been past Oxenholme before speed fell below 60 mph, here we were half-way up Shap itself before going below 50. But unfortunately we were a shade too soon for the signalman at Summit, and although we were still doing 39 mph at Milepost 36¾ the Summit ' distant ' was on, and we had to slow to 15 mph before it cleared. Even so we took no more than 7 min. 52 sec. up from Tebay, and from being 6¼ min. late at Carnforth we were now 2 min. early, signal check notwithstanding. The descent to Carlisle was taken quite easily and we arrived just over a minute early.

During the 12 min. we took in climbing from Milnthorpe to Grayrigg the drawbar horsepower averaged a little under 1,300. Even though the speed was falling from 75 to 50 mph there would probably be not a great deal of variation, as with a constant cut-off throughout the peak output, for a cut-off of 25 per cent comes at about 65 mph. One could estimate a maximum of about 1,400, or perhaps a little more, in the neighbourhood of Oxenholme. The indicated horsepower, on the other hand, varies in relation to the speed—not in exact proportion but something fairly near to it in 25 per cent cut-off. The demand for steam was thus at its highest at the very foot of the bank, where the indicated horsepower was about 2,200; and from this it gradually fell off. Once the fireman had maintained boiler pressure and water level through the initial ' charge ' on the bank, it was an easier matter to sustain them to Grayrigg summit. The boiler was however steaming very freely, and had the occasion demanded it a considerably bigger effort could have been made on the upper part of the bank. On the form shown on this occasion I do not think there would have been any difficulty in clearing Grayrigg summit at 60 mph had it been necessary. At their best the ' Duchesses ' are indeed remarkable engines!

So far as downhill speed is concerned the record of the little 2-4-0 *Hardwicke,* just after midnight on 23rd August 1895, still stands, and is likely to do so. Compared with the really fast descent made with the Midday Scot (Run 3 in the table on page 26) the ' Jumbo ' took 11 min. against 12 min. 35 sec. from Summit to Penrith, and 13 min. against 14 min. 45 sec. from Penrith to the Carlisle stop. On this latter stretch No. 46237 on my recent run was making a continuous 82 to 86 mph from Southwaite to the point of slowing for Carlisle, so Heaven knows what *Hardwicke* was doing! One of the fastest southbound descents I have ever clocked from Shap came more than twenty years ago, on the Midday Scot, before ' Pacifics ' had come into general use. With a Royal Scot, and a load of ' sixteen ' a pilot was necessary from Carlisle to Shap, with a Class 2 4-4-0 on ahead we reached Summit in a little under 40 min.—smart work in itself. Then *Sanspareil* got away, and made the fast descent tabulated herewith. There was, of course, no difficulty in making such times downhill, but it was certainly unusual to see it done at that period in LMSR history, and a most exhilarating experience it was. The engine concerned was, of course, unrebuilt and she has since been renamed.

LMSR : SHAP SUMMIT–LANCASTER

Load 16 cars 498 tons tare 535 tons full
Engine 6126 *Sanspareil* (Royal Scot Class)
Driver G Steel (Crewe North Shed)

Mls		m	s	mph
0·0	Shap Summit	0	00	
2·5	*Scout Green Box*	4	25	71
5·5	TEBAY	6	43	85
7·5	*Dillicar Box*	8	13	75
9·8	Low Gill	10	15	64½
11·5	Grayrigg	12	03	56
15·0	*Hay Fell Box*	15	19	72
18·6	OXENHOLME	18	08	79
22·2	*Hincaster Jc*	20	51	84
24·1	Milnthorpe	22	27	eased 67
28·2	*Milepost 9½*	26	13	61
31·4	CARNFORTH	29	05	74
34·6	Hest Bank	31	52	67
35·8	*Morecambe South Jc*	33	02	60
37·7	LANCASTER	36	00	

LANCASTER–CARLISLE

Run No. / Train	1 — 10 a.m. Euston		2 — 7.30 p.m. Euston		3 — 1.30 p.m. Euston		4 — 11.25 a.m. Birmingham	
Engine No. / Engine Name	46237 City of Bristol		46227 Duchess of Devonshire		46237 City of Bristol		46234 Duchess of Abercorn	
Load tons tare / tons full	385 / 415		491 / 540		497 / 530		514 / 540	
Mls / Station	**m s**	**mph**	**m s**	**mph**	**m s**	**mph**	**m s**	**mph**
0·0 LANCASTER	0 00		0 00		0 00		0 00	
3·1 Hest Bank	2 42	72	2 45	66	2 38	70	sigs 3 50	68
6·3 CARNFORTH	sigs 5 35	58	5 35	71	5 17	73	p w s 10 01	30
9·5 Milepost 9½	8 28	72		62	12 35	69	14 27	49
13·6 Milnthorpe	11 51	62	12 31	72	14 40	72	18 59	15
15·5 Hincaster Jc	13 28	75½	14 22	52½	19 35	51	21 07	49
19·1 OXENHOLME	16 43	69	18 32	69	25 18	62	25 49	39
22·7 Hayfell Box	20 10	64	23 42	56	32 22	51½	30 57	62
26·2 Grayrigg	23 58	56½	30 26	45	39 21	38½	37 00	53½
32·2 TEBAY	30 11	50	36 57	34½	43 30	34½	44 19	41½
35·2 Scout Green Box	33 21	65	40 15	30	49 45	27	48 17	38½
37·7 Shap Summit	sigs 38 03	15	45 50	69½	62 20	53	53 30	32
47·0 Clifton (closed)	47 58		60 27	42	66 18	26	62 50	58
51·2 PENRITH	52 23	69½ (slack)	70 34	21½	70 28	24	66 23	78
56·0 Plumpton	57 18	72	72 44	75	72 14	80½	70 42	71
58·3 Calthwaite	59 30			55		77½	72 40	73
61·7 Southwaite	62 28		sigs 77 06	72	74 55	86½	75 30	75
64·2 Wreay	64 39	73	sig stop 85 44	74	77 05	82	77 37	
67·7 Carlisle No 13 Box	68 10						sig stop 80 37	
69·1 CARLISLE	70 55						87 25	
Net time (min.) : pass to stop	68		78½		77		77½	
Net average speed mph Carnforth—Summit	60		46·8		42·4		45·4	

8 Ceaseless pageant on the Shap Incline: at 6.10 am in June 1960 a stone train, Sandside Quarries (near Arnside) to Kingmoor, stabled overnight at Tebay, toils up, hauled by an ex-WD Austerity 2-8-0 No. 90157, banked by a 2-6-4T.

9 Distinguished visitor climbing Shap in June 1964: an R.C.T.S. Special from Leeds to Penrith (via Ingleton) hauled by rebuilt 'Merchant Navy' class 4-6-2 No. 35012 *United States Lines.*

10 Dillicar troughs, at the northern end of the Lune Gorge, where a respite in the long climb from Carnforth give a chance to pile on some speed ready for Shap itself: a 'Lizzie' No. 46212 *Duchess of Kent* hauling a Euston-Glasgow express in July 1960.

11 The 'Royal Scot' climbing Shap, on a snowy day in February 1960, when limited loads were being carried to permit of overall timekeeping when preparations for electrification were causing heavy delays south of Crewe. The engine, No. 46229 *Duchess of Hamilton* is now preserved.

CHAPTER 4

THE CALEDONIAN LINE

IF ever a great commercial enterprise became wrapped in an aura of
romance it was the Caledonian Railway. I am not suggesting that
there was anything very romantic, or ' airy-fairy ' about the way it
conducted its business; had there been, it would never have sustained its great position in Scotland. But the Caledonian never
seemed to miss a single opportunity for adding touches of beauty,
dignity, and elegance to its business of railroading. The very name
was a masterstroke. Scottish interests had been bitterly divided
over the route to be followed between Glasgow and Carlisle;
English interests and influence were keenly resented, and when the
Annandale route was finally decided upon it would have been quite
easy to devise some grandiloquent, cumbrous, and tongue-twisting
title like The Edinburgh, Glasgow, and Carlisle Junction Railway,
or The Great Carlisle and Central Scotland Direct Railway! No;
it was simply ' The Caledonian Railway.' There was more than a
hint, even in those early days that the accent in the title was on
' the,' and not ' Caledonian.' Not for nothing did the company
adopt the Royal arms of Scotland as its crest, and emblazon the
Royal motto on all its engines! Never mind. It was a splendid
name, and the Caledonian became a splendid railway.

In fighting for the line up Annandale, and up the glen of Evan
Walter, J. J. Hope Johnstone. M.P. for Dumfriesshire, and Charles
Stewart. Factor of the Annandale estates, were looking to a far
broader prospect than those who thought merely of connecting
Carlisle with Glasgow. It must be admitted that the Grand
Junction Railway, which was deeply interested in getting a through
line to Glasgow, had little else in view when Joseph Locke was
sent to survey the country north of Carlisle. This is no place to
try and trace the complicated chain of events that led finally to the
triumph of the Annandale scheme. With variations, in local
details, it followed the pattern of much railway politics in the years
before 1850. But the outcome was that the Caledonian had a

41

direct line striking into the very heart of Scottish industry. The trijunct lay-out set up on the moors of upper Clydesdale, a mile to the south-east of the little village of Carstairs proved a veritable springboard from which Caledonian activities launched out in all directions. It is interesting to speculate, at this late stage, as to why this focal point of the Caledonian did actually take its name from the tiny village of Carstairs, instead of from the larger, and far better-known township of Carnwath, lying almost an equal distance away to the east. But Carstairs it was; and so Carstairs became a household word with travellers to Glasgow and Edinburgh.

At Carstairs business began for the Caledonian. Save for Lockerbie there was scarcely any place larger than a village between the Carstairs–Strawfrank–Dolphinton triangle and the English border, and where through traffic was concerned, everything was to be gained by getting over the intervening distance as soon as possible. And yet in that $73\frac{1}{2}$ miles is to be found one of the greatest obstacles to fast running anywhere on the trunk railway routes of Great Britain. Joseph Locke was not usually afraid of heavy gradients. In defiance of contemporary opinion he took the Lancaster and Carlisle Railway over Shap; but even *he* boggled at the idea of a bank as steep as Shap, but just twice as long! And so he recommended the Nithsdale route from Carlisle to Glasgow; it needed all the enthusiasm and persuasive power of Charles Stewart to get him to reconsider his decision. Eventually he conceded: ' There is every reason to hope that the impediments which inclined planes were at one time supposed to create will, in the continued improvement of the locomotive engine, be still further removed.' Removed indeed! In fifty years—to within a few weeks—from the time the Caledonian Railway Act received the Royal Assent, one of Dugald Drummond's 4–4–0s had climbed the 10 miles of Beattock Bank in $13\frac{1}{2}$ min.

But although construction of the line began at Carstairs it is more logical to begin an exploration at Carlisle, and so with the brisk start traditional of the Caledonian we pass beside the old city walls, beneath the red sandstone cathedral, and across those meadows through which the river Eden makes so majestic a sweep. To west of the main lines at this point are the new freight lines built during World War II, and crossing the river at Etterby Junction on one of the most remarkable viaducts to be found on

British Railways. This viaduct is remarkable neither for its size, nor for its beauty, but for the fact that it was designed to be built by men who had never taken part in bridge construction before, and have probably never done so since. The need for a second bridge at Etterby Junction became urgent when the war was well advanced; our manpower was engaged up to the hilt. Only the very last reserves were left to be scraped together, and yet with such reserves a bridge had to be built over the river Eden to carry a heavy main line traffic. It was not quite a case of employing the halt, the maimed, and the blind, but something very near it! The bridge was designed in reinforced concrete, so skilfully that even with unpromising labour it was built in record time. So, past Kingmoor shed through Floriston woods and away to the Solway Firth.

The marshy, low-lying ground that stretches for miles northeast of the railway forms a vague, ill-defined ' border ' between the two countries—so vaguely defined that for centuries it was a kind of ' no man's land ' where none but the most intrepid ventured far from the roads. Today Mossband signal box stands on the marsh, near to the water troughs installed by the LMS for the Crewe–Glasgow, and Crewe–Perth non-stop workings. The actual border comes not at the Solway viaduct, but at the crossing of the River Sark just to the north of Gretna Junction station, but before the divergence of the Glasgow and South Western line to Dumfries and Kilmarnock. The border is now signposted, as it has been for many years on the East Coast Route by Lamberton Toll; but by the time the Sark is crossed the Caledonian is already climbing, and in little more than a mile comes to that signal box of terrible memories, Quintinshill. The story of the worst disaster in British railway history has been told and retold many times—of the incredible events in 1915 that led to the clearing of the signals for the up troop special. But it was not until I was making some footplate journeys specially for this book that I realised what was probably the crowning tragedy of the whole affair. Both refuge sidings, it will be recalled, were occupied by goods trains, and to clear the line for the ' Midnight ' from Euston the local was propelled back on to the up main line. From the overbridge north of Quintinshill the line is dead straight for nearly three miles and the signal box can be seen through the arch; but from that very bridge a long sweeping curve to the south begins, and, but for the goods in the down siding, obscuring the view on account of the curve, the driver of the ill-fated troop train must surely have seen the massive front of the McIntosh 4-6-0 No. 907 facing him, on his own line. As it was he had no warning, and with all signals clear he came under the bridge at 70 mph.

At Quintinshill, where attention is inevitably drawn to the signal box, one begins to note some of the distinctive detail of the Caledonian Railway scene. It is true that many of the older features are now rapidly disappearing; upper quadrant arms are replacing the old semaphores with their grass-green glasses, that used to show a rather feeble yellowish-green light at night; some of the old boxes have been replaced, and then, to an enthusiast of the stop-watch, there were those unique Caledonian mileposts. At many locations the milepost was treated like a little monument; the walkway beside the track was extended to surround its base, and often the post itself was partly surrounded by a neatly trimmed hedge! The signal boxes, with their great overhanging eaves, and massive uprights between the windows, looked as if they were designed to withstand a siege, compared to the relatively fragile wooden boxes found on so many English railways in pre-grouping days. In the meantime the line is mounting at 1 in 200 through a fine country of rising farm lands. The first summit point is reached some 14 miles out of Carlisle, where the track is high above a picturesque rocky glen of the Kirtle Water. There used to be a block post, Brackenhill, closely marking the summit, but although the actual box still stands it has long been closed.

Speed rises rapidly as the train dips towards Kirtlebridge junction; but then, with the track running due west for a while, we pass on through Ecclefechan, with its memories of Thomas Carlyle, towards the second summit point, near Castlemilk box. It was the North Western rather than the Caledonian that honoured the memory of Carlyle, by bestowing his name upon an engine. But I never pass through Ecclefechan without chuckling over the story of the literary pilgrim from the United States who visited the place in search of local colour; from one of the natives he received this monumental reply: 'Tam Carlyle—ay, there was Tam! He went tae London; they tell me he writes books. But there's his brither Jeems—he was the mahn o' that family. He drove mair pigs into Ecclefechan market than ony ither farmer in the parish.' And so from Ecclefechan, and the beautiful policies of Castle Milk we come to Lockerbie, and at last to Annandale itself. For a time the going is some of the fastest yet on the Caledonian; the track is straight, and slightly favourable, and in these days of the ' Duchess ' class Pacifics, Nethercleugh and Dinwoodie stations are often passed at nearer eighty than seventy miles per hour. But already looking out from the footplate the hills are beginning to close in ahead, and as we sweep down to the crossing of the Annan, near Wamphray station, the green levels of the dale are ringed with greater hills than we have seen so far. Somewhere up there, by the Devil's Beef Tub, in the wild country between Hart Fell and Clyde Law, the shires of Dumfries, Lanark, and Peebles meet.

For a northbound train climbing starts afresh at the crossing of the Annan. At first the gradient is no more than 1 in 200; but just short of the fortieth mile out of Carlisle we come to Beattock. Even today the place is little more than a hamlet, and it can have been a mere clachan when Joseph Locke first surveyed the line of the Caledonian Railway; but among locomotive men the world over Beattock is a name of the utmost significance. For the great bank that climbs for ten miles into the rough country between the Lowther Hills and the heights of Tweedsmuir took its name from the hamlet at its foot. It has always been the Beattock Bank, and the peak where the line tops the 1,000-ft. contour, and then dips down into Clydesdale has always been Beattock Summit. Today the summit, and its slightly higher altitude is posted on the main road as well as on the railway, so that Beattock Summit is a place of significance for motorists, long-distance coach drivers, and lorry-men alike. Although Beattock itself is primarily a bank-engine station, it is also the junction for the short branch to Moffat. The village is a road junction too, for here diverges the highway that climbs over Flocket Hill into Tweeddale. It was near Moffat too, that Joseph Locke came to live in his early retirement; and where, even when life was failing, he would still summon up reserves of energy enough to walk the local gamekeepers off their feet!

Beattock Bank is set in a glorious tract of upland country. At one time there were three intermediate signal boxes in that gruelling ten miles, but two—Auchencastle and Harthope—have now been replaced by remote-controlled colour light signals. Greskine, the exact half-way house, remains, and it is at about this point that the

45

glen of Evan Water begins to narrow perceptibly; the fells on either side begin to close in, and vehicles on the nearby road also begin to notice the gradient. I have ridden up Beattock on the footplate in all sorts of conditions of weather; in the dawn of a cloudless summer day, when the mist rolled down so cold and so thick as to set our great 'Pacific' engine slipping at every hundred yards; in broiling heat, when campers were out sunbathing *à la Lido* by the burn sides, and again on a night of keen frost, when the stars flashed like diamonds. But however fine the day, however favourable running conditions may seem, one can never trifle with Beattock. I shall always remember a trip on the down Birmingham Scotsman, when our engine, a 'Lizzie,' had given a somewhat shaky performance south of Carlisle; but despite a load of 457 tons tare we got away so well from Carlisle and ran so freely north of Lockerbie that our driver decided to take Beattock unassisted. That 10 miles took us $31\frac{1}{2}$ min. There was nothing seriously amiss; the steaming was not as good as it might have been, but speed was allowed to fall too rapidly in the early stages, and doing no more than 20 mph as low down as Greskine the gradient had us in its grip, and there was nothing for it but to hold grimly on. When it was too late the driver tried a considerable lengthening of the cut-off; but the engine wouldn't have it, and although the day was fine and the rails were dry she slipped. Again the hapless driver tried, and again 'Lizzie' said 'no.' Forty per cent was the longest cut-off she would take, and at this low speed it was just enough to hold 14 to 15 mph. Thus although we had covered the $39\frac{3}{4}$ miles from Carlisle out to Beattock in $46\frac{1}{4}$ min. it took us $77\frac{3}{4}$ min. to breast Summit.

Another memory of trouble on Beattock is of 1938, when I had joined the Perth section of the Royal Scot at Carlisle, and clocked a fast run out to Beattock, with a 'Jubilee' and a load of 360 tons. But we stopped for assistance, and with a McIntosh 0-4-4 tank in rear we were going steadily up the bank until we came to Harthope; there we were checked and finally drew to a stop at the starting signal. We were there for 10 min. and then got away very cautiously. In just over a mile, to my astonishment, another train was standing on the down line and from a carriage window I watched while our engine nosed up to its rear and touched buffers. It was the Edinburgh portion of the Royal Scot—six coaches hauled by a Midland compound—and it had stalled within sight of the Summit box! Our engine and our banker thenceforward had the task of propelling the disabled train over the last half-mile, while continuing to haul our own train. Then came one of those curiosities of railway working, the reasons for which are so difficult for an onlooker to imagine. Nothing would have seemed more logical than to couple the six coaches of the Scot on to our train. The ' Jubilee ' could have run the seventeen of them easily down to Carstairs where plenty of engine power would have been available. But no! The unfortunate Scot, engine, train and all, was parked in the siding at Beattock Summit to await a relief engine, while we were allowed to proceed at once.

But although Beattock Bank is a place to be treated with the greatest respect, especially when the wind is high and the winter storms are roaring through the hills, the engines of Sir William Stanier have mastered it with all ordinary loads, and the following chapter tells among other things of a run on the Midday Scot, when the Summit was passed in $3\frac{1}{2}$ min. less time from Carlisle than on the epic last night of the 1895 Race to the North, and with more than five times the load carried by the racing train. Beattock Summit is a bleak and inhospitable place; there are refuge sidings on both sides of the line, and beyond these, on either side, the snow fences tell their own tale. But at once the pace is quickening, and from the footplate Clydesdale is seen opening out ahead. The descent is first of all at 1 in 99, but there is no more than 2 miles of it, and where the line crosses the infant Clyde for the first time there is a short stretch of level. Elvanfoot is the first settlement we have passed since Beattock village, and at one time in very early days the summit $2\frac{1}{2}$ miles to the south was sometimes referred to as Elvanfoot. Now we are speeding on. The hills of Upper Clydesdale are smooth and rounded. In fair weather they are placid and friendly to the point of being quite featureless; but see them on a day of sunshine and storm—when rain sweeps across the valley veiling all in its path, and then the sun burns hot and brilliant, lighting up a dazzling display of blue sky and cloud, and flecking the hillsides with a chequerwork of light and shade.

Crawford and Abington are pleasant and quite sophisticated places, with clusters of modern villas. In Crawford, I was intrigued to find Dunalastair Road, and wondered at the origin of its name.

For Dunalastair itself is an obscure place in the Perthshire High-
lands, and I like to think that that road in Crawford was named
after the blue 4-4-0 ' Dunalastairs ' that became such an institution
in Clydesdale, and everywhere else between Carlisle and Aberdeen
about the turn of the century. I once got into hot water from a
Scots correspondent through a twice-repeated misprint in one of
my books on locomotive performance, and was moved to com-
memorate the incident by a limerick:

> Said an outraged young Scot named McFie,
> ' Yon writer chap Nock's oot at sea.
> For Abington's " t "
> He pits Abingdon's " d "—
> The Sassenach chiel! Lack a'dee!'

The line is winding considerably around Abington, and the speed
is usually restrained to little more than 70 mph; but as the straighter
reaches of the valley are entered, with the great hill of Tinto
dominating the scene to the north-west, engines are given their
heads, and at the crossing of the Clyde just before Lamington
station ' eighties ' can nowadays be recorded. The last miles into
Carstairs are hilly. Here, the exceedingly rural junction of
Symington, in addition to providing occasional connections to and
from Peebles, is a division or linking-up point for the Glasgow and
Edinburgh sections of Anglo-Scottish expresses. It was once a good
deal busier in this respect than it is today, for the Royal Scot called
in both directions, and the up Midday Scot too. The Edinburgh
portions then ran direct from Strawfrank to Dolphinton Junction,
avoiding Carstairs altogether. In the final Caledonian days the
remarshalling of the up Corridor at Symington was typical. Expresses left Glasgow and Edinburgh simultaneously at 1.30 p.m.;
both trains carried portions for Liverpool, Manchester, and London.
At Symington, the London portions were marshalled into one train,
and the Liverpool and Manchester portions into a second; the
Glasgow engine took the London train, and the Edinburgh, the
Liverpool and Manchester.

North of Symington the railway parts company with the main
road to Lanark and Glasgow, and for a while follows more closely
the course of the Clyde; and so, in 73 miles from Carlisle, in a level
tract among the hills, we come to the junctions of Carstairs. There
are water troughs near the intermediate block post of Pettinain,

and then comes Strawfrank Junction. Here, in the days of *Cardean* on the down Corridor, a stop was made to detach the Edinburgh portion, and ever since, a stop at Castairs has been traditional on the down Midday Scot. Even today Carstairs has much of the old Caledonian flavour about it. There are usually engines of pre-grouping vintage to be seen—not only the inevitable 0–6–0 'Jumbo' goods, but the larger McIntosh 0–6–0s, 0–4–4 tanks, and several Pickersgill 4–4–0s. Men from Carstairs shed take a share in working the West Coast expresses on the north road, to Perth; they re-man the heavy 1.42 p.m. from Carlisle and take it forward, and the depot provides the engine and men for the Aberdeen portion of the down West Coast Postal. From the railway, indeed, Carstairs has every appearance of a busy centre. In addition to the running sheds there are capacious sidings for the stabling of passenger stock, long loops for the berthing of freight trains, and a station—albeit a single island platform—equipped in the best Caledonian style. But once clear of that platform, and the cluster of railway workers' dwellings that surround it, and one is immediately out in the wide open country of Upper Clydesdale. Carstairs Junction, more so than Hellifield, Carnforth or even Tebay is a railway colony.

Travelling on, the character of the country begins to change entirely. The Clyde, in making a broad sweep to the south and west of Lanark plunges from the upland strath that we have traversed between Elvanfoot and Pettinain through the beautiful Linn of Bonnington into a deep valley, and the Caledonian line descending less abruptly on its journey to Glasgow stays for a time on the higher ground to the north of the river. For a few miles indeed, from the crossing of the Mouse Water near Cleghorn, the gradient is rising, and at Craigenhill Siding the altitude is less than 300 ft. below the level of Beattock Summit. But by the time one is over Craigenhill, and bearing down towards Law Junction the signs of industrialism are crowding in on all sides. That strong appealing character of railways running through the lone hill country to the Border is giving place to smoking chimneys, black sidings, and all that means good business to the railway manager; and on the curve from Law to Motherwell, at Garriongill Junction, where the original Caledonian line ended and the earliest trains passed, by running powers, on to the metals of the Wishaw and Coltness Railway, we too can appropriately end this chapter.

49

12 Leaving Carlisle for the North in September 1964 a 'Britannia' 4-6-2 No. 70003 *John Bunyan*, crossing the River Lune with a Glasgow parcels train. The tracks on the right, and the new concrete viaduct were built during World War 2.

13 Early on a snowy April morning in 1966, a London-Glasgow sleeping car train passing Kingmoor sheds, and hauled by 'Britannia' 4-6-2 No. 70036 *Boadicea*.

14 At the southern end of Kingmoor's new hump marshalling yard; a southbound freight hauled by '8F' 2-8-0 No. 48151 in June 1965.

15 Kingmoor New Yard, in August 1964: A Manchester-Glasgow express, hauled by the now-preserved 'Scot' No. 46115 *Scots Guardsman* diverted via the goods lines on the extreme west side of the yard.

CHAPTER 5

LOCOMOTIVE RUNNING ON THE CALEDONIAN LINE

ON any main line of railway over which a heavy traffic is conveyed the existence of a major obstacle, such as the Beattock Bank, tends to concentrate the attention of all who study the science of loco-motive performance. Looking back over the records of the past sixty or seventy years it is astonishing to find how little has been published, particularly in the earlier years, about southbound running, whereas work in ascending the Beattock Bank has probably been more fully documented over the years than any other stretch of railway in the British Isles. The work of the Drummond 4-4-0s, and of the McIntosh 'Dunalastairs' certainly tended to draw the attention of all who made a study of engine performance, by the excellence of their work and the outstanding skill and enthusiasm of their enginemen; but today, the changing conditions are tending to put emphasis upon the southbound run. From the authorities of Scottish Region, from whom I have received much kind assistance in the past, I have had the privilege of making a number of journeys on the footplate in the early summer of 1957; and I was fortunate enough to observe the work of four different engine classes in a single day's running.

Beattock Summit lies roughly half-way between Carlisle and Glasgow Central, and the vertical lift in each direction is almost exactly the same. Until the time of nationalisation, however, the day Anglo-Scottish expresses by the West Coast Route conveyed portions for both Edinburgh and Glasgow; on the southbound run combination took place either at Carstairs or Symington, and in consequence the load to be conveyed on the hardest part of the journey from Glasgow to Carlisle was much reduced. On a run I had with the up Midday Scot in 1937, for example, our engine, working through from Glasgow to Crewe had to haul 310 tons tare as far as Symington, 478 tons thence to Carlisle and 532 tons for-ward to Euston. Today, on a train like the up Royal Scot, the locomotive gets its full load from the start, as there are no through portions run from Edinburgh to Euston. Furthermore train schedules over the Caledonian line are now a great deal faster than they were between the wars, or in those now distant days of the Caledonian Railway itself. In 1937 the up Midday Scot was allowed 44 min. to pass Carstairs (28·8 miles) and 52 min. to the Symington stop; after that, 73 min. were allowed for the 66·9 miles to Carlisle, start to stop. Today the up Royal Scot is booked to pass Carstairs in 40 min. with only 71 min. remaining for the 73·5 miles onward to Carlisle. And on the day I was privileged to observe this working from the footplate we had a tare load of 448 tons.

Due to the reduced loads formerly worked over it, the long ascent to Craigenhill summit has not received the emphasis that its severity demands. It is true that for many years very heavy trains have been worked up this gradient on the night sleeper car services, but these latter expresses have not been timed so fast as the day trains—in contrast again to Caledonian days before World War I, when the fastest train out of Glasgow Central for many years was the 10.45 p.m. 'Sleeper' to Euston. After combination with its Edinburgh section at Carstairs, this train was booked to cover the 73·5 miles to Carlisle in 80 min. The climb to Craigenhill begins at Rutherglen Junction, just 4 miles out of Glasgow Central, and in the ensuing 19·8 miles the line rises 685 feet—an average inclination of 1 in 153. There is a brief respite, between Newton and Uddingston, where the line descends for a mile to cross the Clyde; but from Uddingston station the 15·4 miles up to Craigenhill provide a length of unbroken severe climbing considerably harder than the Grayrigg bank on the London and North Western part of the journey north. The gradient over the Uddingston–Craigenhill section averages 1 in 128. Today the up Royal Scot is booked to cover the 52·6 miles from Glasgow to Beattock Summit in 64 min., while in the reverse direction the down Midday Scot is allowed 58 min. for the 49·7 miles to Summit from Carlisle. The respective average speeds, start to pass are 49·5 and 51·4 mph. On the southbound run there are the disadvantages of a 'cold' start for the locomotive, and a speed restriction through Carstairs where otherwise an engine crew could make the most of the falling gradient from Craigenhill to the crossing of the Clyde near Pettinain Box. The Carstairs slack is worth about 2 min. in running.

As if to emphasise the differences between northbound and southbound running today over the Caledonian line, the day's work—or perhaps I should say the day's shovelling!—is practically finished for the fireman of a Glasgow-bound train when Beattock Summit is passed, while on the up journey it needs smart work by all concerned for the 31·1 miles from Beattock station to Gretna Junction to be covered in 27 min. with a heavy train, even though the tendency of the gradients over this stretch is favourable. This has been, I fear, a rather lengthy introduction to a run with the up Royal Scot; but so much 'glamour' has been attached to the northbound ascent of Beattock by railway *littérateurs,* in past years—and with full justification too!—that I felt some 'build-up' for Craigenhill is necessary, even though most of the bank lies outside the region specifically covered by this book. In contrasting past with present I need only add that in the days of *Cardean* on the 2 p.m. up Corridor, the booking was 135 min. non-stop from Glasgow to Carlisle, with a load of 310 to 340 tons. Nowadays the Midday Scot has 110 min., and the Royal Scot a minute more. On my run in the early summer of 1957 we had a load of 13 coaches, 448 tons, and about 475 tons with passengers and luggage.

The Royal Scot is now frequently diesel hauled, and on the same day that I travelled the down train was worked by the two ex-LMS units, 10000 and 10001 together. We, on the other hand, had a steam locomotive, one of the earlier batch of Stanier Pacifics, No. 46209 *Princess Beatrice.* The 'Lizzies,' as these engines are affectionately known by the men, have a tractive effort slightly greater than that of the 'Duchess' class, but their boiler capacity is considerably less, and due to an earlier design of cylinders and valves—not so thoroughly streamlined internally as that of the later engines—they do not run so freely on the faster stretches of line. This was obviously going to be a trip of the greatest interest. On the footplate I was made very welcome by Driver McCart and Fireman McKissack, of Polmadie shed; it was a pleasure too, to have Inspector Muir as my guide and philosopher for what proved to be for me a particularly memorable day's running. To complete the preliminaries I only need to add that the weather was calm and fine with scarcely a cloud in the sky, and so it remained until sundown.

Before starting I had learned from Inspector Muir that our job was to be made considerably harder than normal by the existence of no fewer than *five* permanent-way checks, four of which were to come before Motherwell. In this way we should lose all chances of a 'run' at the long bank. In the ordinary course Uddingston can be passed at 60 mph or even more; but on this occasion not only did we have a 20-mph slack at the very foot of the climb, but we had a further slowing for three-quarters of a mile when we were right on the grade. Prior to this we had had some brief spells of very hard work; from the first check, near Rutherglen, we had thundered away to 39 mph up the 1 in 163 past Cambuslang. The second slowing, near Newton, was followed immediately by the one at Uddingston, and from that one we got away to 34 mph on the 1 in 115 before the fourth and longest of the checks. With cut-offs of 30 to 35 per cent the *Princess Beatrice* had certainly been telling all the world she was coming, and when we finally got away, at milepost 90¾, Driver McCart set the cut-off at 35 per cent, while the big engine pounded her way through Motherwell. Due to these four checks however we were already 8½ min. late: 12·9 miles in 26½ min.; but with such a heavy train, and on such heavy gradients the loss was surprisingly small in the circumstances. Furthermore we were passing Motherwell at a speed much lower than normal; instead of having some useful impetus from a brisk run through Uddingston we were fighting back against the grade from our slack farther north. We held a steady 34 mph on the 1 in 102 past Wishaw, but the increased tractive resistance on the long curve from Garriongill to Law Junction brought us down to 29½ mph at the latter place. The grade eases somewhat above Law Junction, and we topped Craigenhill at 36 mph. The average speed for the 10·9 miles up from Motherwell had been 32·7 mph.

Towards the end of the climb there were signs that the working was beginning to 'beat the boiler'—as the expression goes; while pressure had been nicely held at 225 to 240 lb. per sq. in. as far as Wishaw there developed a definite downward tendency after Law Junction, and we topped Craigenhill, with 205 lb. and a half a glass of water. The downhill stretch through Cleghorn, and the slack through Carstairs gave a welcome opportunity for recovery, and once over Strawfrank Junction, with 240 lb. on the clock, engine and crew were game for anything. The more gradual ascent through Upper Clydesdale was to be taken at top speed; the gradient averages 1 in 306 between the crossing of the Clyde near Strawfrank Junction and Beattock Summit, and here we made an excellent average speed of 55·7 mph. The engine was eased a little on the short descent to the viaduct at Lamington, but otherwise it was hammer and tongs the whole way, with cut-offs varying between 25 and 30 per cent, and regulator absolutely full open. On the open moorland stretches between Lamington and Crawford, where with such working the speed was 57 to 60 mph the roar of the exhaust was tremendous. From Elvanfoot, however, where we crossed the Clyde for the last time, at 58 mph, the firing was slightly eased. After Beattock Summit we should be doing little more than coasting for the ensuing 10 miles, and we certainly did not want a large head of steam in the boiler, which would only result in waste, through blowing off. Nevertheless we topped Beattock Summit at 39 mph, though on account of all the checks we had taken 78½ min. to cover the 52·6 miles up from Glasgow Central.

As we dipped down the steep gradient, and steam was shut off altogether, the scenery as well as the locomotive working changed completely. From the wide open landscapes of Clydesdale we ran through the rock cuttings, over the high embankments, and round the many curves of the glen that leads southwards from Beattock Summit. Speed was restrained at first to little more than 60 mph, but as the glen opened out below the Harthope automatic signals, and the line became straighter, those gentle touches of the brake became less frequent, and below Greskine the engine was given a breath of steam. Speed now rose to 75 mph, but nearing Beattock station it was checked again for we had the fifth, and final permanent-way check ahead of us. The restriction lay near to the crossing of the Annan, and once past this we got away for a good spell of sustained fast running. It was here, however, that we missed the very free running of the 'Duchess' class engines; for although the *Princess Beatrice* gave us plenty of going at 70 to 75 mph she had to be pushed fairly hard to do it. Cut-off was mostly between 22 and 25 per cent, with the regulator varied between the first valve, and about one-half of the main valve. Including the rising stretch from Lockerbie to Castlemilk, we pulled off an average speed of 67 mph from Dinwoodie to Floriston, but we were nevertheless 16 min. late into Carlisle.

THE *ROYAL SCOT*

Load 13 cars 448 tons tare 475 tons full
Engine 46209 *Princess Beatrice*
Driver McCart, Fireman McKissack (Polmadie shed)

Mls		Sch	m	s	mph
0·0	GLASGOW CENTRAL	0	0	00	
1·0	Eglinton Street	3	3	05	
			p w s		20
			7	30	
3·1	Rutherglen		10	33	39
5·0	Cambuslang		p w s		20
			13	20	
6·6	Newton	10	p w s		20
8·4	Uddingston	13	17	08	
10·8	*Milepost* 91½		22	29	34
			p w s		20
12·9	MOTHERWELL	18	26	32	
14·0	Flemington		28	40	34
15·9	Wishaw		32	01	33
18·3	LAW JUNCTION	26	36	43	29½
20·4	Carluke		40	22	39/32
23·8	*Craigenhill Box*		46	33	36
26·0	Cleghorn		49	23	55
28·8	CARSTAIRS	40	52	35	slack
30·3	*Milepost* 72		54	23	54
32·3	*Leggatfoot Box*		56	47	47
33·8	Thankerton		58	24	61
35·4	SYMINGTON		60	18	48½
39·1	Lamington		64	03	66
44·5	Abington		69	21	57
47·0	Crawford		72	00	60
49·7	Elvanfoot		74	58	50/58
52·6	*Beattock Summit*	64	78	27	39
56·9	*Greskine Box*		82	40	75
62·6	Beattock		87	20	62
			p w s		15
67·8	Wamphray		93	24	
70·6	Dinwoodie		97	10	58
73·6	Nethercleugh		100	01	67
76·5	LOCKERBIE	86	102	47	62
79·6	*Castlemilk Siding*		105	53	56
82·1	Ecclefechan		108	27	67
85·6	Kirtlebridge		111	16	75
	Brackenhill				66½
89·2	Kirkpatrick		114	27	73½
92·1	*Quintinshill Box*		116	47	75
93·7	Gretna Junction	101	118	05	72
96·2	Floriston		120	06	73
101·6	*Carlisle No.* 3 *Box*	109	125	02	
102·3	CARLISLE	111	126	50	

Average speed Post 72–Beattock Summit 55·7 mph
Average gradient rising 1 in 307
Average d.b.h.p. 1264

The checks had been crippling, but even with an absolutely clear road I doubt if we should have kept time. With an engine of the ' Princess Royal ' type the crew were up against it on this fast schedule. No. 46209 steamed well, and pulled well on the heaviest grades; but the freedom of one of the later Stanier engines would have made a big difference on stretches like that from Carstairs up to Beattock Summit, and from Dinwoodie down to Gretna. At Carlisle the ex-Southern Region 2000-horsepower diesel No. 10203 was waiting to take on for the non-stop run to Euston. It would have been very interesting to see how this ultra-modern locomotive would have coped with the heavy 13-coach train, but I was due to return north with Driver McCart and Fireman McKissack, and so Inspector Muir and I bade the Royal Scot farewell at Carlisle.

By a coincidence the load of our return train was exactly the same, namely 448 tons tare, but this time made up of 15 vehicles including one four-wheeler. This was the 9.25 a.m. express from Crewe to Perth. At one time one engine worked right through, manned, in the course of the journey, by men from five different sheds, as follows :

Crew No.	Depot	Section of line
1	Crewe	Crewe–Preston
2	Preston	Preston–Carnforth
3	Barrow	Carnforth–Carlisle
4	Polmadie	Carlisle–Carstairs
5	Perth	Carstairs–Perth

The normal engine was a ' Royal Scot,' a locomotive moreover that had arrived in Crewe only four hours before starting time on a through run from Glasgow; but more recently the working has been changed. The engine north of Carlisle is now one that has worked an early-morning stopping train down from Glasgow. In complete contrast to the ' Lizzie ' on which our driver and fireman had come south with the Royal Scot, we had one of the BR Class 6 Pacifics, No. 72003 *Clan Fraser*. This train is booked non-stop to Carstairs in 92 min., but with such a load as 448 tons tare rear-end banking assistance would be essential up Beattock Bank.

The cabs of the BR6 and BR7 Pacifics are ideal for the observer. All features of the working—boiler and steam chest pressure, regulator position, and cut-off can be readily seen, but they can become very hot. So it was on this otherwise delightful summer day. The engine itself was in superb mechanical condition, in fact it was one of the most *puissant* BR Pacifics—Class 6 or Class 7—that I have ever been on. We made a splendid run out to Beattock unassisted with the 475-ton load. Acceleration out of Carlisle was naturally a little slow, with an engine having no more than 27,000 lb. nominal tractive effort; but we were doing 60 mph at Mossband and with 28 per cent cut-off and practically full regulator we held 50 mph almost to the top of the first long stretch of 1 in 200. It was only when our 15 vehicles were strung out round the long curve past old Brackenhill box that speed fell to 48½ mph. We touched 59 at Kirtlebridge, and then went up the second 1 in 200 bank at a minimum of 50½ mph. Thus we kept the difficult 31-min. allowance to passing Lockerbie, 25·8 miles, and went on up Annandale at a good 67-8 mph. Here the cut-off was 24 per cent and regulator eased back to give 140 to 145 lb. steam chest pressure.

Then came the bad slack at the bridge near Wamphray, and instead of charging the lower part of the Beattock Bank, where the gradient is rising at 1 in 200, we had to fight back from a reduction to 20 mph. Using 30 per cent cut-off and full regulator we did well to accelerate this heavy train to 43 mph before stopping at Beattock station for assistance on the bank proper. In such circumstances our time of 47 min. 37 sec. start to stop from Carlisle to Beattock was very fine indeed. No time was wasted in attaching the bank engine, a Stanier 2–6–4 tank, and in a shade under 49 min. from Carlisle we were off again. The two engines climbed the bank in 3 sec. over the even 20 min. For the most part speed was held at 32 mph. On No. 72003 cut-off was varied between 35 and 38 per cent with regulator full open, and steam chest pressure maintained between 200 and 210 lb. per sq. in. As we forged our way up there was ample time to enjoy the fine mountain scenery, and see the unusual sight, in this part of the country, of holiday campers lying out sun-bathing on the grassy slopes, or beside mountain streams that the dry weather had reduced to a mere trickle.

So we came to Beattock Summit, 49·7 miles from Carlisle in 68 min. 58 sec. Booked time for this train is 67 min., but with a Class 6 engine the load is reckoned as 355 tons only. With nearly 100 tons more, the necessity of a stop at Beattock, with a permanent-way check costing a full 3 min. engine and crew had done a grand

SCOTTISH REGION : 1.42 P M   CARLISLE–CARSTAIRS

Load 15 vehicles 448 tons tare 475 tons full
Engine B.R.6 4–6–2 No 72003 *Clan Fraser*
Driver McCart, Fireman McKissack (Polmadie shed)

Mls		Sch	m	s	mph
0·0	CARLISLE	0	0	00	
0·7	*Carlisle No. 3*	2	2	24	
2·0	*Kingmoor No.* 1		4	26	
4·1	Rockcliffe		7	03	50
6·1	Floriston		9	20	54½
7·3	*Mossband Box*		10	36	60
8·6	Gretna Jc	11	11	55	—
10·2	*Quintinshill Box*		13	39	52
13·1	Kirkpatrick		17	03	50
	Brackenhill				48½
16·7	Kirtlebridge		21	20	59
20·1	Ecclefechan		24	55	53½
22·7	*Castlemilk Siding*		27	51	50½
25·8	LOCKERBIE	31	30	55	63
28·7	Nethercleugh		33	33	68½
31·7	Dinwoodie		36	15	63
			p w s		20
34·5	Wamphray		39	01	
36·8	*Murthat*		43	03	43
39·7	BEATTOCK pass :	45	47	37	
	Banker in rear : Stanier 2–6–4 T				
		dep.	48	55	
41·8	Milepost 41¾		53	50	32
45·4	*Greskine*		60	43	32
47·8	*Harthope auto-signals*		65	15	32
49·7	Beattock Summit	67	68	58	30½
52·6	Elvanfoot		72	23	60
57·8	Abington		77	40	60
63·2	Lamington		82	56	63
66·9	SYMINGTON	83	86	35	56
68·5	Thankerton		88	12	64
70·0	*Leggatfoot Box*		89	43	54
73·2	*Strawfrank Jc*		93	00	
73·5	CARSTAIRS	92	94	13	

Net time to Beattock   44¾ min.

job. The descent of Upper Clydesdale was taken quietly. Between Elvanfoot and Abington the curvature is continuous, and speed was not allowed to exceed 60 mph; but the hilly concluding length from Lamington to Strawfrank Junction was run smartly, with a minimum speed of 56 mph at Symington, and we came into Carstairs in 94¼ min. from Carlisle. Engine No. 72003 was then remanned for the continuation run to Perth, while Driver McCart and Fireman McKissack took the Glasgow portion of the train. Normally a 2-6-4 tank is provided for the short downhill run, but on this occasion they finished their day's round on a large-boilered McIntosh 0-6-0 mixed-traffic engine! It would have been highly interesting to have ridden with them on a locomotive that could hardly have contrasted more strongly with the Class 8 and Class 6 Pacifics we had run up till then; but I was going back to Carlisle at 5.5 p.m. on the Liverpool and Manchester express.

This proved to be another very interesting journey, with Driver J. Lindsay and Fireman R. McElvey, also of Polmadie, working through to Manchester on a double home turn. With a slightly easier timing, a load of only 10 coaches, and an excellent Class 6P 4-6-0 No. 45710 *Irresistible,* the four permanent-way checks north of Motherwell had not affected them so severely as they had done to the Royal Scot earlier that day, and the train arrived at Carstairs very little behind time. After combination with the Edinburgh portion we left 2 min. late, with a load of 13 on, 437 tons tare and 470 tons full. The weather remained perfect, and in the late afternoon I saw the hills and dales of the Border country in yet another serenely beautiful light. This train has an easier timing than the Royal Scot, and against an allowance of 24 min. pass to pass for the 23·8 miles from Carstairs to Beattock Summit, the 5.5 p.m. is booked 30 min. start to pass.

I was to see some very smart working with this heavy and well-loaded train. Driver Lindsay did not press his engine at all, as indeed it would have been unwise to do on a long through working of this kind; but every advantage was taken of the favourable stretches of the line, as at Lamington, and the intermediate station working at both Beattock and Lockerbie was very rapid. Thus despite the late start, due to the checks north of Motherwell, and despite the slack at the bridge near Wamphray the train was less than a minute late away from Lockerbie. From the locomotive point of view the most interesting work was naturally that between Carstairs and Beattock. Here almost exact time was kept, with no harder working than 25 per cent cut-off, between Crawford and Beattock Summit. For much of this stretch, too, no more than 15 per cent was used, and on the short downhill length between Symington and Lamington the reverser was pulled up as short as 10 per cent, with the first regulator valve. The engine steamed consistently well, and despite this relatively easy working the resulting performance was a further demonstration of the high standards now required over the Caledonian line. The time between Lamington and Beattock summit may be compared with two pre-war runs with Pacifics, when sectional times were being kept with loads little heavier than this:

Year	1957	1934	1957
Train (ex-Glasgow)	4.10 p m	Royal Scot	Midday Scot
Engine no.	45710	6200	6206
Engine name	*Irresistible*	*The Princess Royal*	*Princess Marie Louise*
Load tons E/F	437/470	465/500	478/515
Time over 13·5 miles, Lamington Beattock Summit	m s 15 50	m s 15 25	m s 16 03
Speeds :	mph	mph	mph
Lamington	64½	61½	60
Crawford (min.)	46½	47½	45
Elvanfoot (max.)	54	55	53
Summit	35½	34½	38

The *Irresistible* was taken very briskly down the Beattock Bank, albeit on next to no steam; but on the next short run to Lockerbie the check at the Wamphray bridge prevented us from keeping the smart booking of 16 min. start to stop for the 13·9 miles. The engine was not pressed here, however, for some recovery time is available on the final stage into Carlisle. I shall, however, always remember this train, and the section south of Beattock, for on it, and as relatively recently as 1933 I clocked my last express run with a Caledonian 4-4-0. One of the Pickersgill engines, No. 95 (then LMS No. 14506) had 290 tons on the second part of the train, and ran to Lockerbie in 15¼ min. The booking was then 28 min. from Lockerbie to Carlisle, and we should have kept this sharp allowance, but for a permanent-way check at Kirtlebridge, and a signal delay outside Carlisle. To return to the year 1957 however, we were running downhill from Kirkpatrick with time very comfortably in hand when adverse signals were sighted at Quintinshill, and again approaching Gretna Junction. But the margin for recovery here was sufficient to offset the reductions in speed, and we came into Carlisle dead on time, at 6.42 p.m., in $33\frac{1}{4}$ min. from Lockerbie. This again was an excellent piece of running.

This indeed had so far been a day of contrasts for me: the big Class 8 engine 'up against it' on the fast and heavy duty coming south in the morning; the 'Clan' putting up a splendid show with an unusually heavy train, and then the 'Jubilee' being worked with skill and economy on a duty of intermediate character. But the greatest contrast was to come on my final run of the day, with the down Midday Scot. The performance on that famous train was such however as to demand a chapter to itself.

16 Quintinshill, a place of tragic memories: in September 1961 the diesel-hauled 'Royal Scot' (loco No. D322) passing the box, with a very heavy Saturday load, including, unusually, two ex-LNER coaches immediately behind the locomotive.

17 Near Harthope intermediate signals on the upper reaches of Beattock Bank in June 1962: a Class '6' 4-6-2 No. 72003 *Clan Fraser* has a bank engine for a nine-coach school special from Carlisle to Glasgow.

18 At Greskine siding, half way up the Beattock Bank: in July 1964 an ex-LNER Class B1 4-6-0 No. 61308 on a mixed freight, banked in rear.

19 A fine action shot of a bank engine, 2-6-4T No. 42693, assisting a Blackpool-Glasgow express past Greskine box, July 1964.

20 Two aspects of banking on Beattock in 1964: a grimed Austerity 2-8-0 No. 90199, steaming well, but hurling out the 'pollution' in spectacular style, (a 2-6-4T in rear).

21 Less spectacular, but nevertheless making a fine picture, a Class 20 diesel No. D8120, also needs the assistance of a 2-6-4T in rear.

CHAPTER 6

RECORD-BREAKING ON THE CALEDONIAN

SIXTY-TWO years ago, almost to the month in which I am writing, the greatest of all railway races that have taken place in Great Britain was working up to its climax. On the West Coast Route the acceleration did not have to be reckoned from week to week; at Carlisle, in the small hours, the North Western brought in the 8 p.m. from Euston earlier and earlier, day by day. Until 19th August they were due at 1.38 a.m., but with various engines of the famous 6 ft. 6 in. ' Jumbo ' type, sometimes piloted by ' Lady of the Lake ' singles, they came in at any time between 1.28 and 1.35; and when schedule was quickened to an arrival at 1.15 p.m., the ' Jumbo ' No. 1683 *Sisyphus* was 14 min. early on the very first trip. But at Carlisle, from 22nd July onwards, one could be sure that the engine forward to Perth would be one of two only—78, driven by Tom Robinson, or 90, driven by Archibald Crooks. Both these engines were of the handsome Drummond 6 ft. 6 in. class, and their drivers vied with one another as to who could do the finest work.

Tom Robinson was the favourite, and in the early hours of 22nd August he covered the 150 miles from Carlisle to Perth in even time, despite the stop then scheduled at Stirling. His load was quoted as ' equal to six '—which would be about 110 tons. On the next night the Stirling stop was cut out, but although the load was reduced to 70 tons (equal to 4½) Crooks did not improve upon the previous best time. Great was the excitement at Carlisle early on the next day, for it was confidently said that Tom Robinson was going to do something ' really special ' when his turn came to run No. 78 non-stop to Perth; great was the disappointment therefore when it was learned that the East Coast had called it off, and the racing thus came to a sudden end. On that last night on which very fast running was made No. 90 covered the 39·7 miles from Carlisle out to Beattock in 39½ min., and climbed the 10 miles of the Bank in 13½ min.; but in 1896 the Tourist express in its normal working had to run nearly as fast as this in order to cover the

117½ miles from Carlisle to Stirling in 125 min., and the McIntosh 'Dunalastair' 4–4–0s used to take loads of 200 tons unassisted over Beattock at speeds equal to or better than the 'racing' time of No. 90. There is a record existing of a run on which a 'Dunalastair,' hauling 170 tons, passed Beattock in 37¾ min. and topped Summit in 52¾ min.; but then as far back as the 1888 race the famous 4–2–2 'single,' No. 123, took a 90-ton load over Summit in 52½ min. from Carlisle.

After the race was over Caledonian locomotive enterprise became devoted to the conveyance of heavier loads, and in due course the series of great 4–6–0 locomotives was turned out from St Rollox works. It is true that many fast and lightly loaded trains remained in the time-table, but attention became focused on the working of *Cardean* on the down 2 p.m. 'Corridor,' then leaving Carlisle at 8.13 p.m., and until the LMS accelerations of the middle 'thirties' really got into their stride the 'Corridor' timing of *Cardean's* day— eighty-nine minutes to the stop at Strawfrank Junction—remained as a yardstick of Caledonian engine performance. With a minimum load of over 300 tons a stop for rear-end banking assistance was scheduled at Beattock, in 44 min. from Carlisle. It must be admitted that on the basis of records that have been preserved *Cardean* did not get to Beattock in 44 min. very often; her time was more usually 45 or even 46 min., though the 2 min. scheduled for attaching the banker were rarely needed, and time could usually be gained in ascending the bank. Thus the summit was passed on time, in 66 min. from Carlisle. Although it was not customary to run fast down the Clyde valley, a little further time could be gained to Strawfrank, so that in general the 89 min. booked was maintained admirably, with loads up to 350 tons.

But in 1937 and in 1938 the old yardsticks went completely by the board. The down Coronation Scot was booked to pass Beattock Summit in 50 min., Symington in 65 min., and Carstairs in 71 min.; while in 1938, the Royal Scot, accelerated to a seven-hour run from Euston to Glasgow was scheduled 40 min. to Beattock, 58 min. to Summit, and 74 min. to the stop at Symington. The Coronation Scot had a regular load of 297 tons tare, and the Royal Scot booking was officially limited to a maximum tare load of 420 tons, with the Stanier 'Pacific' engines. By way of comparison I have set out certain ratios for the Drummond engines, the first 'Dunalastairs,'

Cardean, and the Stanier ' Pacifics,' so that some guidance to their respective working can be obtained:

CALEDONIAN LOCOMOTIVE COMPARISONS

Engine type	4–2–2	4–4–0	4–4–0	4–6–0	4–6–2	
Engine class	No 123	Drummond	' Dunalastair I '	*Cardean*	' Duchess '	
Nominal T.E. at 85% B.P. lb.	12,770	13,750	15,070	21,200	40,000	
Adhesion weight, tons	16	29	31¼	55¾	67	
Load for comparison, tons	90	110	170	350	310	440
Load : T.E. ratio	15·8	17·9	25·2	36·9	17·35	24·
Load : adhesion weight	5·62	3·8	5·45	6·27	4·62	6·
Time to passing Beattock, min.	38½	37	37¾	44*	35	40
Time to passing Summit, min.	52½	51	52¾		50	58

* To stop at Beattock station

From this table it will be seen that in making times of 50 to 53 min. from Carlisle to Beattock Summit the ' Dunalastairs ' on the Tourist express of 1896 had, in relation to their nominal tractive effort, a harder job of it than the ' Duchess ' class Pacifics on the Coronation Scot. On the other hand the latter train was a fairly easy task, and the summit box would often be passed in 46 or 47 min. No-one could say that the ' Dunalastairs ' had an easy job of it with the Tourist! *Cardean,* in relation to her tractive effort, was much the most heavily loaded, and the difficulty experienced with the 44-min. timing to Beattock is thus amply explained. In view of the very limited adhesion weight the performance of the famous single, No. 123, at the climax of the 1888 race, is extremely fine, and altogether astonishing for the year in which it was achieved. This analysis of past records over the Caledonian has been prepared in order that the work done on my recent footplate journey with the Midday Scot may be seen in clearer perspective.

On that July evening in 1957, after the three most interesting trips described in the previous chapter, I was already feeling more than content with the results of my day's running, and in the short turn-round time at Carlisle after the arrival of the up Liverpool and Manchester train there was little time for reflection or day-dreaming upon the changes that have taken place in the working of the down ' Corridor ' since Caledonian days. For although the scheduled times are different, and the circumstances vastly different, this was *Cardean's* old job! Even within the last few days prior to my making the trip there had been an important change in the working. *Cardean's* regular driver, David Gibson of Polmadie, remained in the service long enough to have a ' Royal Scot,' and to participate in the earliest double-home working between Glasgow and Crewe. From the winter of 1927-8 until the summer service of 1957 the ' Corridor ' was worked by Crewe and Polmadie men on alternate days; but now, with the alteration to the up Midday Scot that was tried for a short time, with a 3 p.m. departure from Glasgow, and a non-stop run from Carlisle to Euston, the Polmadie men worked this train to Carlisle and returned the same day on the corresponding down express. Thus I had the pleasure of meeting Driver Tom Currie and Fireman J Brady on the platform at Carlisle before the arrival of the train from the south. She came in on time—engine 46252 *City of Leicester*—and we were gladdened to hear the comment of the Crewe men as they handed over: ' A lovely engine; she'll walk away with the job!' We had twelve on, 367 tons tare, and 395 tons full. This meant that the ratios of load to tractive effort, and load to adhesion weight were 22·1 and 5·8 respectively—not greatly different in either case from the ' Dunalastairs ' on the Tourist, when their load was 170 tons.

There are times when riding on the footplate during a placid run when the quiet even tenor of the going puts the observer in a reflective mood. There is time to note incidental though fascinating detail, to drink in beauty of the passing scene (for there are not many places, even today, where the English or the Scottish countryside is not beautiful!) and time to bring to mind comparisons and contrasts with this or that trip from one's memory. But when a driver like Tom Currie is really ' going for it,' and he has an engine like the *City of Leicester* at his command, every detail of the locomotive performance is worth noting; one looks outside the cab only to sight the mileposts, to note stations and signal boxes, and to scan the line ahead in case an adverse signal should put a check on the running. I was half expecting signal checks in any case, for a relief train had left Carlisle 15 min. ahead of us, and at the pace we developed it seemed more than likely that we should catch it up. For we did make a very fast run. At the time, amid a positive hurricane of note-taking I was vaguely conscious we were breaking records; but it was not until I came to analyse my notes that I realised the full significance of the run.

But let me tell the tale of the run first. Before we were abreast of Kingmoor sheds it was clear that the Crewe driver's eulogy was no mere figure of speech. Full regulator, 20 per cent cut-off, and we were already doing 54 mph past the sheds: 64 mph at Rockcliffe, 72 at Floriston, 77 at Mossband, and we crossed the Border at 76 mph. Up the first long stretch of 1 in 200 we never fell below 62 mph; Kirtlebridge was passed at 76, and here cut-off was reduced to 15 per cent. There was no staying the *City of Leicester*; Castlemilk was cleared at 65, and then with regulator eased right back we swept through Lockerbie at 75 mph. A glance at my notes, to see we had only taken 24½ min. for this first 25·8 miles. On through the Annandale racing ground; a full 80 mph between Nethercleugh and Dinwoodie, and then, fortunately, the engineering work at the Wamphray culvert was finished, and we were able to storm over at 79 mph and to reach 82 at the crossing of the Annan. On to the approach grades of the Beattock Bank, past the now-closed Murthat signal box, and with the speed still 76 mph the driver opened up to 20 per cent cut-off, and put the regulator hard over once more. And so, with thoughts far from stopping for assistance we tore through the little junction at 72 mph. Rarely can the famous bank have been attacked in a more full-blooded charge, and as I jotted down the passing time, what was this— 35 min. 10 sec. from Carlisle ?—we had beaten Crooks, Tom Robinson, and all the giants of the Victorian golden age—with 395 tons behind the tender!

As I came to prepare the log of this very thrilling run, I fell to wondering what conditions were like on the footplates of the little Drummonds, and the first 'Dunalastairs' when those heroic runs were being made. In all probability the going was a good deal smoother, quieter, and more comfortable than one might imagine. Those little engines were kept in beautiful condition, mechanically and otherwise, and having had the opportunity of riding recently on a resuscitated museum-piece and experiencing the smoothness of her riding at speeds in excess of 80 mph I can well believe that the Drummonds and the 'Dunalastairs' rode like true ladies. But as a vehicle also the *City of Leicester* could scarcely have been bettered; she rode with that exhilarating buoyancy characteristic of the best British Pacifics, and without any tendency to roll. The fireman was kept pretty busy, but that is not more than one would expect, in making an average speed of 73·2 mph from Floriston to

THE MIDDAY SCOT

Load 12 cars 367 tons tare 390 tons full
Engine 46252 *City of Leicester*
Driver T Currie, Fireman J Brady (Polmadie shed)

Mls		Sch	m	s	mph
0·0	CARLISLE	0	0	00	
0·7	*Carlisle No. 3 Box*	2	2	02	
2·0	*Kingmoor No. 1 Box*		3	45	54
4·1	Rockcliffe		5	51	64½
6·1	Floriston		7	35	72½
7·3	*Mossband Box*		8	33	77
8·6	Gretna Jc	11	9	33	76
10·2	*Quintinshill Box*		10	53	69
13·1	Kirkpatrick		13	30	64
	Brackenhill				62
16·7	Kirtlebridge		16	50	76
20·1	Ecclefechan		19	40	70½
22·7	*Castlemilk Siding*		21	56	65
25·8	LOCKERBIE	28	24	28	75
28·7	Nethercleugh		26	41	80
31·7	Dinwoodie		28	57	78½/75½
34·5	Wamphray		31	06	77½/82
36·8	*Murthat Box*		32	53	78
39·7	BEATTOCK	40	35	10	72
41·8	*Milepost 41¾*		37	00	58
45·0	*Milepost 45*		41	14	39
45·4	*Greskine Box*		41	53	
46·0	*Milepost 46*		43	02	32
47·0	*Milepost 47*		44	57	31
48·0	*Milepost 48*		46	49	32½
49·0	*Milepost 49*		48	39	33
49·7	*Beattock Summit*	58	49	58	33
52·6	Elvanfoot		53	10	67
				eased	
57·8	Abington		58	28	easy
63·2	Lamington		63	38	73
66·9	SYMINGTON	73	66	48	64
68·5	Thankerton		68	13	72
70·0	*Leggatfoot Box*		69	35	60
73·2	*Strawfrank Jc*		72	47	
73·5	CARSTAIRS	81	74	00	

Average speed Floriston to Beattock, 73 mph
Average gradient rising 1 in 555
Average dbhp 1270

Cut-offs :

Carlisle No. 3–Kirtlebridge	20 %
Kirtlebridge–Milepost 38	15 %
Post 38–44	20 %
Post 44–6	22 %
Post 46–Beattock Summit	30 %

Beattock station. There is a vertical lift of 320 ft. between these two points, equal to an average rising gradient of 1 in 555, and such an average speed meant a continuous output of about 1,300 drawbar horsepower. There was no sign of exertion or sense of effort from the engine proper, though the vigour of the firing, and occasional glances at the water gauge on the tender left one under no delusions as to the magnitude of the effort involved.

The first miles of Beattock Bank made little impression on our speed; by Auchencastle automatic signals we had just fallen below 60 mph, but we travelled another 2 miles on 1 in 75 before our driver lengthened the cut-off from 20 to 22 per cent. By this time however, the Bank was really beginning to assert itself; we approached Greskine box at 39 mph, and the exhaust was now plainly audible. Pressure was showing at a healthy 240 lb. per sq. in. and at the 46th milepost, cut-off was further lengthened to 30 per cent. The job was so comfortably in hand however, that there was no point in pressing the engine on the upper part of Beattock Bank. Had an approximately constant rate of steaming been maintained from Wamphray to the summit the cut-off changes would have been as follows:

Speed mph	75	70	60	50	40	35	30
Cut-off	20	21	23½	26	30	33	36

Actually the rate of steaming was eased off considerably after Beattock station, as speed had fallen to 40 mph before the cut-off was advanced beyond 20 per cent. Thus the engine could have been worked considerably harder on Beattock Bank, had it been necessary, without increasing the rate of steaming above that being used between Wamphray and Beattock station. It is interesting to see, by comparison with the table on page 50, that although the Drummond engines took 37 to 38 min. to pass Beattock they climbed the bank in 14 min. On the other hand our run with the *City of Leicester* corresponded almost exactly with the schedule of the pre-war Coronation Scot; but with a much heavier load. On the final stages of the bank we sustained 33 mph and topped the summit in the remarkable time of 49 min. 58 sec. from Carlisle.

Though there have been faster runs than this with the Coronation Scot, and there may well be faster ones with the Caledonian of today, this run is by far the fastest I have seen, or heard of, with a load of all but 400 tons behind the tender. From leaving Carlisle one minute late we had picked up to 7 min. early at Beattock Summit. After this we naturally went very placidly down the Clyde valley, till Lamington was neared; then a mere touch of the regulator took this grand engine up to 73 mph at the viaduct, and over the switchback grades to Strawfrank in such excellent style that we were once again inside ' level time ' before the slowing for Carstairs began. We were 6 min. early on arrival. Of course, by far the most notable part of the journey from the viewpoint of power output was between Carlisle and Beattock station. The average speed of 73 mph over the rising length from Floriston, equivalent to a continuous output of 1,300 drawbar horsepower on level track, was higher than some Class 8 engines could produce at all, let alone in the course of an ordinary fast run. The ' Duchess ' class locomotives are at their best in sustained high speed working, and all railway enthusiasts will look forward to the publication of the results of the tests conducted on No. 46225 *Duchess of Gloucester* on the Rugby testing plant. It remains to be seen whether they can be set down in history as the greatest of all British express locomotive designs; but after a run like that of the *City of Leicester,* and one at least of those included in the Lancaster and Carlisle chapter, one certainly begins to form rather decided views!

It was an exhilarating finish to a grand day, showing the Caledonian line, its men, and its locomotives at their best. To the drivers and firemen of Polmadie who made me so welcome on their footplates, and to Inspector Muir who accompanied me all day my warmest thanks are due. Since the time of my footplate journeys of 1957 the Caledonian express has fairly got into its stride. The normal load of 264 tons tare does not ordinarily make severe demands upon the locomotives, but when delays occur there are often some very thrilling recoveries of time. One day in August 1958 when Mr W. Robertson was a passenger the same driver who did so well on my footplate trip with the Midday Scot, T. Currie, had engine No. 46242 *City of Glasgow*. There were slight checks, to 42 mph at Floriston, and to 65 mph at Castlemilk; in consequence the times to passing Lockerbie and Beattock were both slightly slower than on my footplate run. But for Beattock Bank the engine was opened well out, with the result that the famous climb was taken at an average speed of exactly 60 mph. The absolute minimum was 52 mph, and as a result the train passed Beattock Summit in no more than 45 min. 47 sec. from Carlisle. With quite moderate speed down the Clyde valley, at no time exceeding 74 mph, Carstairs was passed in 67 min. 40 sec. from Carlisle. In these days it is indeed rare for the speed of the down Caledonian to fall much below 45 mph at Beattock Summit, and one can recall with amusement the early days when the line itself was no more than a project, and men derided Joseph Locke's change of front, in swinging from the Nithsdale to the Annandale route, and involving himself in gradients that it was then believed no engine could climb!

22   In Upper Clydesdale, crossing the river near Crawford, the morning Manchester-Glasgow express at high speed in September 1961, hauled by rebuilt 'Scot' No. 46104 *Scottish Borderer*.

23 In Upper Clydesdale, before modernisation got really under way in June 1965: a Class 47 diesel No. D1638 approaching Lamington with the morning Euston-Perth express.

24 The new era on Beattock Bank, near Greskine, in June 1978: colour light signals and no bank engines. The overnight Newton Abbot-Stirling motorail hauled by electric locomotive No. 81.004.

25 Early morning at the river crossing near Crawford: the Dover-Stirling motorail sweeping round the curve at high speed hauled by electric locomotive No. 86.018.

CHAPTER 7

Newcastle to Edinburgh

Among the three great trunk routes leading to the Scottish Border the East Coast stands apart. The scenery has none of the dramatic quality of Grayrigg, Shap, or the ' Settle and Carlisle '; yet in some ways it is the most fascinating of them all. The crossing of the Tweed, although it does not actually mark the Border, is so well defined and obvious a frontier post, as to provide an outstanding landmark for all save the veriest of dullards, and the railway has for much of its length the attraction of being a truly coastal route. It runs through a countryside steeped in history—a history which, although taking new turns became scarcely less absorbing when the age of railways came. Curiously enough, however, on this route the transition from England to Scotland is, from the railway point of view, the least defined of any. This is not a new phenomenon dating from the time of nationalisation, or even from the grouping. From the year 1869 the North Eastern Railway possessed running powers from Berwick to Edinburgh, and except for a brief period from 1897 the Anglo-Scottish expresses were all worked by North Eastern locomotives between Newcastle and Edinburgh. As long ago as the ' eighties ' of last century the North Eastern were running some of the night expresses non-stop over the 124·4 miles, at that time the longest non-stop run in the whole country.

It is curious in view of the railway political strategy of the North British in Victorian times that there was never a reciprocal arrangement whereby some of the East Coast expresses were worked into Newcastle by North British engines. There was everything to be gained by through engine working. The ' round ' of 250 miles, out and home, formed a good day's duty, but remembering how the North British fought tooth and nail to get a foothold in Newcastle it is surprising that they never attempted to hammer out an agreement whereby some trains were worked by them, and others by the North Eastern. At one time the North British seemed bent upon establishing as many ' bridgeheads ' as possible across the English Border; they forced their way to Silloth, they got as far south as Hexham, and there was also the great project of a line southwards from Kelso to link up with the Blyth and Tyne. Had the North Eastern been less alert at that critical stage they might have found their main line north of Newcastle caught between a pair of North British ' pincers '—the Riccarton–Hexham line on the west, and the absorbed Blyth and Tyne on the east. The North British and the North Eastern were then very far from the close allies and good friends they subsequently became. As it eventually befell, it was not until after grouping that North British engines began regularly working down from Edinburgh to Newcastle.

One could dilate for whole chapters, let alone a few pages upon the historic aspects of both sections of this fine route: how the Newcastle and Berwick might have been built as an ' atmospheric ' line; of the vicissitudes through which the Berwick and Edinburgh section of the North British passed. But this is not a book of railway history, and as the guard's whistle blows for the ' right-away ' at Newcastle, whether it be on the *Flying Scotsman,* the Aberdonian, the Queen of Scots or that enterprising newcomer the *Talisman* we must leave the shades of Hudson, the Stephensons, and even of Brunel behind, the better to see the line and the country-side as it is today. Even before we set out for the Border however there is much to see at our very starting point. The immediate approaches to the Central Station at Newcastle are extremely pic-turesque stretches of railway, not in the scenic sense, but in the lay-out of the junctions, the bridges over the Tyne, and in the possession of such a topographical ' lion ' as the great crossing immediately to the east of the station. For the photographer there are some splendid vantage points, like the signal box at King Edward Bridge Junction and the top of the castle Keep, that stands out so dramatically in the ' V ' of the great crossing.

The accompanying sketch map shows the general layout of the tracks, and from a north-bound train that has come down the Team Valley line the prospect opens out as King Edward Bridge Junction is approached. The bridge itself is utilitarian in aspect, yet from it there is a broad outlook both upstream and downstream. Coming upon it at dusk, and closing one's eyes a little, it is not difficult to imagine what things were like when the railway first came to New-castle, and the Tyne flowed through what was little more than a

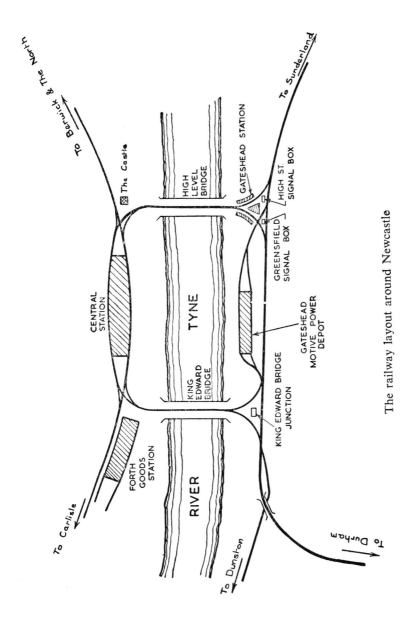

The railway layout around Newcastle

deep ravine. Today, looking downstream, are the High Level Bridge and the new road bridge, with its graceful arch. On many Anglo-Scottish expresses, too, the traveller gets his first sight of the fresh engine that is to take him forward from Newcastle. To avoid congestion at the east end of the station engines of down expresses are kept standing out on the High Level Bridge until the road is clear for them to back straight on to their trains. Even though the bridges are nearly half a mile apart it does not need a pair of binoculars to recognise the familiar silhouette of an A1, A2, A3 or A4 Pacific; it was sometimes much more difficult in the old days to decide at that distance whether the fresh engine was a ' V ' or a ' Z ' Atlantic. The approaches to Newcastle were rendered more picturesque still by the tremendous arrays of semaphore signals. After 1906 these were all pneumatically operated, and the whole area shown on the map formed a most interesting early example of power signalling. But the change-over to modern colour lights is now actually in progress and on the north bank of the River Tyne the old signal boxes at the east end and west end of the Central Station have been taken out of commission and the whole layout brought under the control of a panel like that at York. Similar modernisation is already in progress in the Gateshead side. So, to the North!

The start is like that from many another large city, with lines branching off at frequent intervals in the first miles. At Manors there diverges to the left the branch line running through Jesmond and Gosforth, and then turning to cross our own track at right angles about four miles farther on. At Argyle Street, goes off the electrified line that closely follows the north bank of the Tyne; and finally, at Heaton, the direct line to Tynemouth and Whitley Bay goes straight ahead, while the main line sweeps round to the north. The prospect broadens as we climb on to higher ground past the Benton yards; dotted in every direction are still signs of industrialism, and the familiar *ensemble* of headgear, stack and refuse dump that pinpoint on the landscape many a colliery of the old style. The place-names hereabouts are rich in historical associations with the earliest days of steam locomotives; one has only to mention West Moor, Bedlington, Willington, and above all Killingworth, to turn over once more, figuratively speaking, the pages of Samuel Smiles.

But when studying the map it is striking to see how different the alignment of this part of the East Coast main line might have been if Brunel had succeeded in persuading the Newcastle and Berwick to ' go atmospheric.' One can hardly imagine that on a fast trunk route such as this the man who left Newbury, Hungerford, Devizes, and Trowbridge out in the cold would have agreed to a westward salient in his line in order to pass through Morpeth. No; one can be sure he would have gone due north from Cramlington, and both Bedlington and Ashington would have been on the main line. As it is, the line swings through a full right angle at Morpeth, with the inevitable severe reduction in speed. As the crow flies the distance from Cramlington to Longhirst is 7·6 miles; by the present railway route it is 10·3, and on a first-class run with a heavy train like the Flying Scotsman it would not be covered in less than 11 min. With a straight run through Bedlington—if the line had been made that way—7 min. at the most would have sufficed, and not only would there have been a saving in time on every journey, but what is more important, a saving in wear and tear. The Great Western found it worth while to put in by-pass lines to avoid the speed restrictions at Westbury and Frome; at Morpeth, a line less than two miles long from a point near Clifton Crossing to near the Wansbeck Viaduct would not save much in distance, but it would avoid the speed restrictions and all the expense their careful observation entails. It is certainly one of those ' wrinkles ' in the British railway system that could do with ironing out.

Once across the Wansbeck, however, a northbound express can really settle into its stride, and apart from the need for slight reductions of speed at Alnmouth and Tweedmouth Junction, one is ' right away ' to the outskirts of Edinburgh itself. For the most part we are now sweeping through a fine, open, agricultural countryside; there are glimpses of hill ranges to the west, but inevitably one looks eastward for the first glimpses of the sea, and from Widdrington onwards we are little more than three miles away. Even here we are not entirely clear of collieries, and the branch to Amble now serves little more than the most northerly of these, at Broomhill. At one time Amble Junction, lying almost midway between Chevington and Acklington, had one of those imposing arrays of signal gantries, and overhanging bracket structures that were so characteristic of the North Eastern Railway; but the passenger service to Amble has long since been withdrawn, and the branch is now nothing more than a mineral line. Shortly after Acklington the river Coquet is crossed; although the viaduct is high and the glen is deep, the banks are so densely wooded that one hardly realises that one of the major rivers of Northumberland is here being crossed. Near Warkworth, however, there comes a further glimpse of the sea—a backward look to the mouth of the Coquet, with Warkworth Castle near at hand and the town of Amble stretched out on the far side of the estuary.

The coast is now quite near, and suddenly rounding a slight curve about 1½ miles to the north of Warkworth there bursts upon the eye one of those scenes that a traveller can never forget. The little town of Alnmouth is built on a narrowing spit of land on the north side of the river Aln. Its situation is picturesque, but in almost any conditions of weather it is the colouring that gives such exquisite charm to the scene. The houses are all roofed with vermilion tiles; clustered at the tip of a country that is richly green, backed by the sea, and with the golden sands of the Aln estuary as a foreground it needs only the slightest touch of sun to produce a truly brilliant picture. To an Englishman travelling north, Alnmouth is often seen in the friendly glow of a late afternoon sunshine, but I have also seen it at dawn, and in moonlight from the night trains, and its charms are as varied as they can be colourful. Its station, as junction for the Alnwick branch used to present another of those North Eastern forests of signal gantries, and yet another of those unimaginative track alignments that once characterised so many of our main lines in this country. Immediately north of the platforms the main line bears away to the right, but despite the relative insignificance of the branch the turn-out still requires a slight speed restriction for the fastest trains. This slack has a definite nuisance value, as it is followed immediately by the Longhoughton bank, with nearly five miles of 1 in 170, and it would make things much easier for the locomotives of heavy expresses if they could pass Alnmouth at 75 to 80 mph, instead of the present 'sixty.'

After crossing the fine viaduct over the Aln, the line passes out of sight of the sea, and although there are occasional glimpses eastwards the landscape becomes pastoral again. From Little Mill station, at the top of the Longhoughton bank, the speed is soon back into the high 'seventies,' if not more, and the stretch from Christon Bank onwards to Tweedmouth usually provides the fastest sustained running between Newcastle and Edinburgh. A mile beyond Christon Bank comes Fallodon, always to be associated with one of the greatest British statesmen of the ' old school,' Sir Edward Grey. When in later years he was created a Viscount, it was from his Northumberland home, Fallodon Hall, that he took his title. Before he joined Asquith's Cabinet, and became Foreign Secretary, Sir Edward Grey had been first a director, and then Chairman of the North Eastern Railway; and it was not only as a landed proprietor, and as a business man that he took this honour. He was in every sense of the word a railway enthusiast. After he had largely retired from public life, guests at Fallodon Hall were often astonished when the afternoon's proceedings were interrupted so that host and guests could go to the lineside to watch the down Flying Scotsman pass.

Christon Bank, Fallodon, Chathill, and Newham are all passed at high speed, so much so that there was rarely a chance, at Chathill, to catch more than a fleeting glimpse of those quaint little tank engines that used to work the North Sunderland Railway from Chathill to Seahouses. Between Lucker and Belford are the first water troughs to be laid down by the North Eastern Railway. The company showed great enterprise in scheduling non-stop runs over the 124·4 miles between Newcastle and Edinburgh many years before this facility was available; with the moderate loads and moderate speeds of the eighties and early nineties of last century no difficulty was experienced in spinning out the water supply, but the ' Race ' of 1895 began to reveal the handicap that might develop. In some of the earlier runs drivers were nursing their engines as far as Berwick, or even to Grantshouse, and then piling on every ounce of speed afterwards when they were assured of the water lasting out. Only towards the very end of the ' Race,' with the most expert of drivers, was the running through Northumberland really hard. From Belford down to the seashore at Beal one can record an occasional ' ninety ' today, even with quite heavy trains, and speed rules high beside the dunes of Goswick. And while we have been thus dashing along, we have passed the length of the Holy Island of Lindisfarne. This sacred place of the beautiful name has, however, the appeal of association, rather than of any scenic attraction. Seen from the train it is mostly low-lying; the rocky knoll surmounted by the castle, and the monastery ruins and village near by are too

83

distant for their particular charm to be appreciated. And so, beyond Goswick, the railway begins to climb once more, drawing nearer to the edge of the low cliffs, in a wild, windy, and rather forlorn landscape. Then, as in the approach to Alnmouth, a magnificent prospect opens out.

Although the similarity to Alnmouth is remarkable, the panorama of Berwick is on an altogether vaster scale. It is picturesque beyond words, and as the train comes sweeping down the grade high above the rooftops of Spittal the rapidly broadening prospect across the estuary of the Tweed—Berwick itself, the graceful bridges, and the heights welling up to the north of the town—is apt to take all attention, whereas a locomotive enthusiast would have to dash to the other side of the carriage to view the power on parade outside Tweedmouth running sheds. At one time Tweedmouth housed a great variety of engines. In the days when I knew it most intimately, in the early thirties, there was little except true North Eastern types: ' S2 ' and ' S3 ' 4–6–0s; an occasional ' A ' class 2–4–2 tank; ' M ' and ' R ' 4–4–0s; North British 0–6–0 goods, and usually one or two ' Z ' Atlantics. Tweedmouth then provided an East Coast standing pilot, ready to go in either direction if need be, just as Darlington provided *two,* one up and one down. I remember the Tweedmouth pilot being called out one afternoon when the ' Pacific ' on the up afternoon ' Scotsman,' now the ' Heart of Midlothian,' was in sore straits for steam; the ' Z ' Atlantic No. 2169 was attached as pilot, and the Tweedmouth engine assisted as far as Newcastle in a most spirited recovery.

The station at Berwick-upon-Tweed is built on the site of the ancient castle, on the very edge of the cliff 130 ft. or so above the river. One drives straight off the Royal Border Bridge into the station, as it were. The North Eastern Railway ended at the north end of the bridge, and here one passed in pre-grouping days on to the metals of the North British. The latter company was first into Berwick. Although extending only to Edinburgh at the time, the line was known as the North British from the outset, and the great company that it eventually became—the longest railway in Scotland by some 350 route mile—carried the same coat of arms throughout its existence, a garter encircling the arms of Edinburgh and Berwick. No other towns were ever included. The North British line into Berwick, the first railway to cross the Border, was opened in 1846; it was not until 4 years later that the Royal Border Bridge was opened, and the trains of the then York–Newcastle and Berwick came in from the south. The original Berwick station, owned by the North British might itself have been mistaken for an ancient monument! It was built in masonry largely recovered from the demolition of the castle, and in the Scottish baronial style, but the foundations were unsound, and in the first year of its existence it very nearly collapsed into a ruin on its own account.

From the railway point of view it was a thorough-going nuisance. The platforms were narrow, and generally cramped; the all-over roof closed in offices and waiting rooms typical of the dingiest days of railways in this country, and in the approach the track alignment was so awkward and curved that a speed restriction right down to 5 mph was in force for non-stopping trains. Complete reconstruction had been authorised by the North British Board as long ago as 1914, but on account of World War I work was deferred, and it was not until after grouping that work was started. The present spacious and attractive station was not completed until 1927. In the new lay-out it was not possible to avoid a speed restriction altogether. On the up road there is a reverse curve at the south end, involving a reduction to 30 mph. This is not serious, however, as speed can be quickly regained on the falling gradient across the Royal Border Bridge. On the down road there is no restriction, as the line is practically straight. The only hindrance to down trains is over the facing turn-out at Tweedmouth Junction. The present station consists of a single-island platform, with station buildings in the soft red sandstone of Dumfriesshire.

Once through Berwick the railway climbs high above the sea. At times the track is very near to the cliff edge, and often with a stiff wind coming in from the east the prospect of white breakers as far as the eye can see and great waves crashing against the base of the cliffs far below is something that can rarely be seen from a crack express anywhere else in this country. The famous stretch of the South Devon line between Dawlish and Teignmouth occasionally sees the waves breaking right over the trains, but above Berwick the great panorama is seen from an awe-inspiring height. While in pre-grouping days the frontier point between the North Eastern Railway and the North British Railway was at the north end of the Royal Border Bridge, Marshall Meadows box, a mile north of

Berwick, now marks the boundary point between the North Eastern and the Scottish Regions. One notices, even today, that the mileposts that have so far been on the down side of the line and reading from zero at Newcastle, are now of a new and distinctive design, fixed on the up side and reading from zero at Edinburgh Waverley. From Berwick the gradient has been continuously 1 in 190 against the engine, and at a point about 2½ miles north of Berwick the actual Border is reached. The gaily painted signs erected by the LNER in 1937 leave the traveller in no doubt as to his whereabouts, but otherwise it is a bleak, lonely spot. The A1 trunk road is carried a little higher up the hillside, where the old Lamberton Toll House is passed; but save for a few cottages the line of the Border is hereabouts almost depopulated.

Official gradient profiles show the inclination as continuous from Berwick practically to Burnmouth, but above Lamberton there is a short diversion inland from the original alignment, to keep clear of land affected by a landslip, and on this diversion the gradient eases a little, and then steepens to rejoin the old course of the railway. Nearing Burnmouth the cliff scenery becomes exceptionally fine, with a long view up the coast to the north towards the country of St Abb. The stretch of line between Lamberton Toll and Cockburnspath will however be ever memorable, not so much for its scenery, nor for the heavy demands it makes upon the locomotives of heavy trains, but from the disastrous results of the great cloudburst of 12th August 1948, when, in a length of 28 miles, the line was completely breached at seven bridges and by three large landslips, in addition to being seriously damaged at many other places. I have told in *Scottish Railways* of the havoc caused, and of the civil engineering measures taken to restore communications. Here it is worth recalling what happened to the traffic working on that incredible afternoon. In view of the suddenness of the disaster, and the widespread damage caused to the railway it is indeed little short of a miracle that there were no personal injuries, let alone any loss of life.

The down non-stop *Flying Scotsman* was already north of Alnmouth, running well on time, when news of a minor wash-out south of Berwick led to her being stopped. This news came through in time for those in authority at Newcastle to arrange for diversion of succeeding expresses via Hexham and Carlisle. At this time the idea was to work them over the Waverley route to Edinburgh. The Flying Scotsman had to be drawn back to Newcastle, and it became the fourth of a procession of expresses travelling via Carlisle. The 9.50 a.m. ex-King's Cross was leading, followed by the 10.5, and then by the Queen of Scots Pullman. But while the major effects of the cloudburst over the Lammermuir Hills were felt in the Eye Water valley, and down the Cockburnspath Bank, things were beginning to look very ugly in the glen of Gala Water by the time the 9.50 a.m. from King's Cross had reached Galashiels. This train did actually get through, but when the 10.5 a.m. got to Falahill the driver thought is prudent to stop and telephone control in Edinburgh. A senior officer who had been summoned to the Control Room told me of that phone call: the driver had said that he couldn't get any farther. A somewhat harassed control man demanded to know why, whereupon a plaintive voice came through: ' Ah weel, I'm just up to ma waist in the watter, and there's an awfu' big slip i' the bank aheed!' So the Waverley Route was also closed, and the unfortunate *Flying Scotsman,* which had by that time reached Hawick had to retrace steps to Carlisle and travel via Beattock. Edinburgh was eventually reached at 3.51 a.m. on the 13th, but even this was better than the Queen of Scots, and the 10.5, both of which had to follow the Scotsman back to Carlisle, and make their way through the night to Edinburgh over the Caledonian line.

Today as one travels over the fine inland stretch from Burnmouth to Grantshouse it does indeed seem incredible that a stream like the Eye Water could have swollen to such an extent as to cause such wholesale havoc with the massively built masonry bridges by which it was then crossed by the railway. But it was not the case of a river becoming swollen at all. The rainfall over the Lammermuirs on that amazing afternoon was as though the heavens themselves had opened, and water cascaded down the open hillsides as over a weir. In the trough of the hills, at Grantshouse the flood water rose. It was already surging down the Eye Water valley towards Reston and the sea, but this normal outlet could not take it all. The high ridge at the north end that is pierced by the Penmanshiel Tunnel forms a natural watershed between the Eye Water and the Pease Burn, but on that afternoon Nature was defying all the natural laws of geography, and the water found an alternative way to the sea through the railway tunnel. At one time, it was said the torrent was running to within a few feet of the crown of the arch! The railway has at this point commenced the descent of the Cockburnspath Bank; the gradient is 1 in 96 for more than 4 miles, and farther down, towards the sea, in what is normally a tumbled wilderness of heather and bracken, the biggest of all the landslips in this stricken district made a tremendous breach in the line.

Today, northbound expresses go spinning down the bank with scarcely a wisp of steam. With heavy trains the speed at Penmanshiel Tunnel is usually about 50 mph, and drivers then shut off steam altogether. Engine and coaches coast downhill, and by the time the sea comes into view ahead and we are skimming through Cockburnspath station the speed is nearer 80 than 75 mph. If the day is fair the prospect northwards is fascinating in the extreme. The broad waters of the Firth of Forth stretch almost as far as the eye can see; the Fife coastline, and perhaps the Lomond Hills can be seen on the farther shore, and nearer at hand directly ahead through the cab glasses lies the black, forbidding pile of the Bass Rock. At dusk, as one may see it from ' The Heart of Midlothian,' or ' The Talisman ' the firth is punctuated by flashing lighthouses. Nowhere in Britain, I should imagine, can so many lighthouses be seen in action at once.

Dunbar is a curious station. The platforms are laid in on a sharp curve, but to permit of faster running by non-stopping trains a pair of through lines have been laid avoiding the station itself. The alignment is however no more than half-hearted, if such an expression may be used for a railway track, in that the turn-outs to west and east of the station permit of no higher speed than 60 mph. The best expresses of today are often approaching Dunbar at 75 to 80 mph, and the impetus from such speed would be useful for climbing the rising gradients that follow, in whichever direction one is travelling. As it is, that reduction to 60 mph provides a niggling hindrance just where a little help would be welcome. Once through Dunbar, on a down East Coast express the Border country is left behind, and a fine speed is maintained through the level farmlands of the Lothians. The passing scene is intensely Scottish in aspect, from the massive single-storied cottages, the characteristic stone architecture to be glimpsed in little towns

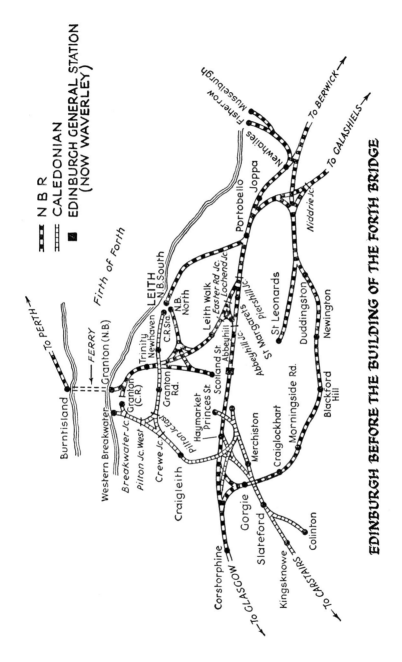

EDINBURGH BEFORE THE BUILDING OF THE FORTH BRIDGE

like East Linton, and Longniddry, while it is not long before the crags of Edinburgh begin to loom up in the picture seen ahead. Near Prestonpans the railway cuts clean across the battlefield of 1745, where the redcoats of Sir John Cope ' ran like rabets '—to quote Bonnie Prince Charlie's own spelling—before the Highland clansmen of the rebel army; and then at Monktonhall Junction we enter upon the complicated railway geography of Edinburgh. The accompanying map shows how the various lines of the North British and Caledonian cross, re-cross, and interconnect. It also shows the important position chosen for the great new marshalling yard at Millerhill, situated alongside the Waverley Route.

It is at Portobello East that the fascinating route from Carlisle joins our present track. Here, again, was another of those incredibly awkward junctions lay-outs that were a heritage from the earlier days of railways. One could perhaps understand why the Waverley Route came in on a bad alignment, but how the main line came to have a double-S, with a 15 mph speed limit might well seem incredible today. Yet so it was, for a period of many years in what might be termed the ' Middle Ages ' of railways. The governing factor, apparently, was the bridge over the Duddingston Road, just to the west of the station. The original alignment was probably straight enough, but when the extensive sidings were laid in on the north side of the line, and the station enlarged, the platforms were pushed towards the hill on the south side. This was economical enough in space, but the down main line had to snake its way round the station, and then back again to the old alignment over the Duddingston Road bridge. Even today, with a much improved alignment, one cannot go through at full speed.

The last miles into Edinburgh are full of interest, railway and otherwise. At St Margarets one passes the site of the old North British locomotive shops, dating from the days when the system extended no farther than from Edinburgh to Berwick. The present running sheds house many of the older engines stationed in the Edinburgh district, including North British ' Scotts ' and ' Glens.' Just beyond, there is a fine view of the palace of Holyroodhouse. Just beyond comes Abbeyhill Junction, now controlled electrically from the big power interlocking at Waverley. At one time Abbeyhill was much more than the junction for Leith, for as the map on page 69 shows this line also serves Granton, at one time the southern end of the ferry to Burntisland by which communication between Edinburgh and the Fife towns was maintained. With the line quadruple now we run through one or other of the twin Calton tunnels and emerge in the Waverley approaches beneath those battlements that have misled hundreds upon hundreds of tourists on their first arrival in Edinburgh. One can heartily sympathise with the enthusiastic Cockney visitor who exclaimed : ' That is the fimous castle of Edinburgh,' for alas, he and his companion were gazing up at the Calton gaol. Nowadays, the Scottish Government Offices have replaced the old gaol, but the battlements are still there! The Castle lies nearly a mile to the west, well beyond Waverley station, and perched so high and sheer above the railway that it can scarcely be glimpsed from the train.

But whether coming from Carlisle or from Newcastle, Waverley is the goal of our journey through the Border country. It is one of the few large stations in Great Britain the fascination of which seems undiminished with the years. The days of the great East Coast ' Atlantics ' are long past, it is true, but much of the old spirit is still manifested in the smart turn-out and splendid performance of the modern Haymarket ' Pacifics.' And now the scene is enlivened by the coming and going of diesel trains. As always in history, Waverley stands for the latest and best in British railroading.

26 Contrasts in freight motive power at Monktonhall Junction: in July 1962, after the diesels had begun to take over, an 'A4' No. 60002 *Sir Murrough Wilson*, hauling a northbound train.

27 Contrasts continued: a tough old North British 'Reid' superheater 0-6-0 (LNER Class J37) No. 64577 on train of southbound coal empties at Monktonhall Junction, in August 1958.

28 Nearing the Border: Kings Cross-Edinburgh express crossing the Royal Border Bridge, Berwick-on-Tweed in July 1966, hauled by 'Deltic' No. D9018 *Ballymoss*

29 Climbing to the summit of the line between Berwick and Edinburgh: in May 1964, a 'V2' 2-6-2 No. 60976 nearing Grantshouse with a heavy northbound freight.

CHAPTER 8

East Coast Express Running

HISTORICALLY, the Newcastle–Edinburgh section of the East Coast Route could not have been regarded as one of the railway racing grounds of this country until about the year 1935. It is true there had been one or two very brilliant flashes in the pan, as in the concluding stages of the 1888 race to Edinburgh, and especially in the early hours of 22nd August 1895; but for the most part the North Eastern was content to jog along with overall average speeds of 50 to 52 mph. Until the water troughs were put in at Lucker there was ample reason for leisurely running. For a time the non-stop run of 124·4 miles was the longest in the world, and the benefits to night passengers in undisturbed comfort were evidently considered to outweigh any prestige that might have accrued from faster start-to-stop averages over shorter distances. At the modest speed of 43 mph booked in the late 'eighties' of last century the little Tennant 2–4–0s did their work economically and well.

Except for a stormy interlude in 1897 this route was always a stronghold of the North Eastern Railway so far as express passenger motive power was concerned. At more than one period in history it was evident that the North British men would have liked nothing more than to show their Geordie colleagues a thing or two. But the opportunity did not come until after grouping; then it was highly amusing to see the way in which the Scottish drivers treated existing train schedules with utter derision. For a time North British 'Atlantics' were working to Newcastle on what is now the up 'Aberdonian,' and night after night they were running through Berwick between 5 and 10 min. early. Integration of the former North Eastern and North British running staffs in Edinburgh was a natural outcome of grouping, though apart from use of the Gresley 'Pacifics' the only pre-grouping engines in regular through passenger service were North Eastern. Occasionally a 'D49' 4–4–0 might work down to Newcastle on a duplicate portion of one of the regular trains, but I have never heard of North British 'Atlantics' from Haymarket being used turn and turn about with their North Eastern counterparts. It was with the introduction of the *Coronation* express in 1937 that really fast running began over this route, and today, such are the habits that have been gradually engendered, any run is as likely to produce speeds of 80 mph or more, whether the train be one of the lightly loaded ' flyers,' or a 500-ton night sleeper.

I was never made more conscious of the change in tempo over the Newcastle–Edinburgh route than on my first run that way after World War II. In common with many others I did very little travelling during the war years, and practically none over the East Coast Route. Then, in the summer of 1945, I had the privilege of a footplate pass for the down *Flying Scotsman*. I joined the train at York, and was not surprised when the load was given to us as ' seventeen—551 tons '; there were no dining cars included in the rake, and those 17 vehicles were packed, compartments, corridors, and brake vans alike. I estimated the gross trailing load as 610 tons at least, probably a good deal more! With a famous ' A4 ' on, the *Golden Eagle*—then No. 4482—we made a magnificent start out of York; but the engine was not steaming well, and from Thirsk onwards we were scraping our way along, often with no more than 150 lb. per sq. in. in the boiler. We did however succeed in winning back 6 min. on the leisurely wartime schedule of 100 min. from York to Newcastle, and this was fully equal to what the North Eastern engines were required to do on the same train in days before World War I. But it is, rather, with the work over the northern division that I am concerned.

At Newcastle we exchanged 4482 for 4483, *Kingfisher,* and the latter engine was in first-class nick. She was so good, and she was driven with such vigour that it is only now, many years after the event, that I can reveal the full extent of what happened! During the later years of the war the LNER was more handicapped than any other of the British railways so far as speed was concerned, by the retention of an overall speed limit of 60 mph. On the other lines this had been generally relaxed to 75 mph, but not so on the LNER. Now, with a load of 610 tons, wartime standards of engine maintenance, and on a most unpropitious afternoon of drizzling rain one might not have expected much more than 60 mph anyway, except perhaps down the Cockburnspath Bank. I certainly did not expect any speeds that I should be asked not to reveal, still less to have that request repeated five years after the run! But from the very start we were going extraordinarily well, so well that on rounding the curve at Morpeth I looked back to make a careful count of the coaches to make sure none had been left behind at Newcastle. We still had 17 on, and towards the coast we were making the usual 60–65 mph pace that one expected in pre-war days on trains like the winter *Flying Scotsman*. But then came a bad relaying slack at Alnmouth—right at the foot of the Longhough-ton bank. The weather, which had been lowering all the way up from the south, was now turning to drizzle, and in trying to regain speed on the 1 in 170 rising gradient *Kingfisher* just could not get a grip on the rails. The driver kept the cut-off at 30 per cent, but every time he opened the regulator a little wider away she went in a thunderous slip. There was nothing for it, but to chug our way patiently up the bank at 25 to 27 mph. Once over the top, however, with the gear linked up to 18 per cent *Kingfisher* was soon into her stride; we swept down Christon Bank, over the level to Lucker troughs, and down to the sea at Beal with speed finally reaching 84 mph. Actually we held 80 mph over the ensuing level to Goswick, and despite a signal check right at the finish covered the 66·9 miles from Newcastle to Berwick in $82\frac{1}{4}$ min. start to stop.

The net time was no more than 75 min., but Authority was ' shocked ' at that 84 mph, at least as far as official utterances were concerned; but privately, to me, they rejoiced that the ' A4s ' could still show their paces after six years of war, and even though they had long since lost their beautiful Garter Blue livery. *Kingfisher,* despite her wartime black and such austerity that even the initials on the tender were then abbreviated to ' NE '(!) showed in parts of the cab interior traces of two earlier liveries. She was one of the batch beginning with *Golden Eagle* that came out in the standard LNER apple-green lined and lettered like the non-streamlined ' Pacifics.' Later when the inconvenience of keeping silver engines for the Jubilee and blue engines for the Coronation became apparent the whole stud of ' A4s ' were painted in blue. Some of the ' A4s ' were to have *four* more liveries, following the wartime black: Garter blue once more, with their post-war LNER numbers; the experimental British Railways Prussian blue; standard ' BR ' blue, and finally Great Western green.

Since that first post-war journey from Newcastle to Edinburgh I have enjoyed many runs over this route, and quite a number of these have been on the footplate. From this collection I have picked four, which are tabulated on page 81. Also, as a tribute to the engines that bore the brunt of the work for so long I have included in the table a run with an ex-NER 3-cylinder 'Atlantic,' which included some good work with a relatively heavy train. In the hey-day of the North Eastern engines on this route the express now known as the North Briton left Newcastle at about 11.15 a.m.— the actual minutes past the hour varied with the years; at its quickest it was allowed 138 min. for the 124·4 miles to Waverley, and the load was about 220 tons gross. The *Flying Scotsman* was slower, and again, while the actual minutes varied slightly, the over-all time allowed was always around 150 min., with a load of about 330 to 350 tons. The run of No. 733 in column 1 of the table on page 81 was made in 1934, when 'Atlantics' had practically disappeared from regular work on the East Coast expresses. The train was a summer Saturday relief that used to start from York immediately after the passage of the non-stop Flying Scotsman, and then run ahead of the so-called Junior Scotsman throughout to Glasgow (Queen Street). No. 733 made a very typical run. The 'Zs' were never at their best in starting, but once fairly on the move they usually ran very freely. From Morpeth the going was excellent, and we might have done even better but for the rather unnecessarily severe slack at Alnmouth, which handicapped the engine in climbing the Longhoughton bank. But then we had a fine burst of speed, with maximum speeds of $71\frac{1}{2}$ mph down Christon Bank, and $76\frac{1}{2}$ at Beal.

The 'Zs' sometimes produced considerably harder running than this in the preceding summer. In that year, during the period when the non-stop 'Scotsman' was running, an 'Atlantic' was regularly used for the 1.20 p.m. from King's Cross north of New-castle, and in attempting to keep the sharp allowance of 36 min., start to stop, for the 32·1 miles from Alnmouth to Berwick the average speeds made by the 'Zs' usually lay between 65 and 67 mph over the 22·7 miles from Christon Bank to Tweedmouth Junction. The load was usually about 340 tons, gross, behind the tender. On that same train, however, by far the finest work I have ever noted was not by a 'Z,' nor yet by a 'Pacific,' but by a 'D49'

4–4–0, No. 249 *Aberdeenshire,* with a load of no less than 435 tons, when the run from Alnmouth to Berwick was made in 36 min. 22 sec. start to stop. I have told the story of that run before,* so must not dwell upon it here, but a partial explanation of the phenomenal work performed is that the driver was none other than the fabulous ' Toram Beg '—in other words Norman McKillop. That run was made long before his name became a household word among locomotive enthusiasts both as engineman, and author. It was made in 1936 while he was still a ' spare ' link man, and as I had to hurry away on arrival in Edinburgh I did not even learn his name until several days later, in correspondence with the Locomotive Running Superintendent. When, many years later, I came to know ' Toram ' well there was an amusing sidelight on this run. At the time I had asked the superintendent if he could supply any details as to how the engine had been worked to achieve such results, and I received a slightly cynical reply to the effect that one could hardly expect a driver to remember how he had worked his engine on a run made a fortnight ago. Fair enough, thought I, and dismissed it from mind. But twenty years later, on one of the occasions I came to enjoy with ' Toram,' he came out, quite casually, with the fullest details. The run was evidently as much a memory in his own footplate career as it is a ' five-star ' entry in my own records!

Reverting now, to the table on page 81, the four runs with ' Pacifics ' are all fairly recent. Nos. 2 and 3 were made on the North Briton, No. 4 on the Heart of Midlothian, and No. 5 on the Flying Scotsman. No. 2 was during one of the coal-shortage periods of post-war years, when temporary curtailment of service led to some alterations in engine workings. On the North Briton engines are normally changed at Newcastle, and the Neville Hill ' A3 ' that has brought the train from Leeds comes off, preparatory to working back with the up Queen of Scots Pullman. At that time the Pullman was one of the trains cut, and so the Leeds engine worked through to Edinburgh, though remanned at Newcastle. The Neville Hill men reported all in good order on their arrival, and on taking over, Driver Magee and Fireman Regan of Gateshead made an excellent run. There was nothing special about it, just good steady work all the way with time being gradually got in hand for

* In *The Locomotives of Sir Nigel Gresley*

the checks that we expected beyond Inveresk. The schedule for this train was then 140 min. so that the crew had ample in reserve by the time Drem was passed. I was on the footplate on this trip, and a very comfortable and uneventful trip it was. Of course a load of 385 tons should not trouble a locomotive of the size and power of an ' A3 ' on a schedule demanding an average speed of no more than 53·2 mph; but the conditions are not always so favourable as this. The very next run in the table, on the same train, was in astonishing contrast.

The date was December 1952, and for several days there had been hard frost in the north-east of England. With brilliantly clear, still nights the fog had come up from the Ouse, and on this particular morning the running of the North Briton was delayed on both sides of York. It was one of the oddest rides I ever remember on the footplate, and we drove northward into an eerie, white world, of mist limiting visibility to less than half a mile, and of hoar frost so intense on the sleepers and in the fields as to make it seem as if they were snow covered. That morning we thanked the powers that be for colour-light signals, for they showed up so well through that white mist that Driver Summersgill was able to take our fine ' A3 '—No. 60074 *Harvester*—along at 70 mph north of Alne. And as we went north the mist gradually dispersed, the weather became less severe, until on nearing Tyneside it had changed to a raw and cloudy winter's day with no sign of the frost remaining. As we ran over the King Edward Bridge we could see, on the High Level Bridge, that our fresh engine was an ' A4 '—*Golden Eagle* once more, as it turned out, but now decked in BR standard blue, and bearing her new number 60023. G. Garthwaite of Gateshead was the driver, with Fireman Regan again, while my good friend Inspector Bob Steadman, of Newcastle, came with us on the footplate.

Golden Eagle backed on to the train with only 200 lb. per sq. in. showing on the clock; I did not take too much notice of this because the Gresley boilers can come up so quickly, and many enginemen deliberately keep pressure down a little to avoid blowing off in the larger passenger stations. But that ' 200 ' on *Golden Eagle* was, this time, not by any means from choice. She proved shy for steam the whole way to Edinburgh, indeed for only 30 min. out of the 132 that we were on the run was the boiler pressure showing more than 180 lb. per sq. in. And yet, following a leisurely start, we made a very fast run. Out to Forest Hall the engine was inclined to slip, and with pressure down to 175 lb. per sq. in. as early as this the driver tried nursing the engine, and shut off steam entirely after passing the summit point near Cramlington. This was not an auspicious start, but after passing Morpeth the driver lengthened his cut-off to compensate for the lower boiler pressure, and with the relatively late admission of 22 per cent—for an 'A4'—Regan managed to keep the pressure around the 180 mark. Then came the two permanent-way checks: a slight one over the Coquet viaduct, north of Acklington, and a further one to 30 mph just by Longhoughton station. By this time the crew had fairly taken the measure of this somewhat temperamental engine, and from now onwards she was made to 'fly' in something resembling the true 'A4' style. It was none too early either, for we had dropped 3 min. on this fast booking to Alnmouth, and another minute went against us to Belford, due, of course, to the Longhoughton check.

Down Christon Bank we went, with regulator full open and cut-off 20 per cent: seventy-eight mph past Fallodon; regulator shut for Lucker troughs, with a drop to 66 mph, then full open again for the fast stretch down to the sea at Beal. The boiler pressure was only 175 mph per sq. in., but we touched 81 mph and cleared the rise on to the bleak Scremerston cliffs at 60. Taking full advantage of the present fine alignment through Berwick we were able to *average* 54·5 mph from Tweedmouth Junction to Marshall Meadows, and to help rally the boiler a bit, where we needed it most, the injector was shut off for about 2 min. This brought pressure up to just 200 lb. per sq. in., which, with 27 per cent cut-off enabled us to clear Burnmouth at 47½ mph. This relatively long cut-off was continued through the Ayton dip, and gave us a good start to the long rise to Grantshouse. The hard work seemed to rally the boiler a little, and pressure rose slightly from 185 at Reston to 190 at the summit. The Cockburnspath Bank can usually be descended without steam at all, and so it was this time; 'Old Man Gravity' must claim the honours for the 81 mph maxima at this point. After Dunbar, where we were practically back to schedule time, Driver Garthwaite threw in all he had, and with 27 per cent cut-off, and most of the regulator we tore through the Lothians in grand style, making an average speed of 71·2 mph from East Linton to Inveresk.

100

The concluding checks were severe, including a dead stop at Piershill Junction, but despite that very shaky start we pulled off a net time of 124 min. for the 124·4 mile run.

The next run was an even greater contrast than between the two journeys on the *North Briton*. It was a sweltering afternoon, and already having footplated up from Peterborough I was not feeling my freshest when I transferred from the ' A2 ' *Owen Tudor*, to the *Empire of India* at Newcastle. Driver Kennedy of Haymarket shed was in charge, and we got away in fairly sensational style. This engine was game for anything, and a maximum of 79 mph *before Morpeth* sounded the keynote of a most exhilarating trip. As on many very fast runs however, extreme caution was shown at the various definite service slacks, and in recovering from the slowing through Morpeth it will be seen we took a minute longer to Pegswood than *Golden Eagle*, the crew of which were of course out to save every second they could during that critical early stage. With *Empire of India* we reached a full 80 mph at the Coquet Viaduct, and Alnmouth was taken rather faster than usual, though in perfect comfort on a somewhat lively riding engine. Down Christon Bank we were doing $83\frac{1}{2}$ mph when adverse signals brought us practically to a stand at Chathill. I fancy the level crossing a mile ahead, at Newham, must have been in use, for we passed nothing else that might have caused an obstruction. ' Eighty ' number three came at Beal, and then, as usual, this driver eased cautiously down for the passage through Berwick.

In recovering, up the continuous 1 in 190, on that fascinating wild stretch overlooking the sea, the engine was not pressed. There was really no point in trying to work up a fierce acceleration, for a very severe slack was in store for us near Ayton. The bridge that carries the line over the ' A1 ' highway was then in course of repair, and a slack right down to 5 mph was in force. But once over that bridge the driver opened out with great gusto. In the short distance from Ayton to the foot of the dip by milepost $48\frac{1}{4}$ we swept up to $58\frac{1}{2}$ mph; a cut-off of 25 per cent was holding this speed on the 1 in 200 rise that follows, but then, at Reston Junction Driver Kennedy advanced from 25 to 30 per cent. On the continuous 1 in 200 climb speed began to rise, and round the succession of curves, over the new bridges built after the 1948 disaster, the *Empire of India* reached 63 mph; several quarter miles indeed were covered at 64, and we topped the summit and entered Penmanshiel Tunnel at 67. As usual the regulator was shut altogether for the descent of Cockburnspath Bank, and as usual speed rose to the region of 80 mph at the foot of the 1 in 96 gradient. From Dunbar onwards however, the speeds run were not so high as on the previous journey, but by this time we were getting comfortably ahead of time. The permanent-way slack near Inveresk was very severe on this trip, right down to 5 mph, but with plenty of time in hand the arrival in Edinburgh was 3 min. early.

Although both this trip and that with *Golden Eagle* on the *North Briton* showed an identical net time there were some considerable differences between the work of the two engines. If one takes an aggregate of the best times made by both engines, the total to Inveresk works out at no more than 110 min. 24 sec. for the 117·9 miles from Newcastle, and an average speed of 66·8 mph over the intervening 110·2 miles from Annitsford. It is astonishing to realise that the aggregate best times of these two runs alone total up to no more than $3\frac{1}{2}$ min. longer at Inveresk than that of the North Eastern 4–4–0 No. 1620, on the last night of the Race to Aberdeen in 1895. She took 107 min., but while it would not take a good 'A4' much to equal that time with the regular load of the *North Briton*, I fancy we are not ever likely to see a repetition of 1620's finishing time from Inveresk into Waverley, when she took 6 min. for the concluding $6\frac{1}{2}$ miles. What with the Newhailes pitfall slack, proper caution at Portobello, and signal checks outside Waverley, the fastest time in my table is 11 min. 12 sec.

The last run was one that I enjoyed as a passenger on the down *Flying Scotsman*, with what used to be the normal winter load, and a 'spare' engine. We began so slowly that I wondered if they were in trouble on the footplate; *Brown Jack* was taken labouring up Benton Bank at only a little over 30 mph, and the speeds over the easier stretch to Cramlington, and down to Morpeth were also much below the usual. But once through Morpeth the going was first class, and the average speed over the ensuing 101·3 miles to Inveresk was $58\frac{1}{2}$ mph. The engine was not unduly pressed uphill, as witness the minimum speeds of 43 mph at Little Mill, and 41 at Grantshouse; neither were the downhill maxima very high. It was a good steady average run, with an arrival in Edinburgh comfortably in advance of schedule.

102

	Run No	1			2			3			4			5		
	Engine No	733			60036			60023			60011			60043		
	Engine Name				*Colombo*			*Golden Eagle*			*Empire of India*			*Brown Jack*		
	Engine Class	NER 'Z' 4-4-2			'A3'			'A4'			'A4'			'A3'		
	Load tons E/F	320/350			363/385			347/365			342/370			463/500		
Mls		m	s	mph	m	s	mph	m	s	mph	m	s	mph	m	s	mph
0·0	NEWCASTLE	0	00		0	00		0	00		0	00		0	00	
1·7	Heaton	4	47		4	02		4	51		3	45		4	50	
5·0	Forest Hall	10	15	38½	8	20	48	9	58	43	8	14	46	10	56	30½
7·7	Annitsford	13	49	53	11	18	61½	13	10	60	11	11	64½	14	57	47
9·9	Cramlington	16	28	47½	13	29	60	15	30	56	13	19	61½	17	59	42
13·9	Stannington	20	32	68	17	13	68½	19	30	64	16	45	79	22	35	60½
16·6	MORPETH	23	20		20	07		22	43		19	37		25	52	
18·5	Pegswood	26	02	47½	22	37		24	50	69	22	52		28	17	54½
23·2	Widdrington	31	00		27	18	60	29	14	64½	27	33	64½	32	49	60
28·5	Acklington	36	17	67	32	20	69	34	04	69	32	05	80	37	52	69
								p w s								
31·9	Warkworth	39	31	60/65	35	37		37	46		34	47	76	40	54	67
					sigs		30									
34·8	ALNMOUTH	42	20	54*	39	47	60	40	48	60	37	12	71*	43	35	64½
39·4	Little Mill	48	16	41	45	03	50	47	03	40	41	28	60	48	57	43
											sigs		83½			
46·0	Chathill	55	08	71½	51	07	74	53	11	78	47	45	5	55	38	70½
49·2	Lucker	58	04	65	53	59	67	55	50	74	53	26	57	58	44	62½
51·6	BELFORD	60	18	63½	56	11	64½	57	56	67	56	10	easy	61	08	58½
58·6	Beal	66	17	76½	62	09	74	63	35	81	62	12	82	67	21	73
63·5	Scremerston	70	54	50	66	37	58½	67	48	60	66	05	66	72	05	49½
65·7	Tweedmouth Jc	73	31	55	68	55	63½	69	59		68	04	69½	74	37	58
66·9	BERWICK	75	35		70	27		71	18		69	37	40	75	54	54
68·0	*Marshall Meadows Box*	4	12		72	10	44	72	31	52	71	03	43	77	03	50
72·5	Burnmouth	13	20	32	78	00	44	78	06	47½	77	03	45	83	34	38
											p w s		5			
75·9	*Milepost 48½*	17	33	58			65	81	18	70½	84	24	58½	87	26	60
78·1	RESTON JC	20	00	50	83	38	58½	83	17	65½	86	40	58½	89	58	51
83·2	Grantshouse	26	59	40	89	27	47½	88	18	58	91	36	63½	96	52	41
87·9	Cockburnspath	32	02	77½	94	12	73	92	35	81	95	41	81	101	56	79
95·2	DUNBAR	38	30	66	101	12	56	97	42	64	102	28	65	108	04	
100·9	East Linton	44	19	53	107	00	58	103	52		107	52		113	20	60
106·6	DREM JC	50	10	62	112	08	70½	108	34	79	112	48	74	118	38	67
111·2	Longniddry Jc	55	13	53/60	116	24	64½	112	25	69	117	10	62/64	123	16	57/64½
114·9	Prestonpans	59	02	57	119	43		115	36	75/71	120	39	66	126	51	64
117·9	Inveresk	62	03	62	122	17	75	118	14	72	123	32	67½	129	40	66
		sigs			sigs p w		15	p w s			p w s		5	p w s		
121·4	Portobello	67	25		129	24		123	00		133	35		134	56	
								sig. stop								
124·4	Waverley	73	15		135	20		131	58		138	45		141	40	
	Net time	75½ + 70			130			124			124			142		

* Max. attained speed after junction

The interesting tests carried out between different designs of
'Atlantic' locomotives in 1923 attracted very little attention at the
time. There was no more than a brief reference to the running of
the North British competitor, engine No. 878 *Hazeldean,* and
although the Great Northern Atlantic No. 1447 was photographed
in her modified condition, with cut-down boiler mountings, it was
not until a few years ago that any of the overall results, so far as
coal and water consumption, and general performance, were published. But the bald details of such tests, important as they are to
the responsible locomotive authorities, can convey little of the
'atmosphere' of such runs; and an atmosphere there certainly was
when Tom Henderson and his Atlantic *Hazeldean* were on the job.
On one particular night, for example, the official record would
read: 'Newcastle arrive 1½ min. early; load 327 tons (tare); number
of checks " one "; conditional stop at Dunbar made.' It would not
tell that the train was within measurable distance of ' even time '
before Dunbar, and that from the restart Alnmouth Junction had
been passed nearly 5 min. early!

Fortunately there is at least one log, compiled in some detail, of
the running of *Hazeldean* in those trials, published some 35 years
ago in *The Railway Magazine* by Mr Cecil J. Allen. The times are
tabulated herewith, and I have added the average speeds in a second
column. To pinpoint more vividly the outstanding features of a
very splendid run, I have tabulated alongside the details of a journey
of my own made in 1952, on the up *Flying Scotsman,* when I was
privileged to ride on the footplate. It is not that this latter run is
a very fast or a spectacular one. At that time the 10 a.m. up from
Waverley was allowed the leisurely time of 150 min. non-stop for
the 124·4 miles to Newcastle. But in all my footplate experience
I have rarely seen a locomotive handled with more precision and
care, both from the driver's and fireman's point of view. Furthermore the technique used by the driver was so diametrically opposite
to the details given in the official report of the North British
'Atlantic' trials of 1923 as to make reading that is almost amusing.
I should add that during the 1923 trials it would appear that the
engines concerned were stationed at Gateshead, since the outward
trips (according to the official reports) were made on the down
Flying Scotsman, and the return trips were made on the 10.50 p.m.
up sleeper. This was a normal Gateshead working. In the table

104

is included a third run, made by the same Newcastle driver, on the up *North Briton*, which by reason of its load corresponds quite closely to the 10.50 p.m. of 1923.

At the time of grouping the colliery subsidence that has compelled the imposition of a heavy slack for so many years between Newhailes and Inveresk had not developed, and with full speed from Portobello the North British ' Atlantic ' was able to make a fast and unhindered start; she drew clean away from the other two engines and $3\frac{1}{2}$ min. ahead of No. 60142 on the *Flying Scotsman* by Drem. More remarkable too was the fact of her drawing still farther ahead prior to the conditional stop at Dunbar. It was only natural that the ' A1 ' Pacific *Redgauntlet* should get away from Dunbar much more rapidly, and her minimum speed of 43 mph up the Cockburnspath Bank put *Hazeldean* completely in the shade by comparison. But the Atlantic was keeping her point-to-point times here, and south of Berwick she drew well ahead, so more could not be expected. The ' A1 ' engines 60137 and 60142 were both handled by a driver who was a consummate artist—W. Hogarth of Gateshead; on run No. 2, with the *North Briton*, which Mr Nelson recorded from the footplate, he was varying the cut-off between 13 and 18 per cent—1 per cent at a time—between Inveresk and Beltonford, and on the Cockburnspath Bank he went up to a maximum of 29 per cent, all with a fully opened regulator. South of Berwick he used between 13 and 20 per cent, until the signal stop at Widdrington.

Of my own run, with engine No. 60142, the point that remains most vividly in my memory is of the wonderfully stable and balanced conditions of working that Driver Hogarth and Fireman Higginbotham succeeding in establishing. The fireman set his injector adjustments so that boiler pressure was kept very even, and just below blowing-off point. The ' A1 's steam very freely, so freely that if a fireman indulges in tactics that are the least bit ' slap-happy,' there is much blowing off and tremendous waste of steam and water. Again, as with engine No. 60137, the driver was using cut-offs as short as 13 per cent, and No. 60142 gave an immaculate performance. It was a time when the Controlled Road System of testing was being perfected at Swindon, and I had made a number of trips in the Western Region dynamometer car, on journeys where an absolutely constant rate of evaporation had been achieved. But here, on No. 60142, amid all the incidents and hindrances of a service run, Driver Hogarth and Fireman Higginbotham were running as near as possible to a constant rate and securing most economical fuel consumption in consequence.

The working of the North British ' Atlantic ' so far as cut-offs were concerned, could not have been more different. Those engines had lever reversers, and the adjustment possible between one notch and the next was very coarse. Successive steps gave cut-offs from the full gear position of 74 per cent, of 67, 60, 52, 44 and 34. All intermediate adjustments had to be made on the regulator. Most drivers with whom I rode on the Aberdeen line preferred the notch giving 44 per cent, but on the 1923 trials between Edinburgh and Newcastle *Hazeldean* was driven at 52 per cent throughout. This apparently had no appreciable effect on the economy, for the North British engine proved the most economical of the three ' Atlantics ' taking part. The results on the service trains were :

Railway Engine No.	GNR 1447	NER 733	NBR 878
Average load tons tare	307	311	345
Average speed mph	49·3	49·0	48·8
Average d.h.p.	393	391	529
Coal per d.h.p. hr./lb.	5·08	4·45	4·12

The North British engine thus showed the best results of all, though on a further trial with a heavier train of 406 tons the North Eastern engine did considerably better, and brought her basic consumption down to less than 4 lb. of coal per dhp hour. *Hazeldean's* figures were virtually unchanged.

Mls	(ex Edinburgh)	1923 · 10.50 p m · No 878 · *Hazeldean* · 327/345 Sch	m s	mph †	1953 · 5.14 p m · 60137 · *Redgauntlet* · 343/360 Sch	m s	mph ‡	1952 · 10 a m · 60142 · *Edward Fletcher* · 416/440 Sch	m s	mph ‡
0·0	WAVERLEY	0	0 00		0	0 00		0	0 00	
3·0	Portobello	6	4 55		5½	p w s 6 58		6	5 53	53
6·5	Inveresk	11	8 30	58·3		p w s 12 16	51		p w s 11 12	60
13·2	Longniddry	19	15 05	61·0		19 32	63½/56½		18 40	69
17·8	DREM JC		19 35	61·4	21½	24 05	72	23½	23 14	60
23·4	East Linton		24 50	64·0		29 17	62		28 29	66
27·0	*Beltonford Box*		28 05	66·5		32 26	74½		32 00	60
29·2	DUNBAR	36	31 30		33	35 24		34	34 03	
0·0	*Oxwellmains Box*		0 00		0	0 00			36 21	55½
2·1	Cockburnspath		5 15	45·5	2	4 46	43½		41 43	64
7·3	Grantshouse	22	11 35	30·5		9 41	68		49 33	27½
12·1	RESTON JC	28	21 00	52·3	16½	15 41	43	50½	55 37	58
17·1			26 45		21	20 32	69½/62½	55½		5
22·8	Burnmouth	40	32 15	62·2		25 38	68		p w s 64 22	
28·3	BERWICK	0	39 00	47·8	33 / 0	31 46		73 / 0	71 45	58
0·0	Tweedmouth		0 00*			0 00			0 00*	
1·2			2 25			2 44			2 03	
								sigs		
8·3	Beal	18	9 45	58·2	16	9 36	74	16	11 07	25
15·3	Belford		17 10	56·6		16 07	58		18 42	53
20·9	Chathill		23 05	56·8		21 29	68½		24 10	66
27·5	*Little Mill*		30 30	53·4		27 46	58		31 14	47
32·1	ALNMOUTH JC	39	35 10	59·3	32	31 54	70/62	33	35 47	63
38·4	Acklington		42 10	54·0		38 02	66		42 12	55/64
43·7	Widdrington		p w s 48 05	eased		sigs 45 03			47 20	eased
50·3	MORPETH	61	57 10		52	49 47		52	53 55	
55·4	Plessey		64 00			59 29	60½		60 44	
61·0	Killingworth		69 40			65 33	70		66 40	
64·4	*Benton Bank Box*		75 30			70 38			70 12	
66·9	NEWCASTLE	83	82 10		75	sigs 73 39 / 80 41		77	sigs 78 13	

* Times from passing Berwick at 20 mph   Times from dead start at Berwick   * Times from passing Berwick at 20 mph

† Average speeds from point to point   ‡ Max. and min. speeds at or near points shown

30 Edinburgh Waverley: in murky weather, for May 1966, The 'A4' Preservation Special leaves Edinburgh for York hauled by 'A4' 4-6-2 No. 60024 *Kingfisher*.

31 A different kind of excursion, in May 1970: the Branch Line Society train at Prestonpans, hauled by a Class 20 diesel No. 8102. The last coach is an ex-Caledonian, preserved.

32 A memorable occasion at Waverley: No. 4472 *Flying Scotsman* leaves on 4 May 1968 on the return non-stop run to Kings Cross celebrating the 40th anniversary of the non-stop 'Scotsman' inaugurated in 1928.

33 Monktonhall Junction in July 1962: a special from Saltburn to Glasgow, hauled by Peppercorn type 'A1' Pacific No. 60116 *Hal o' the Wynd*.

CHAPTER 9

THE SETTLE AND CARLISLE

IT is one of the ironies of our social evolution that through the twists and turns of national and international politics some of the greatest and noblest of man's enterprises are whittled down, if not to the point of redundancy then certainly to the role of playing a very secondary fiddle. Among railway works of this country there is no more poignant case than that of the Midland main line to Scotland. It is however, with no sentiments of nostalgia, or of sighing over past glories that I come to the Settle and Carlisle; for, make no mistake, it is one of the giants of our railway system in this country. Gigantic in its conception, gigantic in the task it set to the men who built it, the Settle and Carlisle is worthy of the tremendous northern countryside through which it runs. That its present owners are not using it to the fullest advantage is, we hope, no more than a brief passing phase. There is no need to cry Ichabod! As this book is so very much a chronicle of personal impressions and experiences, both of Eric Treacy's and my own, I can tell here how it was I came to know the southern end of the line so well.

The whole process of railway evolution has in many instances one could record been halted, reversed, or abruptly ended by amalgamations, grouping, or other processes by which individual concerns passed rapidly into oblivion. In the pages of railway history one finds faithfully entered up how this or that school of locomotive design came to an end; how old liveries were abolished, or how the larger partners in an amalgamation imposed their standard equipment upon the smaller. Little, however, has ever been written about the men affected by such changes. The careers of the higher executives are of course well known, but beneath that level many men experienced a sudden sweeping away of things to which their loyalties had been firmly attached, the need for moving house and home, and a general air of complete upheaval. It was so in my father's case, though not an amalgamation of railways, but of two banking houses. The year was 1916, and due to the presence in the town of a large and well-established branch of the larger partner in the amalgamation his position there became redundant. Although I was no more than a junior schoolboy at the time I can remember it all so well. How anxiously we awaited news on the day Father was summoned to London to hear of his transfer! How anxiously my mother tore open the telegram when it arrived, and how blank she looked at reading the words ' Barrow-in-Furness '! There was a dash for the school atlas, for none of us were quite sure where it was. For all we knew we might well be bound for a foreign country.

One of the incidentals of this family upheaval was of course that a new school had to be found for your humble servant, and when the choice fell upon Giggleswick the apprehensions that a boy of my age felt at changing his loyalties and associations were tempered by the thought of new railways to travel, and the anticipation of seeing ' in the flesh ' locomotives and trains hitherto known to me only in the pages of *The Railway Magazine*. Three years earlier I had become intensely aware of the Settle and Carlisle line. I was on holiday with my parents, at Weymouth, when news came of the tragic collision of two night expresses at Aisgill. Artist correspondents of the newspapers of the day fairly let themselves go in giving lurid impressions of the burning train, with engine No. 446 standing like some black and evil monster in the midst of the conflagration. Descriptions of the lonely moorland countryside where it all happened had impressed themselves upon my boyish imagination, so much so that I had not been very long at Giggleswick before I mentioned the accident to my housemaster when a crowd of us boys were on a long country walk; at the time I remember how amazed I was that he scarcely remembered Aisgill at all, let alone what happened there. He was not to know that on my ' one track ' mind of those days Aisgill had made a far deeper impression than the sinking of the *Titanic*!

The southern end of the Settle and Carlisle line is set in a magnificent countryside. The broad, smiling valley of the Ribble coming up from the Lancashire border is bounded by gentle rolling hills; the white, dry-point, stone walls tell sure enough that we are in a limestone country, but even after the road and railway has passed Hellifield there is not yet a hint of the great change to follow in a few miles. To see it at its finest and most revealing the region of Giggleswick and Settle must be viewed from the hills to south and west of the Ribble. From such a stance, the track of the Little North Western, heading for Wennington, Carnforth, and Lancaster can be seen crossing the level green basin set in front of the limestone ridge of the Giggleswick Scars, and the heights welling up behind Settle. Ribblesdale from being a green, open valley can be seen changing quite abruptly to a mountain glen, and up that glen, with its hint of much higher and wilder country to the north, was carried the Midland main line to Scotland. The point of divergence from the Little North Western—Settle Junction—is $3\frac{1}{4}$ miles from Hellifield; on this stretch trains are coming down from the watershed between the Aire and Ribble valleys, and the brisk start from Hellifield, with speed rising to well over 60 mph in this short distance is a deceptive start to a gruelling piece of railway.

To appreciate the significance of the very heavy engineering works on the line its origin must be recalled. In mid-Victorian days the enterprise of the Midland management knew no bounds. At one time it seemed that the policy of Derby was to watch local railway development, waiting for opportune moments to absorb small concerns that would enlarge its own system without involving the expense of direct capital expenditure on new works. By such means they obtained access to Swansea, and in much later times to Southend, and at one time it seemed as though the Midland route to Scotland might be via the Little North Western, which had duly been absorbed, Ingleton, Low Gill, and running powers over the London and North Western from Low Gill to Carlisle. But by the ' sixties ' of last century the Euston–Derby *entente* of Hudson and Mark Huish days had for some time been a thing of the past, and the North Western made things as awkward as they possibly could for the Midland in the conveyance of any through traffic— passenger or goods—between Carlisle and Ingleton; and so at length, in 1865, the Midland board came to the decision to have an independent line of their own to Carlisle, and to go all out for a major share in the Anglo-Scottish traffic. Not for the first time, and certainly not for the last, did a decision of the Midland board cause a profound stir in many railway circles. There was talk of an amalgamation between the Glasgow and South Western, and the Caledonian; the North Western suddenly became more reasonable, offering revised and quite attractive conditions for conveyance of Midland traffic between Carlisle and Ingleton—on condition that the Settle and Carlisle project was dropped. In face of all this, and particularly in view of the capital expenditure they had already incurred with the London extension the Midland actually presented an abandonment Bill to Parliament.

The pages of history are crowded with ' might-have-beens '! The LMS management from 1923 onwards would probably have been very glad to have dispensed with the Settle and Carlisle, and those who knew their railway history may have wished that the Abandonment Bill had gone through! With careful timetable planning the traffic could have been worked between Carlisle and Low Gill, and a few additional running loops, intermediate colour light signals, and a modernisation of the lay-out at Low Gill to convert it into a first-class main-line junction would have been far cheaper than the maintenance of the Settle and Carlisle. To a railway enthusiast however such talk is pure heresy, and it is amusing to recall that abandonment did not take place because the Midland thought better of it, but because the North British and Lancashire and Yorkshire were determined to keep Derby up to it. Both railways were deeply interested in a route between England and Scotland that should be independent of the London and North Western. Once the Midland attempt to evade the responsibilities incurred under its Act of 1865 had been defeated the project was pushed forward, and, to the credit of the company, in no cheese-paring style. Even though the cost exceeded the estimates by nearly 50 per cent, the line was built in magnificent style throughout. Despite the difficulty of the country traversed there is not one single speed restriction between Hellifield and Carlisle, below the overall limit for the entire route.

To the most casual observer it is evident that the engineering of the Settle and Carlisle is on the grand scale; the lofty embankments, great viaducts, and long tunnels tell their own tale. But the whole conception of the route, particularly over the very difficult section south of Hawes Junction seems to indicate remarkable foresight towards the operating problems of the twentieth century. One would hesitate to suggest that the great Tasmanian engineer Sharland built better than he knew; but the manner in which he contrived that the line should be practically level through Blea Moor

Tunnel has proved a godsend to the locomotive department ever since. Quite apart from the actual scenery the geographical features of the line north of Horton-in-Ribblesdale are outstanding. It is not unusual for a main line of railway to cross, or tunnel under a major watershed; but the Settle and Carlisle traverses, veritably, a general watershed, for a distance of more than ten miles. The Greta, the Ribble, the Dee, the Clough, the Ure and the Eden all have their sources within sight of the line in this short distance. The culminating point, and the point that dictates the summit level of the route lies in the half-mile of open moorland, 1,150 ft. above sea level, that separates the rivers Ure and Eden. The place is now well known among the railway fraternity as Aisgill, but actually the tiny cleft in the side of Wild Boar Fell from which the name is taken, Ais Ghyll, lies more than a mile to the north, and there are half a dozen other ghylls in the neighbourhood from which a name for the summit box might have been taken. But whatever the name, unless a long tunnel was to be bored there was no escaping the summit level of 1,150 ft., or thereabouts, at this point; the fascinating study is rather the way in which Sharland worked up to it from the south.

From the head waters of the Ribble and the Greta to the point where Wensleydale turns north towards the Aisgill watershed two great ridges had to be cut through—the eastern flanks of Whernside, and the high upland between Dentdale and Garsdale, modestly called Rise Hill. Naturally the engineer wished to keep the length of tunnelling to a minimum, as the conditions in both bores were likely to be severe; and so he took the line to a high altitude at Blea Moor, and on the north side of the tunnel traversed first Dentdale and then Garsdale on practically level track. Above Horton-in-Ribblesdale the rise could have been made more gradual, and the incline continued through the two long tunnels; but as things turned out it was fortunate that Sharland built as he did. Blea Moor Tunnel is a wet, horrible place, and had there been an appreciable rising gradient the locomotives of northbound trains would inevitably have been handicapped by slipping. As it is, the long bank from Settle Junction can be fought in the open air, and even though the storms lash down from the fells, wind and rain at the speeds express trains climb this grade are not too serious a handicap. Furthermore the level stretch high on the southern slopes of Garsdale enabled the Midland Railway to lay down water troughs—a very useful institution, not far from the midway point between Leeds and Carlisle.

Enough of preliminaries however, though it is hoped this rough survey of the countryside will help towards an appreciation of the railway and of the mountain grandeur in which it was built. One last point before we set off for Carlisle: Sharland was instructed to build a fast express route; there could be no deviations to lessen the cost in avoiding natural obstacles. There was no question of swinging into the hillsides, horseshoe-wise, in crossing the deep ghylls; likewise if a rocky bluff lay in the track of the railway there was only one course, to blast clean through! Once through the quaint old town of Settle, and with some last glimpses of the green, open valleys we have travelled whether coming from Leeds or by the Lancashire and Yorkshire line, the hills close in on either side; speed is falling off noticeably, as indeed one would expect, for by the time we pass the Stainforth Lime Works the gradient has been 1 in 100 for 5 miles continuously. There is a short tunnel here, and we pound on through a narrowing gorge. Then quite suddenly it seems, to a traveller in the train, the landscape opens out to a broad prospect over the moorland wastes of Horton, with the striking mountain Pen-y-ghent dominating the scene to the north-east. For half a mile past Helwith Bridge the gradient does lessen; but then, as a result of Sharland's constructional tactics the line continues on 1 in 100, climbing higher and higher above the course of the Ribble. There is an intermediate signal box at a bleak spot called Selside, and hereabouts the traveller gets his first sight of the second, and finest, of the Ribblesdale mountains, Ingleborough.

Beside the giant peaks to be seen from express trains in Switzerland, or even against some of the breath-taking vistas on the Callander and Oban, and West Highland lines in Scotland, the Ribblesdale trio, Pen-y-ghent, Ingleborough, and Whernside, might statistically seem very small beer, with no point over 2,400 ft. among them. But see Ingleborough from the footplate, as a southbound express emerges from Blea Moor Tunnel, and comes sweeping round the curve over Batty Moss Viaduct, and it has a form and a grandeur that compensate for anything in the way of mere height. 'Muckle flat-topped hill' indeed! So it was apostrophised by Jeanie Deans, in her ever memorable tramp from Edinburgh to

115

London in *The Heart of Midlothian,* a century before a train of that same name would have taken her in little more hours than the weeks she took to walk it. Whernside, the highest of all the fells ranged round Ribblehead is seen to the least advantage from the train; it appears as a long, rather featureless backbone of a ridge to which the sedgy moorlands beside the railway at Blea Moor are rising.

At the north end of Blea Moor Tunnel the train emerges to traverse a stretch of line that is surely unparalleled for wild grandeur anywhere in the north of England. It has none of the breath-taking vistas of Alpine railways or even of the West Highland line in Scotland; it is England's own peculiarly characteristic combination of rolling moorland and deep valley, dry-point stone walls, and brawling mountain streams, but all on the mightiest scale, and seen moreover from a relatively high level. We are no sooner out of the tunnel than we are skimming across Denthead viaduct, a hundred feet or more above the dale; then northwards, well on the hillside, with a double line of snow fences higher still above the track of the railway. It was here, during the extraordinary winter of 1946-7, that Hubert Foster went to take photographs of the snow blocks— photographs that went before the Cabinet, and revealed more than reams of written report the extent to which Nature had seized in a stranglehold some of the greatest arteries of the nation's transport. But even studying Eric Treacy's photographs, in these pages, taken as they were on fine summer days, it does not need much imagination to picture how inhospitable this wild countryside can become when the winter storms begin to rage.

Dent Station is 650 ft. above the village, and a weary trudge of 5 miles at that; but is still smartly kept, and its newly-pasted posters exhort the occasional travellers to see Britain by rail. In all seriousness there is no finer way of seeing the grand country between Settle and Appleby. Before leaving Dentdale however, and driving on north through Rise Hill tunnel, I must spare time to retrace steps for a mile or so. For the northern approach to Blea Moor Tunnel is extremely fine. Seen from the footplate of a south-bound express the line ahead swings out from the shoulder of the steep hillside on which we have been running from Dent, strides high across the head of the dale, on Denthead viaduct, and then plunges straight under Whernside. High up the mountain slopes can be descried one of the ventilating shafts of the tunnel, usually with a plume of white smoke drifting from it.

In high rugged country such as this one usually imagines the passage of an express train to be slow: frequent applications of the brake, a constant sensation of travelling round curves, and an occasional swing, even in the best of track that causes a mild flutter in the dining car. But there is nothing of the sort on the 1,100 ft. 'plateau' of the Midland between Blea Moor and Aisgill. The train sweeps along at an effortless 60 to 65 mph; for the undulations of the track are little harder than dead level, and as for the alignment, the speed could be 75 or 80 mph all the way if circumstances demanded such haste. At the north end of Rise Hill Tunnel another great prospect is revealed, of Garsdale far below, and stretching away to the south-west. But this dale rises quickly to its head, and we are now approaching the moorland watershed where the infant rivers Clough, Ure, and Eden are all so close to each other, and yet flowing eventually to Morecambe Bay, to the North Sea, and to the Solway Firth respectively. Here, too, is the station known for so long as Hawes Junction, but renamed Garsdale by the LMSR. Hawes itself is six miles away, and was reached by the Midland on its own metals. There, however, the branch line made an end-on junction with the North Eastern branch coming up Wensleydale from Northallerton.

At Garsdale, to west of the line, can be glimpsed the turntable that is surrounded by a palisade of old sleepers—a reminder of that ferocious day of storm, when the wind catching an engine and tender on the table put the whole thing beyond human control, and engine, tender, and table just went round and round! But a reader who did not know Hawes Junction in the old days might wonder why it should be necessary to have a turntable at all at such a bleak unfrequented outpost—perhaps just for North Eastern engines coming across from Northallerton; but then, again, if so why put it on the western side of the Midland main line? In actual fact that turntable had a pretty busy time of it. In Midland days there was always a serious shortage of really powerful engines on the Settle and Carlisle line. Apart from the ten Class 4 simple 4–4–0s of the '999' class reliance was placed almost entirely upon Class 2 engines, many of them non-superheated, and as the maximum unassisted load for Class 2 was 180 tons there was much double-

117

heading. It was evidently found more convenient to pilot up to Aisgill from both north and south, and send the assistant engines back light to Carlisle or Hellifield as the case might be. The Midland rarely sent the pilots right through as the North Western did between Oxenholme and Carlisle. And so all the Midland pilots whether from north or south came to Hawes Junction to turn. At the busiest times, in the early afternoon and in the early hours of the morning it was not unusual for Hawes Junction to be positively congested with light engines, queueing for the turntable, and afterwards waiting their turn to proceed in twos or threes, to their home stations.

At times of the heaviest traffic the presence of so many engines together with the frequent passage of express trains on the main line could become quite an embarrassment, and it was in such circumstances in the early hours of Christmas Eve 1910, that the stage was set for the tragic collision just south of Shotlock Hill Tunnel, $1\frac{1}{4}$ miles to the north of the junction. The details of the accident are well enough known—how the signalman made what might appear as quite an elementary mistake in forgetting the two Carlisle engines standing on the main. But just imagine Hawes Junction on that night! At one time there were no fewer than nine light engines standing either in the yard, or in the station: three 2–4–0s, Nos. 42, 247 and 249; four unrebuilt Johnson 4–4–0s, Nos. 312, 313, 314 and 317; and two rebuilt, but unsuperheated 4–4–0s, Nos. 448 and 548. There were entries in the train register on an average once every ten minutes from 4 a.m. onwards, quite apart from the various local movements involved in manoeuvring the light engines, and when the drivers of the two Carlisle engines failed to remind the signalman that they were held up on the main line, awaiting the clearance of the advanced starting signal, by carrying out Rule 55, it only needed the momentary forgetfulness of the signalman at the height of his busyness to complete the moves necessary for the disastrous ending. But even then a tragedy was not inevitable. If the two light engines had got smartly away from the advanced starting signal instead of drifting away in the most leisurely style, they would have been on a long open stretch of line where their tail lamp could have been seen in good time by the enginemen of the Glasgow express. This latter train was also double-headed and would in any case have been slowing down to stop at Aisgill and

118

put off its pilot. But as things were disaster was made a certainty. North of Hawes Junction the line passes through two short tunnels in succession, first the Moorcock and then the Shotlock Hill, and at first the line is on a long gradual curve to the left. It was not until the express was clear of Moorcock Tunnel that its enginemen saw the tail lamp of the engines in front, and then they were so close upon them that a collision was unavoidable.

As Aisgill summit is approached the bold outline of Wild Boar Fell towers up immediately ahead; but as soon as the summit is passed, and the line dips down on a 1 in 100 gradient the beginnings of the Eden valley are seen as a vast and deepening cleft in the earth's surface. For a split second one may well puzzle as to how so mere a trickle of a stream could have worn out so great a V among the mountains. But while the prospects are as wild and bold as those south of Blea Moor the tempo is now of the swiftest: Mallerstang siding, Birkett Tunnel, Kirkby Stephen, Crosby Garrett follow with speeds usually held at 75 to 80 mph. So, down towards a gentler, greener countryside. The main northern ridge of the Pennines, with the high fells behind Brough dominating the picture to the east, lies some distance away from the railway; but a lineside name hereabouts is a reminder that this stretch, with its long adverse gradient from Ormside viaduct up to Aisgill can be just as trying to the enginemen, and as just a subject to wild weather as the line south of Blea Moor, and across the table-land between Hawes Junction and Denthead. Helm Tunnel!—so named from the Helm wind, that is sometimes a phenomenon of these parts. A cloud cap on the ridge of the Pennines is usually a sign that the ' hurricane ' is about to break. Cool winds from the North Sea sweeping over mile upon mile of gradually rising moorland suddenly meet on the crest of the Pennines, with the warm air of the western vales. The outcome is the so-called Helm wind, that sweeps down into the Eden valley with the force of a miniature tornado.

Helm Tunnel really marks the end of the fell country, and for the next 15 miles or so we are racing on, over gradients that are generally favourable through the rich farming lands of the Eden valley. But the Pennines are never far away, and by New Biggin and Culgaith we are only five miles from the summit of Crossfell, which only just fails to top the 3000-ft. contour and is the highest English mountain outside the Lake District. By Langwathby and

Little Salkeld the speed is often into the eighties once more, and then comes that supremely beautiful stretch where the line is carried on the western side of the gorge through which the Eden forces a way to the Solway Firth. The length between Lazonby and Arma-thwaite can be compared on equal terms with such scenic gems as the Pass of Killiecrankie, and Symonds Yat; but as with most parts of the Settle and Carlisle line it is passed all too swiftly. Even with a south-bound train the heaviest of the initial climbing out of Carlisle ends at the summit once marked by Low House Box; the speed rises to a full 60 mph by Armathwaite, and the rise at 1 in 220 through Armathwaite and Barons Wood Tunnels is taken in the locomotive's stride. North of Low House the line comes out into the open country, and with the North Eastern line from Newcastle soon coming into view the city of Carlisle is neared. Midland trains approach Carlisle over North Eastern metals from Durran Hill Junction. Near this point were the Midland engine sheds, though these, like those of the G & SWR at Currock Road have now been closed and power for the Settle and Carlisle line is provided from the former North Western shed at Upperby Bridge. Today, on expresses to and from the sou'west, locomotives work through between Leeds and Glasgow, and it is only on trains for the Waverley route that engines are changed at Carlisle.

34 Gresley 'Pacifics' on the Midland Scotch Expresses: Class 'A3' 4-6-2 No. 60038 *Firdaussi*, on the down 'Waverley', passing Bell Busk in June 1962.

35 Settle Junction: a westbound freight diverging to the 'Little North Western' line, hauled by '8F' 2-8-0 No. 48454 (Swindon built) and remarkably for July 1961 fitted with a snow plough!

36 Climbing southwards towards Aisgill, in August 1964, the up 'Thames-Clyde Express' passing Kirkby Stephen, hauled by 'Peak' class diesel No. D87.

37 An invaluable diversion route, now threatened: in August 1965 the up 'Royal Scot', on the Settle and Carlisle line approaching Aisgill summit with the escarpments of Wild Boar Fell an impressive background. The locomotive is a Class 40, No. D231.

CHAPTER 10

A Famous Test Route

A ROUTE with the physical characteristics of the Settle and Carlisle breeds naturally a high standard of locomotive performance and traditions of first-class enginemanship among individual crews. Yet some marked vicissitudes are to be noted in the history of the line over the eighty years of its existence. From the outset the working had to be smart. It was built to compete with the well-established East Coast and West Coast routes to Scotland, and some of the best of all Midland express engines were put on to the job. As the service developed and train loads increased, larger and more powerful types were introduced until, in 1902, there came the first of the 3-cylinder compound 4–4–0s—not, it is true, in the form they are so well known today. The first two of the Smith-Johnson engines, Nos. 2631 and 2632 as they originally were, ran exclusively north of Leeds in their early days. The ingenious, though complicated controls were similar in effect to those used on the De Glehn compounds in France, and enabled the driver to admit live steam direct to the low pressure cylinders, not only when starting, but at full speed if desired. 'Reinforced compound' working, as it was sometimes called, was intended to provide extra power for short periods, as on the last miles up to Blea Moor, or Aisgill where the pace might otherwise be flagging with a heavy train. With engines 2631 and 2632 confined to regular drivers, who got to know all their peculiarities, some remarkable uphill work was often done, and in those early years of the present century there seemed every likelihood of Midland motive power developing towards a big-engine policy, and there was a prospect of our seeing really heavy trains taken over Aisgill unassisted.

Within a very few years all had changed. As a result of a new policy dictated by the top management of the Midland Railway the locomotive department was compelled to ' make do.' Little or no money was forthcoming for new and larger engines, and the best that could be done was to rebuild a number of the older 4–4–0s with larger boilers. At first these ' rebuilds ' were not even superheated. Thus, on the Settle and Carlisle line there came a period in which a tremendous amount of double heading was necessary, and when, in 1913, Mr Cecil J. Allen published in *The Railway Magazine* a series of 13 runs from Hellifield to Carlisle no fewer than 6 of these had pilot assistance up to Aisgill; and except for one journey made at a holiday period no train had a heavier load than 285 tons. At the time when I was at school at Giggleswick, and had many opportunities of observing the locomotive workings I must say that piloting had become comparatively rare; but in that period, 1916 to 1921, the schedules had been very much eased out, and for a time there were no dining cars on the Scotch expresses.

At the time of grouping, in 1923, the maximum tare load permitted to an unpiloted 4–4–0 engine of Class 4, whether a ' 999 ' class simple, or a 3-cylinder compound, was 240 tons; and since at the same period North Western engines of similar capacity were taking trains of 375 and even 400 tons over Shap unassisted, comparisons were not to the advantage of the Midland. But then, what a change came over the scene in the ensuing two or three years! The Settle and Carlisle line is an almost ideal route for testing locomotives. The long drag from Settle Junction up to Blea Moor can be a devastating test of steaming capacity, while from the northern side, the combination of hard slogging gradients, with considerable lengths of easier ascents where there can be no let-up and a high rate of evaporation must be continued, can be one of the most gruelling stretches of express route to be found anywhere in this country. As with most stretches of this kind, speeds scheduled in the downhill direction permitted of running under the lightest of steam. In 1923, on expresses booked to cover the 113 miles from Leeds to Carlisle non-stop in 135 min., at an overall average speed of 50·2 mph, the allowance for the 48·3 miles down from Aisgill to Carlisle was 49 min., whereas the corresponding up expresses were allowed 68 mins. to pass Aisgill from the dead start.

Very occasionally the fullest use was made of the splendid alignment and favourable grading north of Aisgill, and then the times really were spectacular. There was a run in October 1902 that perhaps may stand as a record for all time. It was made on the 9.30 a.m. from St Pancras, with a load of 320 tons behind the tender.

The engine was one of the Johnson 'Belpaires,' No. 2607, after-wards better known as 'Class 3' and numbered in the 700s; pilot assistance was taken up to Aisgill, and it was from the restart, near the summit box that this astonishing speed exhibition took place. The accompanying log has been prepared from recordings taken at every milepost, with some half-miles and quarter-miles in addition. The result was a start-to-stop run of 41 min. 55 sec. from Aisgill to Carlisle, while for 45 miles, between mileposts 262 and 307, the average speed was 76 mph, and below Kirkby Stephen, and again near Ormside the speed reached 90 mph. It was a magnificent run indeed, as fine a tribute to Sharland's survey and constructional work through mountain country as it was to the free running of S. W. Johnson's beautiful 4-4-0 engine.

But I must bring the story rapidly forward more than 20 years, from the exploit of old 2607 to the days when locomotives of the constituent companies of the LMS were tested against each other between Leeds and Carlisle. At the time railway enthusiasts and the travelling public knew little of what was going on. Dyna-mometer car trials were being conducted on the night expresses, and for the first group of tests between engines of Class-4 capacity the loads were fixed at 300 tons tare. This was well above the old Midland limit, but was no doubt established in response to the West Coast plea that 240 tons was scarcely worth pulling with a Bowen Cooke 4-6-0 of the 'Prince of Wales' class. The engines concerned were:

    (a) Midland 4-4-0, No. 998 (simple)
    (b) Midland 4-4-0, No. 1008 (compound)
    (c) L & NWR 4-6-0, No. 388 ('Prince of Wales' class)

To the surprise of the Derby authorities all three engines made short work of the job. On one occasion, indeed, No. 1008, with 306 tons tare passed Aisgill in 63 min. from Carlisle, while the '999' also ran well ahead of time. It was, on the other hand no surprise at Crewe that No. 388 did extremely well also.

The work of the latter engine, and also that of the Midland compound No. 1008 was so good, and so obviously within their maximum capacity, that further trials were arranged with tare loads of 350 tons. Although some very hard work was involved both these engines gained time to Aisgill. On the heavy initial climb from Carlisle to Low House box the two engines practically dead-heated; then the compound got away to make faster running over the more gradual ascent between the summit point 13·5 miles out of Carlisle, and Ormside. Over this latter stretch, 19·7 miles, the averages were 56·2 mph by the 'Prince,' and a remarkable 61·6 mph by No. 1008. At Ormside the compound was leading by 2¼ min., but then the North Western engine did some magnificent work up the heavy final stage to Aisgill. The compound took 24¼ min. to climb this last 15·1 miles, while No. 388 took 23 min. 40 sec. With the 'Prince.' the absolute minimum speed was 29¼ mph leaving Birkett Tunnel, and topping the longest stretch of continuous 1 in 100. The compound was doing 27 mph at this point, but it is evident that the North Western engine was giving of her finest, for on the easing of the grade to 1 in 302, for 3/4 miles past Mallerstang box, she accelerated to 40 mph and the last 3 miles of 1 in 100 up to Aisgill were cleared at 32¼. The compound recovered to 37½ mph at Mallerstang, and topped Aisgill at 27¼ mph. The overall times from Carlisle, of 66 min. 10 sec. with the 'Prince,' and 64 min. 35 sec. with the compound were indeed superb, with gross loads amounting to 370 tons in each case, but one could no more expect such efforts to be reproduced regularly in ordinary service than one would expect a Great Western 'King' to work 25-coach trains of 800 tons at normal West of England express speed.

So far as provision of motive power for the Settle and Carlisle was concerned these first trials seemed inconclusive. The Midland Class 4 engines had their load limits raised, but even at 300 tons there were still trains that needed double heading. Furthermore, with grouping there was no longer any need for Carlisle to be a frontier point, and already there were ideas of through locomotive workings between Leeds and Glasgow, and Preston and Glasgow. Accordingly a further series of trials was conducted, in which Midland compounds were pitted against Caledonian Pickersgill 4–4–0s and a North Western 4-cylinder 4–6–0 of the 'Claughton' class. The dice were rather loaded against the Caley engines. Although nominally Class 3, and therefore expectedly inferior to the compounds, and the '999' class, the inferiority was absolute by reason of their smaller boilers and fireboxes. On the climb from Carlisle to Aisgill nothing could make up for lack of steaming capacity, and although the total heating surface of the Pickersgills and the ' Class 4 ' Midlands was much the same, the much larger grates (28·4 against 21 sq. ft.) and a working pressure of 200 lb. per sq. in. against 170 made all the difference. It is no surprise that the Pickersgill engines could barely manage 300 tons unassisted over Aisgill.

The ' Claughtons,' on the other hand, had a handsome margin in reserve, even with 350-ton trains and if sometimes they were heavier on coal than the compounds it did seem that they might provide the answer to the motive-power problem of this route. At that time however, the whole stud of 130 engines were fully engaged on their own line; together with the Hughes 4–6–0s from the Lancashire and Yorkshire they were the largest and most powerful passenger engines then available on the whole of the LMSR. Further trials with the compounds, some in very bad weather, showed that the 350-ton loads taken so magnificently by No. 1008 in the first series of tests could not be taken as an all-the-year-round proposition, and pending the introduction of new engines on the West Coast main line it was evident that the former Midland engines would have to carry on between Leeds and Carlisle, assisted when loads exceeded 300 tons. Piloted, or not, the working was extremely smart, and one experience of my own on the 2.42 p.m. up from Carlisle in 1927 was characteristic of the times.

The day was a Saturday towards the end of the summer, and we had a load of ' twelve ' out of Carlisle—seven through from St Enoch to St Pancras, three from St Enoch to Manchester (via Hellifield) and the two coaches off the 12 noon Edinburgh Waverley: 382 tons tare, and packed with passengers, fully 415 tons full. We had one of the then—new 6 ft. 9 in. compounds, No. 1070; these engines were built in the Midland tradition, and originally had right-hand drive. The pilot up to Aisgill was a rebuilt and superheated Class 2, No. 444. Never shall I forget the way those two engines set about things up the initial ascent out of Carlisle. The maximum tonnage then allowed to Class 2 engines was 180 tons, and dividing our load in the ratio of this latter to the compound rostered maximum gives 260 tons to No. 1070, and 155 to No. 444. I have tabulated this run in detail, and in comparison with the fastest of No. 1008's brilliant test runs 1070 and her pilot were leading by *three minutes* as early as Lazonby. No. 1008 had

320 tons against No. 1070's share of 260 tons. The combined roar of the two engines as they accelerated to 39 mph up the initial 1 in 132 to Scotby still lingers in my memory. A permanent-way check at Culgaith, and the stop at Appleby makes comparison with the test runs more difficult thereafter, but between Ormside and Mallerstang, 11·6 miles, 444 and 1070 together took 15½ min. against the 16 min. 4 sec. of No. 1008 with 320 tons, even though the double-header accelerating from the Appleby stop was doing no more than 58½ mph at Ormside viaduct, while No. 1008 crossed at

LMSR (MIDLAND) 2.42 p m CARLISLE–HELLIFIELD

Load 13 cars 382 tons tare 415 tons full
Engine 4–4–0 Compound No 1070
Pilot to Aisgill ' Class 2 ' 4–4–0 No 444

Mls		m	s	mph
0·0	CARLISLE	0	00	
2·7	Scotby	5	20	39
3·9	Cumwhinton	7	10	40¼
6·8	Cotehill	10	50	50½
8·1	*Milepost 300*	12	28	45½
10·0	Armathwaite	14	30	62½
13·1	*Milepost 295*	17	45	54
15·5	LAZONBY	20	05	68
18·4	Little Salkeld	22	45	64
19·8	Langwathby	24	12	54½
		p w s		30
23·4	Culgaith	28	40	
24·7	New Biggin	30	55	41
27·9	Long Marton	34	45	60
30·8	APPLEBY	38	35	
0·0		0	00	
2·5	Ormside	4	15	58½
5·3	*Griseburn Box*	7	48	41
7·5	Crosby Garrett	10	55	51
10·7	Kirkby Stephen	14	50	45
14·0	*Mallerstang Box*	19	45	38/45
16·8	*Milepost 260½*	23	55	37½
17·5	*Aisgill Box*	arr. 25	20	
		dep. 26	25	
20·6	Hawes Jc	31	50	58½
23·8	Dent	35	25	53
25·9	*Denthead Box*	37	35	63½/56
28·7	*Blea Moor Box*	40	20	66
30·0	Ribblehead	41	28	72½
32·4	*Selside Box*	43	23	76½
34·8	Horton	45	25	69 (slack)
36·4	*Helwith Bridge Box*	46	46	76
40·8	Settle	50	35	60 (slack)
42·7	*Settle Jc*	52	15	72½
44·8	Long Preston	54	10	60
		sigs		
46·0	HELLIFIELD	57	15	

Net times : Carlisle–Appleby 36 min.
Appleby–Hellifield 56 min.

$69\frac{1}{2}$ mph. Approaching Aisgill on my run, the absolute minimum was $37\frac{1}{2}$ mph.

The Midland Railway had developed to a fine art the operation of detaching pilots at Aisgill. On the six runs published by Mr Cecil J. Allen in *The Railway Magazine* in 1913 the average duration of the stop was 69 sec., and on this run of mine, in 1927, the time was 65 sec. In this time the fireman of the pilot had to climb down and uncouple; the engine had to draw ahead, and then set back into the siding. To do this in so short a time, involved the slickest of movement, and complete co-operation between the driver and fireman of the pilot, and the signalman. On this run of mine we covered the 6·6 miles up from Mallerstang and onwards to Hawes Junction in 12 min. 5 sec., stop included. Further comment is unnecessary, seeing that a 415-ton train was involved. No. 1070 went brilliantly across the high table-land stretch, passing Blea Moor box 11·2 miles in 13 min. 55 sec. from the fresh start. There was a brisk descent of the long bank, and at Long Preston—27·3 miles in $27\frac{3}{4}$ min.—we were getting near even time. In all my years of travelling over the Midland line I have never had a better run than this.

With the introduction of the ' Royal Scots ' on the West Coast main line some ' Claughtons ' could be released for regular Midland Division duties, and by 1928 a number of them were in service north of Leeds. The pioneer engine No. 5900 *Sir Gilbert Claughton* was one of these, and I shall always remember the positively immaculate condition in which she was kept. Surely no Midland engine, even in the most ornate of Johnson's days was groomed, cleaned and burnished more than No. 5900; but fine though she looked in Derby red, to one who loved the North Western it was an alien livery, just as much as the neo-Crewe style of British Railways looks utterly alien on a Midland compound. I had a good run behind *Sir Gilbert Claughton* on the up Thames–Clyde Express in 1931; with a load of 335 tons we passed Aisgill in 66 min. 2 sec. Throughout the climb there was every impression that things were being taken quite comfortably, the lowest speed at any point was $31\frac{1}{2}$ mph, and after such good uphill work very leisurely running downhill and eastwards from Hellifield brought us into Leeds 3 min. early, in 140 min. exactly from Carlisle. When occasion demanded it, the ' Claughtons ' could really ' fly,' and I shall always

remember a trip on the up afternoon ' Scotsman ' later that same
year when No. 5960 with a similar load of 330 tons, had lost a little
time to Aisgill, in very bad weather.   Then down from Blea Moor
we came like a thunderbolt, passing Ribblehead at 78, Selside Box
at 82½, and reached 88 mph, before a touch of the brakes near
Horton.

It was in 1937 that a remarkable series of tests were conducted
on four successive days with the Stanier ' 5 X P ' 4–6–0 No. 5660
Rooke.   The four stages were : Bristol to Leeds; Leeds to Glasgow;
Glasgow to Leeds; and Leeds to Bristol.   The load was one of
9 vehicles, having a tare weight of 302 tons, and it was on the return
trip from Glasgow that a phenomenal climb was made from
Carlisle to Aisgill.   The 48·4 miles were covered, start to pass, in
48 min. 36 sec., with the summit box passed at the astonishing
minimum speed of 46½ mph.   On the previous day, in the northbound direction a very stiff timing of 117 min. had been laid down
for the 113 miles from Leeds to Carlisle.   Due to permanent-way
checks the test schedule was not bettered in any way as far as
Hellifield—36·2 miles in 42 min.; but there was no lower speed
than 46 mph at any point climbing to Blea Moor, and the 14 miles

MIDLAND RAILWAY

AISGILL BOX–CARLISLE

Load : ' = 17½ ' : 320 tons gross
Engine 4–4–0 No 2607 (Johnson Belpaire)

Mls		m	s	mph
0·0	*Aisgill* (post 259½)	0	00	
3·7	*Mallerstang Box*	5	12	70
7·1	Kirkby Stephen	7	51	82
10·3	Crosby Garrett	10	13	80
15·3	Ormside	13	49	90
17·8	APPLEBY	15	36	77
20·7	Long Marton	17	46	82
23·9	New Biggin	20	10	77½
25·2	Culgaith	21	10	80
28·8	Langwathby	23	57	75
30·2	Little Salkeld	25	02	79
33·1	LAZONBY	27	16	75
35·5	*Milepost 295*	29	24	64
38·6	Armathwaite	32	07	71
40·5	*Milepost 300*	33	51	63
41·8	Cotehill	35	01	
44·7	Cumwhinton	37	24	76½
45·9	Scotby	38	22	69
47·5	*Milepost 307*	39	52	
48·6	CARLISLE	41	55	

130

up from Settle Junction were covered at an average speed of 51·4 mph. It is interesting to recall, however, that on the downhill run from Aisgill, the speeds were nothing approaching those of the Midland 'Belpaire' No. 2607 on that run of October 1902, and from passing Aisgill to the stop at Carlisle engine No. 5660 *Rooke* took 44 min. 26 sec. against the 41 min. 55 sec. start to stop of the earlier run.

Since nationalisation the Settle and Carlisle line has become the regular road-testing ground for locomotives put through their paces on the Rugby Stationary Testing Plant. Controlled road tests with the dynamometer car have been conducted with, among others, the following diverse collection of locomotives:

(a) ER Class 'B.1,' 4–6–0, No. 61353

(b) BR Standard Class 5, 4–6–0, No. 73008

(c) BR 'Britannia' Class, 4–6–2, No. 70005

(d) LMR 4–6–2, No. 46225, *Duchess of Gloucester*

(e) The English Electric 3,300 hp 'Deltic'

It is interesting to compare runs made under severe test conditions with those made on the earlier LMS trials. Unfortunately, published details of the various tests do not necessarily cover the same stretches of each run. In the test bulletins obviously the more interesting features are brought out, and with the 'Britannia' for example the section shown diagrammatically is that farther north, not including the final ascent over Aisgill. I have tabulated on page 106 details of some of the recent test runs, in comparison with earlier efforts:

The striking similarity between the work on runs 1, 2, 3, 5, and 6 will at once be noted, and no less that between the high-speed run of the Stanier engine *Rooke*, and the 'Deltic.' The 'B1,' although worked hard, was not pressed to the limit of the boiler. The feed water rate on this trip was 18,020 lb. per hr., and although the limit of the exhaust steam injector fitted to this locomotive is a feed rate of 20,000 lb. per hr. the boiler was steamed, on stationary tests, to 25,000 lb. per hr. The average drawbar horsepower between Ormside and Aisgill, as actually recorded in the dynamometer car, was about 900. In comparison with this, the Stanier '5XP,' making

APPLEBY-AISGILL SUMMIT (pass to pass)

	1 998 MR '999' 320		2 1008 Compound 370		3 388 LNW 370		4 5660 '5XP' 305		5 61353 ER 'B1' 405		6 73008 'BR5' 560		7 'Deltic' E.E. Co. 642	
Run No / Engine No / Engine Class / Load (tons gross)	m	s	m	s	m	s	m	s	m	s	m	s	m	s
Mls														
0·0 Appleby	0	00	0	00	0	00	0	00	0	00	0	00	0	00
2·4 Ormside	2	32	2	29	2	38	1	59	2	30	2	50	2	20
7·5 Crosby Garrett	9	06	9	22	9	32	6	50	9	10	10	00	7	18
10·7 Kirkby Stephen	13	36	13	54	14	12	10	05	13	55	14	30	10	25
17·5 Aisgill Box	25	58	26	44	26	18	18	16	26	10	27	05	18	20
Speeds (mph)														
Ormside	65¼		64½		62½		77½		68		60		73	
Griseburn Box	38½		37		36¾		58		40		37		56	
Smardale Viaduct	48		47		47		62¼		50		47		63	
Birkett Tunnel	30		27		29¼		48		32		31		51	
Mallerstang	38		37½		40		53		39		39		55	
Aisgill	28		27¼		32¼		46½		30		29		49	
Average speed Ormside–Aisgill	38·6		37·4		38·4		55·8		38·4		37·4		56·7	

much faster times with a lighter load, registered an average dhp of 1054 between Ormside and Aisgill. The working of the two engines must have been very similar. On the ' B1,' with constant changes in cut-off, to keep the rate of evaporation constant throughout the ascent, the variations ranged between a very brief 28 per cent when crossing Ormside Viaduct at 68 mph to a maximum of 40 per cent. On the ' 5XP ' the range of cut-offs was between 35 and 40 per cent. In view of the earlier LMSR trials, and the fact that the minimum speed on the entire ascent usually occurs at the south end of Birkett Tunnel, it is interesting to see that it was here that the maximum cut-off was needed on the controlled road test with the ' B1.' The lever had been gradually dropped from 30 per cent crossing Smardale Viaduct, to 40 per cent in the tunnel; it was then eased back, 1 per cent at a time, to 35 above Mallerstang, and advanced finally to 37 for the last mile up to Aisgill.

The very close correspondence of the times and speeds made on the earlier trials to those of the ' B1,' enables an estimate to be made of the power exerted by the compound and the North Western ' Prince of Wales ' class 4-6-0. It would seem that these two engines were each exerting about 825 dhp between Ormside and Aisgill. The average gradient over this section is 1 in 118, and to obtain a truer comparison of the way in which these locomotives were working, relative to their size, the performance needs to be assessed by the equivalent output on level track. The comparison works out thus:

Locomotive	Equivalent dhp
Midland Compound, No. 1008	1,005
LNWR ' Prince of Wales,' No. 388	1,115
LMSR ' 5XP ' 4-6-0, No. 5660	1,400
ER ' B1 ' 4-6-0, No. 61353	1,150

Passing over for the moment one's astonishment that the older engines, of Class 4 capacity, could do such magnificent work, there is also the modern ' BR5 ' mixed-traffic 4-6-0 to be brought into the comparison. The 560-ton-load test, tabulated in column 6 of the table on page 106, required a feed rate of 23,000 lb. per hr. The actual drawbar horsepower on the climb appears from the published graphs to have averaged about 1,125, and the ' equivalent,' related to performance on level track, would be about 1,375.

133

Inevitably one wishes to carry the comparisons still further, and to see how the power outputs compare with the relative sizes of the boilers, cylinders, and nominal tractive effort, and I have prepared the accompanying table:

DRAWBAR-HORSEPOWER RELATIONS—37–8 mph

Engine Class	Midland 7-ft. Compound	LNWR 'Prince of Wales'	LNER 'B1'	BR Clas
dhp sustained :				
Ormside–Aisgill	825	825	900	1,125
Equivalent dhp	1,020	1,030	1,150	1,375
Total heating surface, sq. ft.	1,607	1,897·5	2,005	2,019
Grate area, sq. ft.	28·4	25·0	27·9	28
Nominal T.E. lb.	22,650	21,600	26,878	26,120
Weight, engine only, tons	61·7	66·25	71·15	76
Rates :				
Equivalent dhp per sq. ft. of H.S.	0·633	0·543	0·574	0
per sq. ft. of grate area	36	41·2	41·2	47
per lb. of nom. T.E.	0·045	0·048	0·043	0
per ton of engine wt.	16·5	15·5	16·2	18

Except for the ' BR5,' which was being worked practically ' flat-out,' there was surprisingly little in it. The ' BR5 ' was given cut-offs of more than 40 per cent before Crosby Garrett. There was an easing to 38 over Smardale Viaduct, but then the percentage went up till it was 48 on emerging from Birkett Tunnel. One rather suspects that by this time the boiler pressure was flagging somewhat, because on the final climb to Aisgill no less than 52 per cent was needed in order to sustain the power output required. The flogging necessary to achieve this performance was reflected in the coal consumption. Between Ormside and Aisgill the ' B1 ' was taking 66·3 lb. per mile, while the ' BR5 ' was taking no less than 90 lb. The comparison of these two runs does however present a striking commentary on modern locomotive performance, in that our latest designs do not become wildly extravagant when they are ' thrashed.' The coal consumptions of the ' B1 ' and the ' BR5,' making almost identical speed are in exact proportion to the loads hauled.

And what of the ' Deltic '? Its outstanding feature is of course the tremendous power output in relation to its weight. Until the building of the Western Region diesel hydraulic locomotives it was by far the lightest of any of the large internal-combustion loco-motives now running in this country, and yet its performance may be thus compared with the 2,000 hp diesel-electric No. 10203:

Loco.	Nominal hp	Max. dhp at 70 mph	Max. db Pull at 70 mph	Total Weight, tons	Pull: Weight, tons
10203	2,000	1,200	3·0	132·8	0·0226
'Deltic'	3,300	2,400	5·8	106	0·055

In other words, the 'Deltic' gives 2½ times as much drawbar pull per ton of engine weight as No. 10203. On the Settle and Carlisle line the 'Deltic' did much of her work with the ex-LMSR Mobile Test Plant, in which the equivalent of very heavy loads can be obtained by electrical braking devices. All this gives us some glimpses of the shape of things to come on British Railways, and one must heartily applaud the mechanical engineering genius that has been packed into the 'Deltic.'

But out there on the moors by Birkett Tunnel and Mallerstang, the sight of that sleek blue 'shape' gliding up the bank at 50 mph with 642 tons behind her could not conjure up the same sense of human endeavour and human achievement. With 'Deltic' the work has been done on the drawing boards, and in the shops. The enginemen have merely to 'turn on the taps' so to speak. Instead, picture the still dark night up among the fells—still, that is, till the roar could be heard of 1008 coming up from Kirkby Stephen. No-one who has participated in a really hard dynamometer car trial can fail to experience the feeling of intense pride and enthusiasm of all concerned, and men who have had to work hardest of all, the firemen, have gloried in showing what they could do when engine, coal, and all else were in their favour. Whatever future may be in store for the Settle and Carlisle, the enthusiast with a touch of fantasy in his heart may yet imagine the long and varied cavalcade of steam locomotives that have been flogged to their limit climbing to Aisgill, passing in ghostly procession amid the age-old fells of Mallerstang Common.

38 Appleby, Settle and Carlisle line, June 1961: a mechanical-stoker-fired '9F' 2-10-0 No. 92167 with a heavy southbound freight makes a strong bid for the air pollution championship!

39 An impressive rearward shot of a '9F' No. 92017 climbing the last miles up to Aisgill, with an Anhydrite train from Long Meg quarries to Widnes in May 1967.

40 Bleak scenery: magnificent engineering. The northbound 'Royal Scot' diverted via Settle in April 1967 here seen crossing Arten Gill viaduct, near Dent, hauled by a Class 47 diesel No. D1855.

41 Southbound over Arten Gill viaduct: the up 'Thames-Clyde Express', hauled by 'Peak' class diesel, No. D20. The masonry work can be appreciated from this striking picture.

137

CHAPTER 11

THE WAVERLEY ROUTE

ALTHOUGH it is now more than thirty years ago I can still remember vividly the thrill and eagerness with which I looked forward to my first trip from Carlisle to Waverley. Before that I had several times watched the comings and goings of North British engines at Carlisle, but the opportunity to travel that way had not come. Then the family decided on a holiday at Nairn, and my journey from London was planned so as to include the maximum of new railway sightseeing, and what I hoped would be interesting loco-motive performance. So instead of taking the ordinary route, and entering a through carriage at Euston that would bring me to Nairn in time for a late breakfast with the family I took the Waverley sleeper from St Pancras, and sat up most of the night recording the locomotive work. The Midland did me proud. However tired I may have been I was kept wide awake by the interest and excellence of the running north of Leeds, and there was no time to think of what lay in store on the continuation of the journey north of the Border. So, in the coldest and darkest hour of an early autumn night, we came into Carlisle, and is so happened that the coach in which I was travelling stopped almost abreast of our fresh engines. Momentarily I was disappointed to realise we were going to be double-headed, since we had come single-headed over Aisgill; but at that time through carriages were run nightly from Bristol to both Edinburgh and Glasgow by the Midland route, and during the height of the season traffic from the West of England was heavy enough to warrant running a separate train throughout to Carlisle. There the Edinburgh and Glasgow sections were separated and attached respectively to the 9.15 and 9.30 p.m. expresses from St Pancras. Thus the 4.25 a.m. out of Carlisle, by which I travelled, was loaded to over 400 tons, and piloting was essential. And there on the centre road stood *Waverley* and *Rob Roy,* gleaming and polished to the last split-pin.

Never before—and I would be almost inclined to say never

138

since !—have the proportions, the lines, the *massif* of a locomotive design impressed themselves more vividly, more instantly, and more lastingly upon me than did *Waverley* that morning, only half seen in the station lights of Carlisle. The ' Scott,' coupled behind, had all the grace and distinctive appeal of her class; but one needs to borrow a phrase from the Great Western to describe those North British ' Atlantics '—' might and majesty.' Soon we were away again, into the intense darkness that preceded a cloudy September dawn, and at once I was wrestling with the intricacies of rail-joint timing over a strange route. I had been warned beforehand that it was not the straightforward job that I knew so well over the 60-ft. rails of the old North Western, or yet the 45-ft. rails of the Midland, or even the 44 ft. 6 in. of the Great Western. The North British, I had been told, used 24-ft., 30-ft., 40-ft., and 48-ft. rails, and I had carefully worked out the numbers I had to count with each to make up a quarter mile. What I was not prepared for was frequent changes in the rail lengths. Often one stayed on the same length for little more than a mile at a time; in the darkness, with no mile-posts to check by, it was almost impossible to distinguish between 24 and 30 ft., or between 40 and 48 with the result that my attempts at speed recording went completely haywire. Baffled and frustrated I fell dead asleep soon after Longtown, and did not awaken until we were over Whitrope summit and coasting down the bank into Hawick. That train was then allowed 67 min. for the 45·4 miles from Carlisle, and on my first trip I was treated to a characteristic piece of Waverley-route precision in timekeeping, for we took 66 min. 50 sec.

The North British Railway had perhaps the most fascinating of the lines running north from Carlisle. Far more so than either the Caledonian or the old Sou' West it is a line of the Border. It does not pass from Cumberland into Roxburghshire until the train is more than 20 miles out of Carlisle, and even when as far north as Riccarton Junction the nearest point of Northumberland is less than three miles away. But long before Riccarton is reached, long even before the crossing of the Border the keynote of travel on the Waverley route has been sounded. While the Caledonian trains get away from Carlisle in a straightforward dash for Gretna, the North British have fairly to box the compass, taking the sharp curve to the left at Caldew, travelling south-west for a short time, and then swinging round again in a full right angle to the north-wards at Canal Junction. There is a fine panoramic view of the Caledonian sheds at Kingmoor as we approach and cross the West Coast main line, and then, for about 9 miles, comes the only stretch on the whole route when the line is anything like straight. Occasionally one may record speeds approaching 70 mph near Lyneside and Longtown, but usually 60 is about the maximum, even here.

We are speeding across the Debatable Land, that vaguely defined no-man's-land between the old historic Border fortresses of England and Scotland, and at Scotch Dyke station an early defence work is recalled. From tide water at the Solway Firth the actual Border is at first marked by the small river Sark, which the Caledonian line crosses at Gretna Junction; but some four miles to the north, striding the gap between the rivers Sark and Esk, are the remains of the old Scots Dike, an earthwork constructed along the line of the Border after the final settlement of the boundary in 1552. The purists may well be shocked, but the North British named their station ' Scotch Dyke,' and so it has always been since. The Border is now within sight of the railway, and lies on the west bank, first of the Esk, and then of the Liddel. With the windings of the rivers the line is many times almost upon the east bank, but it is not crossed by a bridge on the main line until beyond Kershopefoot, and by that time the county on the Scottish side has changed from Dumfriesshire to Roxburghshire.

Even through the Debatable Land the line, as seen from the footplate is far from straight, and the curve at Riddings Junction, where the branch to Langholm goes off, is enough to need a per-manent speed restriction, and to provide a bad start to the climb of Penton bank. Here climbing high above the Liddel Water, the scenery is changing rapidly from the Solway flats to that of a fine upland glen. We are indeed heading up Liddesdale, and high fells rising to over 1,500 ft. are beginning to block in the prospect seen ahead through the cab glasses. Hereabouts the gradient has eased to the extent of including a short length of descent, and before Kershopefoot the speed is usually about 60 mph. This village takes its name from the Kershope Burn, which comes down from the heights of Caplestone Fell away to the north-east. The course of this tiny burn marks the border between England and Scotland,

140

and the local names of the hills clustered on either side are in some way reminders of the days when such names stood not for individuals, but for well-organised, warlike clans: Elliott's Pike, Wilson's Pike, and significantly, Bloody Bush, while the knolls—here called 'knowes,' include Watch Knowe, which gives an unrivalled look-out over the 'enemy' country towards Brampton.

And so, in crossing the Kershope Burn just by Kershopefoot station, we enter Scotland. The railway is still by Liddel side, but nearing Newcastleton this river is crossed for the only time, and soon afterwards the great climb to Whitrope begins. From the locomotive point of view the respite between the top of Penton bank and Newcastleton is somewhat similar to the downward sweep of the Caledonian from Dinwoodie to the crossing of the Annan before Beattock Bank is commenced; but as everywhere on the Waverley route the performance is set in a more minor key, and while Beattock is often charged at nearly 80 mph the speed through Newcastleton is usually little more than 50. Thereafter the line toils up the western slopes of Liddesdale. The outlook grows increasingly bleak and wild, and the curvature is constant and often quite severe. In such country it is remarkable that an absolutely constant gradient has been engineered. The mileposts give the distance from Edinburgh, and from post 73, just a mile north of Newcastleton, the 1 in 75 ascent is unbroken for practically 8 miles. Above Steele Road the line begins to turn northwards out of Liddesdale, and to make for the watershed between the streams flowing towards the Solway and those of the Teviot and the Tweed; and soon, high up on the hillside to the right of the line, is seen the old North British branch that makes a long and winding course in the valley of the North Tyne to Hexham.

This fascinating, beautiful, but long-unremunerative by-way recalls the tremendous drive of the North British management in early days, long before the East Coast alliance meant more than an uneasy 'agreement'; when Hodgson, sometimes referred to as 'the Scotch Hudson,' was bent on the establishment of as many North British footholds in England as he could. He secured running powers from Hexham to Newcastle; he built a branch line from Redesmouth eastwards to Morpeth, and pushed another branch northward from this, and parallel to the North Eastern main line, from Scots Gap to Rothbury. There was a further scheme to con-

141

nect Rothbury and Kelso, and so obtain a *third* trunk route into
England; but in this case the North Eastern got in first, and tapped
the traffic of the intervening district with a line of their own from
Coldstream to Alnwick. Today, one of the most poignant relics of
the expansionist activities is of the North British to be seen at
Riccarton Junction, high up in the Cheviots, away from all main
roads, ' an out-and-out railway colony.'

Any present-day reader, coming across the article under the
above title in *The Railway Magazine* of May 1912, and learning that
there, up in the Cheviots, was a village with positively no approach
by road might well be disposed to toss the curiosity on to one side
with the comment: ' Oh yes, but that was in 1912.' So it was; but
the astonishing thing is that Riccarton still has no road approaches
today! Even though its role as a junction has largely disappeared
the inhabitants are still entirely dependent upon the railway for all
their contacts with the outside world. Bread groceries and other
provisions arrive daily by train from Hawick; children over ten
years old travel by train to school, either to Hawick or Newcastleton
while the refreshment room on the station serves as the ' local pub.'
At the present time this isolated railway community musters about
120 men, women and children. They have no doctor of their own,
and special railway arrangements are in force to get the nearest one
there quickly in case of emergency. If a train is not immediately
available a pilot engine is sent to fetch him. For the most part the
villagers seem to make their own amusements, but on three evenings
a week a late train is run from Hawick which gives the Riccartonians
a chance to go to the cinema. Neither did the North British Railway neglect to provide for the spiritual needs of its ' colony.' On
alternate Sundays a Church train was run from Riccarton to Newcastleton, or Hawick, and free tickets were issued for the journey.
Now, instead, there is a visiting minister from the village of Saugh-
tree, on the Hexham line, and he has a walking permit to reach the
village by way of the railway.

I saved the checking over of this chapter for an evening when I
was travelling south by the up Waverley ' sleeper,' and I dotted the
i's and crossed the t's to the accompaniment of a characteristic
syncopated roar from our Gresley ' A3 ' Pacific, as she toiled up the
bank from Hawick. It was intensely dark up there in the hills, and
when we came to the summit the lamps in the Whitrope box shone

out like beacons. Then we came to Riccarton. Brakes hard on, for the curve is sharp; although it was nearly midnight there were lights in the cottages, and railway folk, if I know them aright, would involuntarily look at their clocks, or watches, with the mental comment, ' There goes " the St Pancras " on time.' The London expresses are the only passenger trains that do not stop at Riccarton, and with the sound of its wheel beats growing fainter as it coasts down into Liddesdale another day ends in the life of this ' out-and-out railway colony.'

In the last 1½ miles up to the Whitrope Box the gradient eases a little, to 1 in 80; but the country is bleak in the extreme, and after the grind round the Riccarton curves there is seldom any recovery in speed before the tunnel is entered. There would not be much point in pounding hard at this stage, to snatch a few odd seconds; for the long descent to Hawick is at hand, with plenty of opportunity to pull the boiler round if the steaming has been ' shy ' on the way up from Newcastleton. Down the bank speed is mostly held in to 50 mph or even less. I once clocked a maximum of 67 behind a North British ' Atlantic,' many years ago, but that was quite exceptional. Very quickly, the bleak uplands of the Cheviots give place to a smiling, wooded glen, though here, beside the Slitrig Water, as on Teviot and Tweedside, the plantations are of relatively recent origin compared with the more ancient forests of Scotland. In contrast also to the Newcastleton bank the gradients are constantly changing, with the steeper pitches at 1 in 72, 75, 77, and 80. The curves are, if anything, still more severe, and nowhere more so than in the immediate approach to Hawick. Rounding a curve to the right, the busy industrial Border town is seen across a high embankment, packed in between the hills; but two more reverse curves must be traversed before the train comes in to the station.

This is indeed a land of folklore, despite its modern occupations. The ancient war-cry of the young men of Hawick—' Teribus ye Teri Odin ' (' May both Tyr and Odin have us ')—gave its name to one of the North British ' Atlantics,' No. 906 *Teribus,* while another engine name springs from the next station northward, Hassendean, immortalised in one of the great ballads of the Border, *Jock o' Hazeldean.* Engine No. 878, of the first batch of 'Atlantics,' was named *Hazeldean.* There is some fairly stiff climbing out of Hawick, as we cut across high ground north of Teviotdale; but soon after

143

Hassendean, the Eildon Hills begin to dominate the scene ahead, and by St Boswells we are on Tweedside, in a land where the memories and associations of Sir Walter Scott are evergreen. ' Wizard of the North ' indeed! Today, perhaps, we can scarcely realise the almost overwhelming impact of the Waverley novels upon the cultured public of the day, and how the effect of that impact was sustained for scores of years afterwards. Could one imagine, by way of comparison, a popular novel of the present time giving its name to a great airport, or to an ocean terminal of many shipping lines; or of airliners, motor-cars, diesel-electric locomotives, or even a great trade route all taking the same name ? Yet that in effect is what actually happened a hundred years ago.

Walter Scott as a relatively young man visited the ruins of the earliest Cistercian monastery in England, the beautiful Waverley Abbey, near Farnham in Surrey; with his skill in choosing euphonious and arresting names for his characters he took the name of the abbey as the surname of his hero in the first of the novels that brought him immortality. They became known as the Waverley novels. Later works were sometimes styled as ' by the Author of Waverley.' The name was on everyone's lips, and so, on the North British Railway there was a Waverley station, a Waverley route, and both a locomotive and a steamer named *Waverley*. So far as locomotives were concerned the North British did not have the first *Waverley*. There was a broad-gauge Great Western 7-ft. 4-4-0 bearing the name built by Stephenson's in 1855, and the North Western followed in 1863, with engine No. 806 of the ' Lady of the Lake ' class. When the North British began engine-naming in earnest, after the arrival of Dugald Drummond in 1875, the titles chosen were topographical, in the Brighton style, and the very fine ' 476 ' class 4-4-0s of 1876, built specially for the Waverley route mostly had uninspired names like *Carlisle, Hawick, Galashiels,* and *St Boswells.* Two of the class, allocated to the line north of Dundee, were originally named *Aberdeen* and *Montrose,* but after the fall of the Tay Bridge in 1879 and the consequent alterations in engine workings, these two engines were transferred south of Edinburgh, and it was then that they were renamed *Eskbank* and *Waverley* respectively. One suspects, however, that in the fashion of the day engine 487 was named *not* after Sir Walter's hero, but after the station!

Matthew Holmes had no use for the Brighton style of naming, and when he succeeded Dugald Drummond the names on all North British engines so adorned were painted out. Naming was revived however, in much happier style with the building of the Reid 'Atlantics' in 1906, and then, what a change for the better! *Abbotsford* and *Waverley* reappeared; but among those appropriate to the Waverley route we had also *Dunedin, Midlothian, Liddesdale, Hazeldean, Tweeddale,* and *Borderer.* In the later batch, put into service in 1912, there were added *Holyrood, Teribus,* and *Buccleuch.* This has been, I fear, rather a digression from the Waverley route itself; but between St Boswells and Galashiels, running in the shadow of the Eildon Hills, and passing Melrose, one may be forgiven, in an age of intense propaganda and publicity, for letting thoughts wander to the man who did more than anyone else in history to publicise and glamourise Scotland and Scottish history. That Tweedside by Melrose and Abbotsford is very beautiful goes almost without saying, and even the busy town of Galashiels, set tight among hills at the junction of Gala Water with the Tweed, is not distasteful to see.

From the railway point of view I shall always associate Galashiels with that incredible summer and autumn of 1948 when storms of unprecedented fury caused such havoc on the East Coast main line between Dunbar and Berwick, and made it necessary to divert all the London and Edinburgh traffic via the Waverley route as far south as St Boswells, travelling thence via Kelso to Tweedmouth Junction. The heavy Anglo-Scottish expresses stopped at Galashiels to take water, including even the nominally non-stop King's Cross–Waverley flyer, then named 'The Capitals Limited'; the water stop was made until one enterprising Haymarket driver made an all-out attack on the tremendous climb up to Falahill from the north side, got up successfully without the rear-end banking assistance that was always available at Hardengreen Junction, and judged he had enough water to get through to Tweedmouth and Lucker troughs without stopping at all. After that, on seventeen runs in all, eight down and nine up, the King's Cross–Waverley trip was made actually non-stop via Galashiels, a grand tribute to the enginemanship of the crews concerned, and to the economy in coal and water of the Gresley 'A4' Pacific locomotives. The trains concerned were carrying a gross load of about 460 tons.

145

Resuming the journey towards Edinburgh, still in what might be called the Border country, the line climbs the glen of Gala Water, through fine country, though neither the gradient nor the scenery is so severe as that south of Hawick. The curvature is much the same as usual on the Waverley route, precluding anything in the way of fast running downhill—indeed the speeds of ascending trains in the neighbourhood of Stow and Fountainhall is often much the same as that of southbound expresses. Although the general gradient is 1 in 150 there are several short stretches of dead level that make the aggregate effect of the bank much less severe than it would otherwise be. I have recorded speeds of between 55 and 60 mph on northbound trains on this stretch. The last miles up to Falahill summit bring us to an altitude of 880 ft. above sea level, a bleak spot certainly, but with the line in cutting a passenger does not gain quite such an impression of wilderness that is so apparent in the approaches to Whitrope, whether going north or south. At Falahill we are less than 18 miles from Edinburgh, and the ensuing descent is very steep. At first the line traverses wild upland country, and the ruin of Borthwick Castle tells its own tale of the stormy history of Scotland; but soon the wide prospects give way to evidence of increasing industrialism. From the railway point of view one of the most interesting is the work connected with the great new marshalling yard at Millerhill. Since nationalisation of the railways much of the through freight traffic from Scotland to the south has been put over the Waverley route, and the Millerhill yard will act as the concentration and remarshalling point for traffic coming from many parts of Scotland.

The familiar crags that flank Edinburgh on the south are now close at hand. At Niddrie South Junction the Waverley route turns to the right and descends on a 1 in 80 gradient, and in a moment more we are joining the East Coast main line, at Portobello East. Such is an impression of the Waverley route; a fine road; a fascinating road, but no place for weak or ailing engines!

146

42 Out in the Border Marches May 1965: a northbound freight between the great marshalling yards of Kingmoor and Millerhill, in level country not far out of Kingmoor, hauled by 'V2' 2-6-2 No. 60970.

43 New style Waverley Route goods near Newcastleton, hauled by two Type 1 Clayton-built diesels Nos. D8570 and D8573.

44 In the beautiful scenery of the Border Country in June 1966: a northbound goods climbing from Galashiels to Falahill, near Fountainhall, with Class 40 diesel locomotive No. D366.

45 Climbing southbound to Falahill; freight between the yards, Millerhill to Kingmoor, in May 1962, hauled by 'V2' 2-6-2 No. 60933.

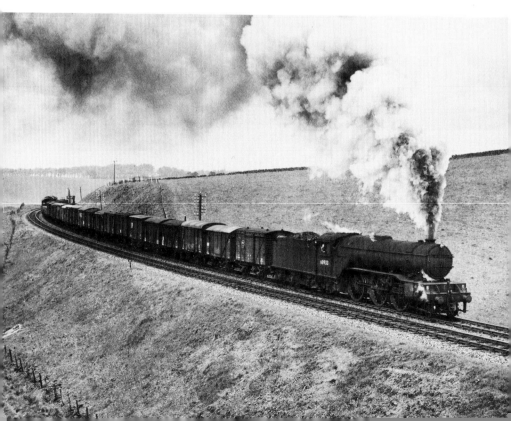

CHAPTER 12

IN no possible stretch of the imagination could one consider this wild, fascinating, heavily graded railway as a fast express route. A study of the gradient profile alone gives no more than a partial clue to its unique character. Locomotive enthusiasts travelling as ordinary passengers and clocking the speeds have sometimes expressed disappointment to me that time is not made up, after late starts from Carlisle, when there appears to be ample engine power and a clear road; but when riding on the footplate the reason is obvious. The 'Waverley Route' must contain the most constant and continuous curvature of any 'crack' main line anywhere in the country. A locomotive engineer once summed it up by saying: 'It's a case of slogging uphill at 30 mph, and doing 60 where you can downhill and on the level—no more!' There are indeed numerous curves where speed has to be reduced to 50, 45, or 40 mph, and on a southbound run for example, after descending the Steele Road Bank it is very far from a straightforward run from Newcastleton to the outskirts of Carlisle. If by piling on additional engine power—steam, diesel, gas turbine or what you will—we could run uphill as fast as is nowadays run in the descending direction, and we could climb from Newcastleton to Riccarton in 10 min. instead of 16, and from Galashiels to Falahill in 19 min. instead of 23, this saving of 10 min. is about all one could hope for throughout from Carlisle to Waverley. The curves preclude anything more.

For a short time in the summer of 1901 there were the makings of a third Railway Race to the North, when the Midland and North British booked the 9.30 a.m. from St Pancras to arrive at Waverley at 6.5 p.m., or ten minutes ahead of the *Flying Scotsman*. Although the North Eastern could not leave Newcastle before time every effort seems to have been made to beat the Midland and North British into Edinburgh and on several occasions the arrival was 12 or 13 min. early. Although certain newspapers 'splashed' these runs, and talked about 'A great Railway Race,' the challenge was never really taken up. The North British share in the working of the accelerated service from St Pancras was to cover the 98¼ miles from Carlisle to Waverley non-stop in 135 min. The intermediate times were very much the same as they are today, such as 54 min. from Carlisle start to Whitrope Box, compared with 52 min., and 24 min. from Galashields to Falahill, as compared with 23 min. today from a standing start. The downhill speeds were generally higher, but even then 65 mph was about the maximum to be noted. Before the decelerations occasioned by World War I the summer 9.30 a.m. from Waverley to St Pancras was still faster, with a schedule of 131 min. to Carlisle; but in the period between the two wars non-stop running was never revived. Today the down 'Waverley' is allowed 2 hr. 42 min. with stops at Hawick, St Boswells, Melrose and Galashiels, while the corresponding up express is similarly timed.

Coming now to locomotive power, the Reid 'Atlantics,' in their non-superheated days were assisted when the tare load exceeded 250 tons. Superheating made a wonderful difference to them, and the load limit was afterwards increased to 290 tons. The heaviest train I ever personally observed with one of them unassisted loaded to 285 tons gross, and details of this are tabulated alongside a very smart 'Atlantic' run with a load of under 200 tons, and with a run I was privileged to make on the footplate in 1953, with a 'Pacific.' Three of the Gresley 'A3' class are stationed at Canal Junction shed, Carlisle, namely:

60079	*Bayardo*
60093	*Coronach*
60095	*Flamingo*

The first two of these have at various times participated in workings over the East Coast main line; but *Flamingo,* as LNER No. 2749, went to Carlisle when brand new, and so far as I am aware she has never worked from any other shed. Referring to the table on page 129, *Saint Mungo* had the 12 noon express, in the summer of 1927; both *Holyrood* and *Bayardo* had the 10.5 a.m. The schedules of all three trains were approximately the same as far as Newcastleton; from there southward in 'Atlantic' days the timings were faster, with 27 and 28 min. for the last 24·3 miles into Carlisle, against 32 min. when I rode on *Bayardo* in 1953.

Although *Saint Mungo* had a load that would have been con-
idered fairly light for an ' Atlantic ' in 1927 the uphill work was
xtremely smart; the sharp staccato beat of the exhaust, the rapidity
f acceleration the moment there came any easing of the gradient,
1ade the obvious mastery of the engine over its task exhilarating
ɔ record. The average speeds of 48 mph from Niddrie South
unction to Newtongrange, and of exactly 30 mph from Gorebridge
ɔ the summit, over stretches where the gradient averages 1 in 150
nd 1 in 75 respectively, were the fastest I have ever seen, except
ɣith some of the very light loads taken on expresses of the pre-1914
ra. *Holyrood*, with an additional hundred tons of train also did
ome hard excellent work. There was a permanent-way check
ɔ 23 mph most awkwardly, on the 1 in 80 from Portobello up to
√iddrie South Junction, and the engine lost a good minute, as com-
ɩared with *Saint Mungo* here; but it was splendid work to recover
ɔ 52 mph at Hardengreen Junction, and to average 26 mph from
ɔorebridge up to Falahill. There was however no attempt to regain
he lost minute on the downhill stretch to Galashiels, in fact a
urther 40 sec. was dropped due to the cautiousness of the running
ɩn the curves. This was, of course, thoroughly typical of ' Waverley
₹oute ' running.

On the third run, a load very little greater than that conveyed
ɔy *Holyrood* might have been thought to provide an easy task for
ɩ ' Pacific '; but riding on the footplate I was very soon under no
lelusions about the arduousness of the job. For *Bayardo* was flailed
ɩlong good and hard, with regulator full open and cut-off rarely less
han 40 per cent; and far from gaining an impression of a ' Pacific '
1aving an easy time of it, I thought of *Holyrood* once more, and
ried to picture what was happening on her footplate when she was
naking relatively similar times, with a load nearly as great.
Although I rode several of the ' Atlantics ' on the Aberdeen route
˙ never had the opportunity of riding one down to Carlisle. With
₹ayardo we came thundering up the 1 in 80 to Niddrie South
Iunction at 37 mph, and with cut-off kept at 40 per cent we got
ɩway to nearly 50 mph at Hardengreen   The roar of the exhaust
ɣas by this time tremendous, and as we came on to the long stretch
ɔf 1 in 70 ascent our driver dropped the lever first to 42 and then to
15 per cent. The boiler pressure had fallen somewhat at this critical
itage, and instead of the full 220 lb. per sq. in. the needle was

hovering around the 175 mark. Falahill is always a gruelling business. There is no chance to get the fire gradually into good shape, no chance for any gentle warming up; after the brief down hill run to Portobello the engine is at it, hammer and tongs, fo nearly half an hour on end. It is really no surprise that the steaming tends to flag a little by the time the train is out on the high embankment overlooking Borthwick Castle! *Bayardo* got down to 25½ mph at one stage, but for the last two miles our drive increased cut-off to no less than 50 per cent, and we topped Falahill at 27½ mph.

The care taken in running downhill over the constantly curving stretches of the Waverley route could not be more clearly empha sised than by the details of these three runs. Here were three journeys made in the years 1927, 1928, and 1953, and yet the maximum variation between the fastest and slowest times was 6 sec over the 4·7 miles from Falahill to Fountainhall; 20 sec. over the 7·2 miles from Fountainhall to Bowland, and 55 sec. over the las 3·7 miles into Galashiels. The fact that *Saint Mungo* was slightly ahead of time no doubt explains the very slow approach her drive made to this stop. Between *Holyrood* and *Bayardo* there was a modest 8 sec. in it!

Over the central section of the journey, on Tweedside, through the land immortalised by its associations with Sir Walter Scott there is always some really hard running between stops; there are sharp rising and falling gradients, and with the modern ' Pacifics there can be no pulling the reverser back to 15 per cent cut-off, or so, and allowing the engine to make its own pace. With *Bayardo* boiler pressure had been worked up again while we stood a Galashiels, and we left with 210 lb. per sq. in. on the clock. The driver quickly linked up to 35 per cent, and in about 100 yd. from the dead start reduced further to 27 per cent, with regulator now full open. The gradient is now falling at 1 in 120 for nearly a mile out of Galashiels, and we swept into speed; but after Selkirk Junction, now remotely controlled, there is a rise at 1 in 200, and we did not exceed 50 mph before the stop at Melrose. *Holyrood* obviously worked hard, made slightly better times here, while *Saint Mungo* for once was the slowest of the three—again, however, by no more than a few odd seconds.

Out of Melrose, where there is no favourable grade until almos within sight of St Boswells station, *Bayardo* was driven harder than ever, with cut-off at 40 per cent at first, and 35 sustained to Ravenswood Junction, where speed was up to 45 mph. Here, indeed, the 'Pacific' did show up to advantage over the two 'Atlantics,' though on both the latter runs the working was smart enough by any ordinary standards. Over the final 'leg' of the central stage of the journey, the 'Pacific' was working to a sharper timing than the other two engines. The allowance of only 15 min. for the 12·2 miles from St Boswells to Hawick is indeed tight, and despite some excellent running it was not quite kept. The schedule for the trains worked by the 'Atlantics' was 17 min. in each case. Due to the station overtime at St Boswells *Bayardo* was a minute late into Hawick, but both the other trains were dead on time, and by smart station work on the most recent journey that odd minute was regained, and all three trains left punctually for Carlisle.

The climb from Hawick to Whitrope is perhaps the worst of the whole journey. It begins right off the platform end at 1 in 75, and except for an easing to 1 in 112–123 over the second mile, and 1½ miles at 1 in 117–121 approaching Shankend, the gradient is between 1 in 72 and 1 in 80 for 10 miles continuously, to the northern end of Whitrope Tunnel. The last three-quarters of a mile through the tunnel to the summit box is at 1 in 96. Bookings of 25–6 min. for this 10·9 miles from the standing start at Hawick leave no margin with heavy trains; the curvature is continuous and severe enough in places to require check rails, but a slight concession is made by banking trains just out of the platform at Hawick. In accordance with the practice then prevailing, *Bayardo* was re-manned at Hawick, Driver Watson and Fireman Hadley, of Canal Junction shed, Carlisle, relieving Driver J. Chapman and Fireman J. Elliot, the Hawick men who had worked us down from Edinburgh. The practice of remanning at Hawick has now been discontinued, and on the 10.5 a.m. from Edinburgh, now happily titled 'The Waverley,' Carlisle men work through.

Bayardo got away well from Hawick, but by Stobs pressure was beginning to fall, and with the continuous use of 32 to 37 per cent cut-off, with full regulator the needle was showing around 185 lb. per sq. in. Consequently the 'Atlantic' *Holyrood*, which had dropped behind somewhat on the first gruelling pitches from the start was gaining steadily by Stobs. On the easier length before

Shankend she reached $34\frac{1}{2}$ mph against *Bayardo's* maximum of 31, and on the last toiling ascent to the mouth of Whitrope tunnel, out among the lone, windy heights of the Cheviot Hills, she held $25\frac{1}{2}$ mph, and recovered smartly to 32 inside the tunnel. On *Bayardo* pressure fell still further. My notes show a number of readings above Shankend ranging between 165 and 180; cut-off was advanced to 40, and finally to 42 per cent and we entered the tunnel at $22\frac{1}{4}$ mph. By this time *Holyrood* had forged well ahead, but even with her fine work time had been dropped to the tune of 20 sec. By comparison, *Saint Mungo* on the 12-noon train fairly sailed up. Her time is the fastest I have ever seen recorded with a load of 185 tons, unassisted. The nearest was a time of exactly 22 min. from Hawick to Whitrope, with 170 tons, by engine No. 868 *Aberdonian* in the early days of World War I.

Prior even to that period, when the summer 9.30 a.m. up from Waverley was booked non-stop to Carlisle in 131 min., one of the non-superheater ' Scott ' class 4–4–0s, No. 899 *Jeanie Deans,* made a remarkable ascent, from passing Hawick at about 30 mph. The 10·9 miles to Whitrope were climbed in $18\frac{3}{4}$ min., with a load of 170 tons. The time from Stobs to the summit box was 12 min. 10 sec., against the 12 min. 50 sec. of *Saint Mungo,* and definitely places the honours in the lap of the non-superheater 4–4–0. In making such a comparison I am not suggesting that the ' Atlantic ' could not have substantially bettered her own times had it been necessary. She left Hawick on time, and passed Whitrope $3\frac{1}{2}$ min. early, while the 4–4–0 due to signal checks farther north was $5\frac{1}{4}$ min. late through Hawick, and gained $3\frac{1}{4}$ min. on the pass-to-pass schedule of 22 min. then laid down. Even on this journey of long ago when the driver was so obviously out to regain all the time he could, no chances were taken downhill, and the point-to-point times onwards to Carlisle were strictly observed. So it was on all the three journeys tabulated; the schedule times of the three trains were 65, 66 and 71 min. respectively, so that timekeeping was generally accurate.

Turning now to the north-bound run on page 126, this was quite a recent experience on the down ' Waverley ' when I was privileged to ride on the footplate. I had travelled through from St Pancras, and it had been a journey of contrasts. To Leeds I rode passenger, and on the non-stop run to Nottingham we had had some really high speed; but between Normanton and Leeds we were sorely delayed. Most of the loss would however have been made up by some spirited work over the Settle and Carlisle line. We had one of the incomparable Stanier 'Class 5' 4–6–0s, piloted by a Midland 7 ft. 4–4–0, and a hard ride it had been for me. Splendid motive-power units though they are, the 'black fives' are no Rolls-Royces when it comes to riding, and with much running at 75 to 80 mph north of Blea Moor I reached Carlisle feeling somewhat shattered. But then, what a change! In all my years of footplating I never remember riding on a locomotive in more perfect mechanical condition than the Gresley 'Pacific,' *Flamingo* which took over haulage of the 'Waverley' that day. She had run just over 11,000 miles since her last visit to Doncaster, and was an absolute joy to experience. When the Midland engines had coupled off, she drew ahead and set back on to the train like some ghost machine, and as we got away and took the sharp curves at Caldew and Canal Junction she just floated round, with an ease and silence that was almost uncanny.

As we bowled along, and the hills of the Border country began to loom up ahead on this autumn day of lowering skies and high wind, this, I reflected, was the steam locomotive at its very finest, 'a machine of precision,' as Mr K. J. Cook so significantly called it in his Presidential Address to the Institution of Locomotive Engineers in 1955; and this engine, superbly repaired and well maintained subsequently, was certainly a tribute to his works at Doncaster. For a time, by Lyneside, we were running on no more than 13 per cent cut-off, but after passing Scotch Dyke there comes a first taste of the real character of the Waverley route, in the climbing of Penton Bank, with nearly 4 miles at 1 in 100. With the lever in 27 per cent we sustained 38½ mph here, hauling 325 tons: the engine was as strong as she was 'sweet.' On the slightly favourable stretch past Kershopefoot and over the Liddel Water into Scotland, we just touched 60 mph, but then came Newcastleton, and the tremendous climb to Whitrope.

This bank is really worse than Beattock. It is almost as long, just as steep, and has the great additional disadvantage of much curvature. One cannot go charging through Newcastleton at 70 to 75 mph and get a run at it; the most one can hope for is about 55. Throughout the ascent the line is completely exposed, mounting steadily up the open hillside, though at speeds of 30 mph or so, a high wind cannot offer so serious an increase to the tractive resistance as on fast-running sections of a railway. All the same it can be a very wild and rough spot amid the winter storms. On this trip we passed Newcastleton at 53 mph, with the lever in 17 per cent cut-off; in the first mile the gradient stiffens from 1 in 200 to 1 in 125, and then at the 73rd milepost from Edinburgh, a mile beyond Newcastleton, the 1 in 75 begins. It continues without the slightest

SCOTTISH REGION

4.12 p m CARLISLE–EDINBURGH

'The Waverley'

Load 9 cars 309 tons tare 325 tons full
Engine Class 'A3' 4–6–2 No 60095 *Flamingo*
Driver Moffat, Fireman Lamb (Canal Jc Shed)

Mls		Sch	m	s	mph
0·0	CARLISLE	0	0	00	
1·5	*Canal Jc*	4	4	05	
6·6	Lyneside		11	17	54
9·6	LONGTOWN JC	13	14	44	50
11·9	Scotch Dyke		17	37	54
14·1	Riddings		20	12	
16·6	Penton		24	01	38½
21·1	Kershopefoot		29	29	60
24·2	NEWCASTLETON	31	32	47	53
28·8	Steele Road		40	11	30
32·3	Riccarton Jc	47	47	10	31
34·5	*Whitrope Box*	52	51	13	33½
38·4	Shankend		56	12	
41·5	Stobs		59	53	
45·4	HAWICK	68	65	52	
0·0			0	00	
4·3	Hassendean		7	13	51/49
7·6	Belses		11	07	60 (max)
12·2	ST BOSWELLS	16	16	20	
0·0			0	00	
3·4	MELROSE	6	5	40	55 (max)
0·0			0	00	
3·7	GALASHIELS	6	5	48	55 (max)
0·0		0	0	00	
3·7	Bowland		7	55	42
			p w s		5
6·8	Stow		13	50	43
10·9	Fountainhall		18	40	52½
14·4	Heriot		22	49	47½/49
15·6	*Falahill Box*	23	24	19	47
25·2	*Hardengreen Jc*	36	36	22	58 (max)
			p w s		
29·1	*Niddrie S. Jc*	43	42	54	
30·5	Portobello	45	45	22	
33·5	WAVERLEY	51	51	15	

Net time Galashiels–Waverley 48¾ min.

break for 8 miles. At once Driver Moffat lengthened the cut-off to 26 per cent and a mile later he increased still further to 30 per cent. By this time the exhaust of the engine was plainly audible, and a beautiful, regular, and even beat it was. The Gresley three-cylinder ' syncopation ' was quite absent, and from the way the engine was climbing it is evident that the valve-setting was extremely accurate. At milepost 71 we were down to $33\frac{1}{2}$ mph, and the cut-off was further advanced to 33 per cent, and this setting, despite the wind which was catching us furiously broadside from the east, took us to within sight of Riccarton Junction. For mile after mile above Steele Road speed was held absolutely steady at 30 mph. This is a tribute no less to Fireman Lamb, who without blowing off was keeping pressure just at ' sizzling ' point. The valves blew off at about 212 lb. per sq. in., and I watched with pleasure how the gauge registered 208, 205, 209, and so on, all the way up the bank. The combination of a well-nigh perfect engine and a supremely competent crew was exhilarating beyond words.

In readiness for the Riccarton curves Driver Moffat increased cut-off to 35 per cent at the 67th milepost, and instead of falling on that sharp swing to the left when nearing the station we were accelerating a little, and on the last $1\frac{1}{2}$ miles to the Whitrope box where the gradient eases a little to 1 in 80, we worked up to $33\frac{1}{2}$ mph. It was indeed a grand climb. After passing Whitrope the power demanded from the locomotive ceased altogether for a while, but no part of the Waverley route could be called dull; and there is fascination in watching from the footplate the ceaseless windings of the track down into Teviotdale. After the bleak uplands of Liddesdale the trees in the glens by Shankend and Stobs, rich in their autumn colours brought a warm and friendly air to the countryside. Speed was at no time allowed to exceed 55 mph, and so we came round the curve on a high embankment into the grey old Border town of Hawick.

In the locomotive yard beside the station there was a strong flavour of the old days. The ' Scott ' class 4–4–0 *Norna* was alongside, and on the shed there was not a single engine in sight that was not North British—not even LNER, let alone British Railways. Getting away again we had the usual very smart running between the Border towns, though with *Flamingo,* the driver was able to get back to 15 or 17 per cent, once the engine was well into her stride. On both of the short stretches after St Boswells we reached 55 mph before the next stop. Due to signal checks in the immediate approach to the Citadel station we had left Carlisle 16½ min. late; the arrears had been reduced to 13½ min. on arrival at Galashiels, and by smart station working there we were away only 11½ min. late. The immediate start is up a gradient of 1 in 120, which steepens almost immediately to 1 in 110; but above Bowland the ascent becomes easier, and between Stow and Fountainhall the speed is normally well into the ' fifties.' But on this trip, after a splendid start up to Bowland we were brought down to 5 mph for a severe engineers' slack through the tunnel just north of Bowland station. The gradient was now 1 in 175, and up the glen of Gala Water the engine was accelerated magnificently back into her stride. The cut-off was first of all 45 per cent; then 40 per cent and next 35 for well over a mile. Stow station, 2½ miles from the site of the slack, was passed at 43 mph, and with cut-off further reduced to 25 per cent we reached 52½ mph at Fountainhall. The gradient at the point is 1 in 150, but interspersed with one or two strips of level, that make the aggregate climbing of much the same severity as the unbroken 1 in 175 between Bowland and Stow. For the last 2 miles up to Falahill, at 1 in 100–132, Driver Moffat dropped the lever slightly to 27 per cent, and we cleared the summit at 47 mph. Despite the severe check at Bowland we had climbed the 15·6 miles up from Galashiels in 24¼ min., or only 1¼ min. outside schedule.

Although we were now less than 18 miles from Waverley the character of the line still has that wild, romantic aura of the Border country, and we dipped down the very steep gradient past Tyne-head, and round the long curve overlooking Borthwick Castle at 58 mph. But the stacks, and gaunt head-gears of collieries began to crowd into the landscape. The Lothian coalfield was at hand, and we were entering industrial Scotland. So to Millerhill, to observe a lengthy engineers' slack beside the site of the great new marshalling yard. A little extra time has been put into the schedule to compensate for this slow running while work in connection with the new yard is in progress. At Niddrie North Junction, 29·6 miles from Galashiels in 42 min. we were exactly on our point-to-point time, and a careful and unchecked run down through Portobello and along the East Coast main line through St Margarets, brought us into Waverley at 7.2½ p.m., 11½ min. late, and in just over 51 min.

Mls	Station	Year	1927 12 noon 9873 Saint Mungo 174/185		1928 10.5 a m 9904 Holyrood 265/285		1953 10.5 a m 60079 Bavardo 288/305	
			m s	mph	m s	mph	m s	mph
0·0	WAVERLEY		0 00		0 00		0 00 (p w s)	
3·0	Portobello		4 50	57	4 40	22	5 40	
4·5	Niddrie S. Jc		6 45	42	7 25 (p w s)		7 59	37
8·2	Hardengreen Jc		11 35	53½	13 00	52	12 55	48
9·7	Newtongrange		13 25	50	14 55	44	14 53	
12·7	Fushiebridge		18 40	31	21 30	25	21 00	30
16·0	Tynehead		25 30	28	29 20	24	27 26	27/25
17·9	Falahill Box		29 30	31	33 55	30	31 39	27½
22·6	Fountainhall		35 25		39 45		37 28	
29·8	Bowland		43 20		48 00		45 24	
33·5	GALASHIELS		48 50	60 max	52 35		50 07	
0·0			0 00		0 00		0 00	
3·7	MELROSE		5 50		5 30		5 37	
0·0			0 00		0 00		0 00	
3·4	ST BOSWELLS		6 00		6 15		5 47	
0·0			0 00		0 00		0 00	
4·6	Belses		7 25		7 25		6 31	62½ max
7·9	Hassendean		11 25	58½ max	11 45	62½ max	10 18	
12·2	HAWICK		16 45		16 40		15 33	
0·0			0 00		0 00		0 00	
3·9	Stobs		8 45	37/31	10 10	33/25	9 38	30/23
7·0	Shankend		14 20	40	16 55	34½	16 40	31
10·9	Whitrope Box		21 35	30	25 30	25¼	26 49	22¼
13·1	Riccarton Jc		24 40		28 30		30 15	
21·2	NEWCASTLETON		34 50	61 max	37 40	61 max	40 31	57 max
31·3	Riddings Jc		45 50		48 30		52 16	
35·8	LONGTOWN JC		50 40		53 15		57 30	20
41·0	Harker		55 35	66	58 40	62½	64 51 (p w s)	51½
43·9	Canal Jc		58 30 (sigs)		61 45		69 58 (sigs)	20
45·4	CARLISLE		62 05		65 25		74 33	

Net times :
Waverley–Galashiels: 48¾ | 51½ | 49
Hawick–Carlisle: 61¼ | 65½ | 70

Note—On Run No 3 engine was remanned at Hawick

from Galashiels. It had been such a beautiful run—far removed, it is true, from the high-speed exploits for which the Gresley 'Pacifics' will be remembered as long as there are railways, but memorable in the comfort and quietness of the riding, and in the sterling uphill performance. And, after all, hard slogging uphill is the only kind of power output that really matters on the Waverley route.

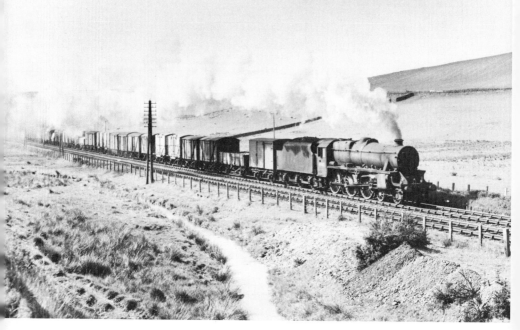

46 The northbound approach to Falahill: a freight from Carlisle to Millerhill Yard, in June 1965, hauled by ex-LMS 'Black Five' 4-6-0 No. 45082.

47 Falahill summit, in May 1962, showing signalbox and sidings: a local train

Edinburgh to Carlisle is hauled by a Class 27 diesel No. D5316.

48 Leaving Millerhill Yard for the south: in February 1965 the 'Black Five' 4-6-0 No. 44899 is fitted with a small snow plough.

49 'Pacifics' on freight on the Waverley Route in April 1964: a Millerhill-Kingmoor mixed goods hauled by Class A3 4-6-2 No. 60042 *Singapore*, near Eskbank.

CHAPTER 13

THE SOU' WEST 'LONG ROAD' TO CARLISLE

THE men of the Glasgow and South Western must have been among the greatest creators of nicknames, for trains, locomotives, and for their fellow men, to be found anywhere in the British railway service. The Irish boat train from Carlisle to Stranraer was the Paddy; among enginemen at various times one found 'The Mool,' 'The Calculator,' and 'Th' Auld Juck,' while the night express freight train to the South was always 'The Long Road Goods.' It is from this latter nickname that I have 'lifted' the title of this chapter, though curiously enough the main line from Kilmarnock south to Dumfries and Gretna was scarcely ever known as 'The Long Road' in any other connection. Still when entering upon Sou' West metals one must do as the Sou' West men did, and nicknames there must be.

The early history of many railways is one of intense conflict and competition with their neighbours. The Glasgow and South Western is certainly no exception, for the extension to the south of the old Glasgow, Paisley, Kilmarnock and Ayr—the GPK & A as it was known—was born out of the intense rivalry between the two great schemes for building a main line from Carlisle to Glasgow. If Joseph Locke and his sponsors of the Grand Junction Railway had alone been responsible for choice of route the Caledonian would have gone through Dumfries, and up Nithsdale. In the early days of that great project Glasgow, and Glasgow alone was the ultimate goal of the English promoters who so skilfully contrived to get Locke introduced and commissioned to do the work. Purely Scottish interests in Glasgow and the west formed a fairly shrewd idea of what was behind this move, and the rival party fought tooth and nail to effect a link-up via Kilmarnock. Then local interests in Annandale stepped in, and began to stress the advantages, as they saw it, of a route farther to the east. Viewed in the light of the eventual ramifications of the Caledonian Railway in Lanarkshire, and its connections northward via Larbert and Stirling these are now obvious enough; but the mere suggestion of a change of

163

plan was enough to rouse Nithsdale and the west to fury, and it was not merely a case of two alternative railways schemes, but of one dale against another.

The Annandale party carried the day, and the Caledonian went through Lockerbie and over Beattock summit, and although in due course the Nithsdale route was also built, time saw no burying of the hatchet. The two rival companies were deadly enemies down to the last day of 1922, when both were swallowed up in the LMS system, and even then enmity did not begin to vanish. It was a rivalry not merely of policy and major operational tactics, but a plain distrust, and scorn which filtered down to the humblest employees on either side. All this came vividly back to my mind one night in the spring of 1958 when I was driving to Euston to catch the midnight express to Glasgow. With what triumph, I reflected, would men of the old Sou' West have hailed a day when one of the crack North Western Scotch expresses would regularly travel over their route from Carlisle, and not over the hated 'Caley'! It would be daylight by the time we crossed the Border, and so I asked the sleeping-car attendant to bring my early morning tea at Carlisle, so that I should see once more as much as possible of the Sou' West countryside. Many times before I had travelled this way to Glasgow, but not until now in the early dawn when it was light enough to see.

One always felt that rivalry between the Scottish companies was kept well stirred up on the Glasgow and South Western side more than on any other, and it may have arisen from a vague inward feeling of inferiority complex in the situation at Carlisle; for not only was the city reached by running powers over $8\frac{1}{2}$ miles of the Caledonian, but having arrived, the G & SWR locomotives had to traverse a length of the Maryport and Carlisle Railway in order to reach their running shed at Currock Road. Today all is changed. The integration of the Caledonian and G & SWR motive-power studs at Carlisle was one of the earliest developments after grouping, and it was naturally at Kingmoor, and not at Currock Road that the combined power was stabled. At one time, there were certain duties on which one Stanier 'Pacific' engine worked through between Euston and St Enoch, but now engines are changed at Carlisle on such of the West Coast expresses as are routed over the Sou' West line north of the Border. Cyclic engine diagrams are now in force by which Scottish locomotives work some trains over the Caledonian line, and some over the Sou' West in the course of a single round of duties, while to add towards the complete obliteration of the one-time individuality of the route, not a single one of the G & SWR locomotives now remains in service.

Only the country itself remains as of old, save in the very few places where new building sites have been developed, or factories erected, and the wistful, early-morning beauty of the Solway Firth across to the Cumbrian mountains, and the gentle rising landscapes of lower Nithsdale must have looked much the same from my sleeper window, as travellers in the old night 'Pullman' from St Pancras saw them seventy or eighty years ago. The leftward turn of the Sou' West, at Gretna Junction, takes the line near to the Solway shore for some fifteen miles, giving a prospect to the south that can be fascinating or forlorn according to the degree of visibility over the firth; and then, as the train turns a few points northward, by Cummertrees and Ruthwell the scene across the Lochar Moss to the Nith estuary brings the fine hill Criffel prominently into the picture. As yet the immediate countryside is undistinguished, characteristic of the farm-lands of the border marches, but without the grandeur of the hills as a background. So, in 33 miles from Carlisle, we come to the fine old town of Dumfries; a railway junction of some importance.

From here to the westward goes the line to Castle Douglas and Stranraer, while from the north came a branch of the Caledonian, from Lockerbie. In view of what I have already written about the cat-and-dog state of affairs existing between the Caley and the Sou' West, one might have imagined that here in Dumfries was a fine source of contention and feud, with the Caledonian thrusting a small but impudent figure into a stronghold of the G & SWR. But the railway situation from Dumfries westward to Stranraer was far more delicately balanced than in the districts around Glasgow and the Clyde estuary, where no quarter was shown by either company in its dealings with the other. Here, in the south-western corner of Scotland the two lines were actually *partners,* in working the Portpatrick and Wigtownshire Joint Line. This may well seem to be a very strange state of affairs, seeing that the joint line, terminating on the eastward at Castle Douglas was separated from any part of the Caledonian Railway by the line of the former Castle Douglas and

Dumfries Railway, which was pure G & SWR. The situation out in Galloway arose from one of those highly competitive manoeuvres of early railway politics that frequently left strange sequels.

The Portpatrick Railway, an independent concern incorporated in 1857, approached both the Caledonian and the G & SWR with the idea of one of the larger companies working the line; of the two, the Sou' West tried to strike a harder bargain than the Portpatrick could meet, and so the Caledonian jumped in. From the outset the London and North Western was interested in this venture of its Scottish partner, and went so far as contributing to the Portpatrick Railway capital. So the Caledonian secured a firm, but very isolated foothold in what would otherwise have been reckoned exclusively G & SWR territory. This arrangement lasted for twenty years, when the Portpatrick company was eventually sold, and became a joint concern of the London and North Western, the Caledonian, the G & SW and the Midland. Responsibility for operation as from August 1885, was vested jointly in the Caledonian and the G & SWR. And so the Sou' West had to remain content with Caledonian interests cutting right across their main line at Dumfries, and deep into their own territory in Galloway. Right down into the nineteen thirties a relic of the strong Caledonian interest in that line remained in the running of through carriages between Whithorn and Edinburgh Princes Street. I well remember one journey on the morning Liverpool and Manchester Scotsman when, to our already overloaded compound the two-coach Whithorn portion was added at Lockerbie, sending us forward from there with 480 tons!

Dumfries is indeed rich in historical railway associations, no less than in its more famous ties with Scottish history and literature; but it is time we were away to the north. Before leaving however, it is worth mentioning that the one-time Glasgow, Dumfries and Carlisle Railway, the eventual outcome of the GPK & A determination to have a route to the south through Nithsdale, was opened only as far as Dumfries, from Carlisle, in 1848, yet from the outset, and though at first completely detached, it was worked by the GPK & A. Once away from Dumfries the main line enters a beautiful upland countryside; the hills rise gradually, there are no dramatic or frowning profiles, while in the foreground the farmlands are rich and fair with much picturesque woodland. From Holywood the gradients are steadily rising. Although running in

166

a dale parallel to that of the Caledonian and no more than 10 miles away the profile of the two lines is quite distinct. While the Caledonian climbs at once from Gretna, and then runs roughly level for 15 miles north of Lockerbie, the Sou' West is level, in the aggregate, right through Dumfries, and then begins to climb in earnest only when deeply ensconced in Nithsdale. By Auldgirth the hills are beginning to close in, but the gradient is still no steeper than 1 in 200, and such is modern power on the G & SW that with the 540-ton down *Night Scot*, our ' Duchess ' class 4–6–2 was purring her way up the bank at 52 mph.

Between Auldgirth and Closeburn there is a slight easing of the gradient, so much so that on the recent journey of mine we reached all but 60 mph; but then comes the worst part of the ascent: 6 miles continuously at 1 in 150, to the south end of Drumlanrig Tunnel. Well can one appreciate Joseph Locke's preference for this route, over one which gave the alternative of the Beattock Bank! And despite the easier gradients the Sou' West has a route that is far more beautiful, scenically. At Thornhill, the heights of Queensberry, and Ballencleach Law are blocking in the prospect to the north-east, though it is not the hills themselves, but the glorious woodlands that bring the more gentle, softer beauty to Nithsdale that the harsher grandeur of Beattock lacks. As the train climbs the last few miles to Carronbridge station, with speed usually dropping into the middle forties, the fine seventeenth-century mansion of Drumlanrig Castle may be glimpsed among the trees far below and to the left of the railway. This country seat of the Duke of Buccleuch remains a magnificently preserved example of a Scottish baronial home in the grandest manner. The fair prospects to be seen from the train are cut off as the tunnel that takes its name from the castle is entered; but then one emerges with the speed noticeably quickening, into a scene that must rank as one of the finest to be enjoyed from a fast express train anywhere in Britain.

The line has now entered the narrow gorge of the Nith. The river runs deep between lofty moorland heights, but its course is thickly bounded on both sides by luxuriant woods. The railway runs high enough on the eastern side of the valley to look down upon the trees, and the effect, as the train snakes its way round the numerous curves at 60 mph is exquisite. The Glasgow and South Western Railway was always very proud of its permanent way, and whatever may have been felt in other directions there were no inferiority complexes on this score when it came to comparisons with the Caledonian! And here, in the gorge of the Nith, the old Manson 4–6–0s used to go streaking round the curves at 70 mph and more. Unlike their rivals in the next valley, the G & SW enginemen always practised the art of coal saving; they took their engines very quietly uphill, and then fairly let them loose on the downgrades. 'Were you going hard ?' asked Manson once, of a driver who had survived an alarming derailment due to a faulty point blade. 'Oh aye, but no' as hard as I would like to ha' been goin'!' And this was a man who once ran the 37 miles from New Cumnock down the grade to Dumfries in the level half-hour!

Climbing begins again near the crossing of the Mennock Water, that little burn that comes down from the Mennock Pass leading through the Lowther Hills to Wanlockhead, and the terminus of the Caledonian branch from Elvanfoot. The country is noticeably bleaker hereabouts, though to be sure Sanquhar is a snug enough little town, characteristic of the dales of the border country. Four miles rising at 1 in 180 terminate near this station; speeds of northbound trains are rarely much below the middle fifties, and, again in complete contrast to Caledonian topography, the higher one rides up Nithsdale, the easier the road becomes. Above Sanquhar, too, the direction of travel is almost due west, and with speed little below 60 mph a high, level stretch among the moorland heights is reached. Climbing positively ends at Upper Cairn box, and on the dead-level track beyond the LMSR installed water troughs. The scene is also tending to become less fair, for there is coal hereabouts, and several new sinkings have been made in recent years. The town of New Cumnock, astride the infant Nith, lies just on the southern fringe of the level watershed that extends several miles to the north and from which the country then falls abruptly to the valleys of the Ayr and the Irvine.

Although the rise from Dumfries has for the most part been gradual, it has been continuous nevertheless, and near New Cumnock it reaches a summit level of 616 ft. above ordnance datum. In some ways it could be more trying than the Caledonian, for once away from Dumfries there is no stopping for rear-end assistance, and many a driver of our own times coaxing a lame duck, maybe through from Leeds, will have been glad to see the

168

glint of the water troughs on passing Upper Cairn box. In Glasgow and South Western days there was always a great deal of piloting with the heavier of the Midland Scotch expresses; conversely some of the trains were excessively light. On the other hand the crack Glasgow expresses of the Caledonian were not unduly fast and the 2 hr. 7 min. of the 8.13 p.m. from Carlisle—*Cardean's* regular job —over 102½ miles to Glasgow Central was little superior to the 2 hr. 22 min. of the 1.30 p.m. from St Pancras to St Enoch, over 115½ miles. The open stretches of line in Upper Nithsdale, down as far as Drumlanrig Tunnel in fact, are subject to wild weather, and the section needs as careful patrolling as any in Southern Scotland when the snow is drifting. It was down at the Mennock siding, in 1882, that the 5 p.m. up mail from St Enoch, double-headed with two Stirling 4–4–0s, collided with a freight, the engine of which was well and truly stuck, with the ashpan all clogged up with snow. The depth of the drifts probably saved the lives of the men of the leading engine of the mail, for they were catapulted, as it were, clean out of their cab and landed practically unharmed in the snow, one on either side of the goods train.

The actual summit point, north of New Cumnock is marked by the tiny signal box of Polquhap (pronounced *Polhap*). Then the long descent to Kilmarnock begins. But the coal workings have taken their toll here, and there were usually one or two speed restrictions in operation, due to subsidences. As far as Mauchline there is no stretch steeper than 1 in 150, but roughly 3 miles north of Auchinleck there comes the engineering *pièce de résistance* of the Glasgow and South Western Railway—the viaduct over the river Ayr, at Ballochmyle glen. It is, however, a topographical 'lion' that travellers and the great majority of railway enthusiasts have to take on trust. It comes on a relatively fast stretch, and apart from a fleeting glimpse of a deep wooded gorge below there is no suggestion of what manner of bridge carries the railway over the glen. The impression is no deeper when riding on the foot-plate, for the line is almost straight and the parapets are massive. It was built by the GPK & A, on the first stage of its extension to the south. This had been authorised as far as Cumnock—Old Cumnock that is—in 1845, and work at the site of the great viaduct began in March of the following year.

For magnificence of conception and superb workmanship it is

fit to rank with any works constructed in the grandest of railway pioneer days. Although consisting of seven masonry arches it is the centre one, striding clean across the glen that commands outstanding attention. This arch is a complete semicircle of 181-ft. diameter, carrying the rails about 160 ft. above the bed of the stream. At the time of its construction it was the largest masonry arch in the world; in all probability it still retains that distinction. Earlier photographs, taken from deep in the glen revealed no more than the central part of the main arch, carrying the railway, it is true, at an awe-inspiring height above the water; but at the time of its centenary, in 1948, photographs taken from a much higher level on the eastern side revealed to many enthusiasts, for the first time, the full extent of this remarkable viaduct. Not the least notable feature of its construction has been its longevity, without anything in the way of heavy repairs for over 100 years. It is built of locally quarried red sandstone, with the arch rings of a harder stone.

By the time the Ballochmyle viaduct is crossed we are in the heart of the country immortalised by Robert Burns. One might almost say that Burns was a G & SW man! Certainly, while the North British were making capital out of their associations with the land of Sir Walter Scott, in Liddesdale, Tweedside, and by the naming of their great station in Edinburgh after the immortal Waverley, the Sou' West 'adopted' Burns, and he appeared on their posters, in their brochures, and even on one time-table cover. It is a pity in some respects that the Sou' West did not name locomotives, for I feel sure that here was a railway, if ever there was one, where the names would have really meant something to the drivers and firemen. To LMS men the pioneer Pacific was 'sixty-two hundred' not *The Princess Royal*; talk of *Rooke,* and they would look blank, while 'fifty-six-sixty' would immediately touch the most responsive of chords. But name a green Glasgow and South Western engine *Bonnie Jean, Tam o' Shanter* or *Mary Morison,* and the effect might well have been electrifying. I shall always remember a footplate journey from Crewe to Glasgow with a wee Scots driver whom I had put down as taciturn by the time we reached Carlisle. But once over the Border, what a change: he sang, he whistled, and as we pounded our way up Beattock he was reciting Burns! If a Caledonian man could do that, imagine the driver and fireman of a Sou' West *Highland Mary*, riding the Ardoch and Mennock curves!

At Mauchline we are travelling well beyond the Border country; the direct line to Ayr goes off to the west, and after cutting through the ridge between the Ayr and Irvine valleys, by the Mossgiel tunnel the main line drops abruptly at 1 in 100 for four miles. At Hurlford, we are on the outskirts of Kilmarnock, and entering upon industrial Scotland. All down the years it has needed good going to cover the 58 miles between Dumfries and Kilmarnock, in either direction, and it is now time to ring up the final curtain and see something of Scottish engine performance over a route that has changed much with the years. One could hardly say Sou' West, or G & SW performance today, for the driver of the Thames-Clyde express is always a Midland man from Leeds, and many other trains are worked by Polmadie or by Kingmoor men. The times when one could hear the broad Cumberland accents of the Currock Road men in St Enoch are relatively few today, though one of the most interesting runs I have to describe in my final chapter was with one such worthy. So, then, to Kilmarnock, for some running over 'The Long Road,' to Carlisle.

50 Parallel movement at Mauchline June 1961: a Dumfries to Glasgow 'stopper' hauled by 'Black Five' 4-6-0 No. 44783 pulls out abreast of a Barony Pit to Ayr coal train, hauled by Horwich 2-6-0 No. 42745.

51 Empty stock train off the G&SW line passing through the Floriston woods between Gretna Junction and Carlisle, hauled by Class A3 4-6-2 No. 60070 *Gladiateur* (July 1963).

52 Glasgow-Carlisle stopping train in the Drumlanrig Gorge of the River Nith, July 1964, hauled by 'Black Five' 4-6-0 No. 44726.

53 Climbing south from Kilmarnock, the up 'Thames-Clyde Express', near Bowhouse, in July 1958, hauled by 'Black Five' 4-6-0 No. 44899 and '5XP' 4-6-0 No. 45677 *Beatty*.

CHAPTER 14

Running on the Glasgow and South Western Line

My first experience of locomotive running on the Sou' West line was very mild. I had been working at St Enoch for over a week, in connection with the preparations for colour light signalling—at times in an improvised drawing office in an old shed on one of the platforms, at times out on the line measuring up. Each day I saw the goings and comings of many trains, and in the year of grace 1930 there were still a considerable number of pre-grouping engines at work. The Manson 4–6–0s had long since been displaced from the Midland Scotch expresses, but they still worked on the slower of the coast trains, while the 4–6–4 tanks were still much in evidence. When the time came to return south I took the 12-noon express to St Pancras, and with the usual 9-coach train we were double-headed as far as Kilmarnock. Thence a Midland compound, No. 1067, carried on unassisted with a 295-ton train, and kept, to the second, the 72-min. timing for the 58 miles to Dumfries. At the time there was a very bad slack over the viaduct at Hurlford, giving a difficult start to the climb to Mossgiel Tunnel; but although passing Mauchline 5 min. late in consequence, the loss was steadily made up and Dumfries was reached on time.

For a compound, with slightly less than 300 tons of train it was an easy task. It did not require a sustained speed of more than 25–6 mph up the 1 in 100 to Mossgiel Tunnel, and over the 33½ downhill miles between New Cumnock and Holywood we took 32½ min. It was however no more than charactestic of the old G & SWR that the maximum speed of the whole journey occurred on the winding stretch in the gorge of the Nith, between the Mennock and Ardoch signal boxes. Here we skated round the curves at 72 mph, but so smoothly I should add, that it was not until I rode over this line on the footplate many years later, that I realised how relatively sharp those curves are. Net time for the 58-mile run from Kilmarnock to Dumfries was 69 min.

At the end of their career on the main line the Manson 4–6–0s were not cutting a very brilliant figure. Some locomotives, like the Great Northern ' Atlantics,' the Southern ' King Arthurs,' and the North British ' Glen ' 4–4–0s, seemed to be rising to their greatest heights just as the time comes for them to be replaced; but not so the Manson 4–6–0s. There were two exceptions, the superheater engines 128 and 129, which became LMS Nos. 14673 and 14674. In view of the great success of these two engines ever since they were put into service in 1912, it has always been a matter of surprise to observers that the older non-superheated engines of the 4–6–0 type were not similarly equipped, especially as they were all rebuilt by Whitelegg after World War I. I have always understood, however, that the original engines were not entirely sound structurally, and that there was trouble with the cylinders working loose. This would partly explain why drivers were disinclined to thrash them hard, uphill, while so many other Glasgow and South Western engines were shown no such mercy. Enhancement of their capacity for power output would merely have exaggerated the trouble, and Whitelegg's rebuild was evidently little more than a ' patch up.' But 14674 not only continued to do great work on her own line; she carried the prowess of Sou' West engines on to the Caledonian. In 1928 the LMSR authorities were busy integrating the former Caledonian and South Western locomotive workings between Glasgow and Carlisle, and the top link enginemen of both sections were learning each other's road. The Sou' West men took their own engines with them, and 14674 did some excellent work on the Caledonian line. On one recorded occasion she ran the 73 miles from Strawfrank Junction to Carlisle in 84 min. start to stop, with a load of 365 tons.

It is a far cry from the Manson 4–6–0s to the Stanier ' Pacifics,' but one of my first post-war journeys over the G & SW line had at least one so very strong link with the old days that it does follow on naturally. During the war we were constantly being exhorted not to travel. Instead of the friendly ' Skegness is so bracing,' ' Speed to the West,' ' South for Sunshine,' and so on, the station hoardings scowled: ' Is your journey really necessary ? ' ' Give your seat to a shell,' and ' There isn't even half an engine to spare '! Trains were crowded, accommodation was limited, and as for sleeping berths, well—they almost became a commodity for the Black Market. Imagine, therefore, the consternation of a harassed bona fide traveller from London to Glasgow finding that, ahead of the packed regular night train from Euston, another, not in the time-table at all, slipped furtively out into the night, and conveying a goodly number of first-class sleeping cars! Was this a Black Market train ? Eventually questions were asked in Parliament, for it became known that this train ran every night, Saturdays and Sundays included. It then transpired, and was made public, that this was a servicemen's special, very much on the lines of the famous Naval Special of World War I, that ran daily from Euston to Thurso. The Glasgow trains of World War II became known, for a time, as the Ghost Trains, albeit very substantial ' ghosts.'

So far as I can trace, these two trains, leaving Euston at 8.40 p.m. and St Enoch at 9.27 p.m. represented the first regular working of ' Pacifics ' over the G & SW line. One engine worked throughout, with remanning taking place at Carlisle. Shortly after the end of the war I was privileged to make a footplate trip on the south-bound train, between Glasgow and Carlisle, and in every way it proved a most fascinating experience. First of all there was the undoubted thrill of travelling on a train not available to the public; there was the business of getting through the barrier on to the platform at St Enoch, and of seeing this ' train of mystery,' as one of the daily newspapers had called it, in the flesh. The load was fully up to expectations—fourteen, for a tare load of 463 tons; while with the passenger accommodation full, and all sleeping berths reserved the gross load must have been at least 490 tons. The engine was one of the first LMS streamliners, No. 6224 *Princess Alexandra,* but in 1945 painted black—so far as could be discerned through the coating of austerity grime! But we had a first-rate crew, and it was with them that there was so strong a link with old times. The moment the driver greeted me, in a rich Cumbrian brogue I realised that here was one of the ' old brigade ' from Currock Road; and in name as well as dialect and association, he could not have hailed from anywhere but the mighty region west of the main line over Shap. J. J. Cartmell, ' Johnny ' to his fireman: I wonder what nickname the men at the Scottish end of the Sou' West had for him! His fireman, T. Johnstone, was a Borderer, who spoke the robust English of Carlisle.

Heading out into a murky night we made a grand start from Glasgow, but a signal check brought us practically to a stand on on the 1 in 69 gradient of Neilston Bank. We could not have been checked in a worse place, but the way in which we got under way again with our 490-ton train showed up the quality of the engine and driver. This was only by way of a curtain-raiser, however, for in this book I take up the story at Kilmarnock. During the last years of the war some remarkably tight schedules were in force over this route. The morning express to St Pancras was allowed no more than 68 min. for the run of 58 miles to Dumfries, compared with the 72 min. of the 12 noon up when I made my first run, in 1930. The ' Ghost' train, although timed easily south of Carlisle, was allowed 72 min. to Dumfries, and to discourage anything in the way of downhill fast running this schedule was divided in the proportion of 30 min. for the heavily adverse 21·1 miles up to New Cumnock, and 42 min. for the downhill 36·9 miles to Dumfries. Over the G & SW line this train ran only a short distance behind the ordinary 9.15 p.m. up ' Sleeper ' to St Pancras, and was liable to delay from it; but on this trip of mine, apart from the Neilston check, we encountered adverse signals only in the immediate approaches to Kilmarnock and Dumfries stations. From Dumfries, the ' Ghost' train ran nominally non-stop to Watford Junction, 314 miles, though this included the stop to change enginemen, abreast of Upperby sheds.

We left Kilmarnock 3 min. late, and I was interested to see at once that Cartmell was doing the exact reverse of the old traditions; he was going hard for the New Cumnock ascent, and was not reckoning on gaining time downhill. In harmony with these tactics Johnstone fired, practically without intermission the whole way from Kilmarnock up to Polquhap. It was not heavy firing, but all the way up he was steadily at work, piling it in just under the door, packing the back corners, gradually building up. The rate of firing per mile between Kilmarnock and Polquhap, namely at 100 lb. per mile, sounds terrific, but once over the summit the doors were shut, and the fire was not touched again till we were leaving Dumfries. The injectors were skilfully managed so that the engine never once blew off, although the steaming was very free, and the soft Scottish coal reasonably good. The engine, despite her dingy appearance was in first-rate nick, and riding very comfortably. Cartmell was a ' full-regulator man.' Once we were under way, and on the slightly favourable start from Kilmarnock, down to

Hurlford and over the viaduct this meant in less than half a mile, the regulator was put hard over, and all further adjustments of power output made on the reverser.

We were doing 39 mph when we struck the 1 in 100 ascent to Mossgiel Tunnel; cut-off 20 per cent, but immediately the driver began dropping the lever—to 28 per cent at once, and soon afterwards to 35. For a modern locomotive this was quite strenuous going, and it was reflected in a minimum speed of 30 mph on the 1 in 100 gradient, and a minimum, moreover, that occurred some considerable distance before the summit. The effect of the 35 per cent was to accelerate the pace well before we reached the easier grades leading into the tunnel. As on the Neilston Bank, where we were so nearly stopped, the engine was a joy to hear, with her deep, beautifully even exhaust, smooth action, and free steaming. From the southern end of the tunnel, through Mauchline, and on to Ballochmyle viaduct the gradients undulate, with an aggregate effect that is practically level; with the reverser back in 20 per cent we touched 59 mph on this stretch, and then, as we crossed the viaduct, and resumed the ascent, Driver Cartmell at once lengthened cut-off to 25 per cent. This took us up the 3 miles to Auchinleck, including substantial lengths of 1 in 150 and 1 in 180, without falling below 50 mph; there was a rise to 53 on the easier pitch past Old Cumnock, and then with cut-off advanced to 28 per cent we took the last 3 miles up to Polquhap—continuously at 1 in 145–175—at an absolute minimum speed of 49 mph. With a 490-ton load this was grand work, showing an average speed of 44·3 mph throughout, over the 16·9 miles from Hurlford to Polquhap. Once on to the level at the summit speed rose swiftly, and New Cumnock, 21·1 miles from the start, was passed in 29½ min., at 60 mph.

The quality of the performance can be further appreciated by comparison of the speeds between Hurlford and Polquhap made on three other runs of which I have very complete details, as follows:

Engine No	Engine Class	Load tons full	Average speed Hurlford–Polquhap mph
1067	Compound	295	39·0
46133	' Converted Scot '	385	37·4
5565	' Jubilee '	410	40·5
6224	' Duchess '	490	44·3

178

On the Ghost train, having made such splendid time to New Cumnock the rest was easy. We had nearly 40 min. left for the 36·9 miles to Dumfries, and after reaching a maximum speed of 70 mph near Kirkconnel the engine was allowed to coast. From our experience outside Kilmarnock it was evident we were not far behind the St Pancras train, and if we were much ahead of time nearing Dumfries we would almost certainly be held up again. In the meantime I was enjoying the spectacle of the gorge of the Nith by night. The sky was dark and heavily overcast, but the main road runs lower down the hillside, and the headlamps of cars and lorries constantly lit up the woodlands to give an extraordinarily beautiful effect as we looked down from above. For ourselves Sanquhar (31·9 miles) had been passed in 39¾ min. and in spite of a relaying slack at Carronbridge we had plenty in hand to make Dumfries on time. But as we had half expected, the road was not clear—in fact so long was our wait outside that we were 14 min. late in. Our net time from Kilmarnock was, however, no more than 67 min., despite the leisurely running after Kirkconnel. Had we run really hard downhill, which would have been easy enough to engine and crew, we could, with a clear road have made the 58-mile run from Kilmarnock in about 61 or 62 min. It was entirely a measure of the work uphill from Hurlford to Polquhap, where the capacity of the Stanier ' Pacific ' was so splendidly shown.

The last stages of the run were badly delayed. We left Dumfries 16 min. late, and in other circumstances one might, with such an engine and crew, have looked forward to some handsome regaining of time, seeing that the schedule was a leisurely one of 48 min. for the 34 miles to Carlisle No. 12 Box. We got away briskly, and passed Annan, 15·5 miles, in 19½ min. But then, to the train in front was added further congestion from traffic on the Caledonian line at Gretna Junction; checks came thick and fast, and eventually we were stopped outside the Citadel station at Carlisle. Booked time to passing the station was 46 min., and in the circumstances we did well to wriggle through in 47½ min., while eventually we drew up at No. 12 Box, in 50¼ min. from Dumfries. The relief men were waiting, and Cartmell and Johnstone were able to hand over to them reporting all in first-class trim. Although the schedule for the long non-stop run through the night was not a difficult one, 280½ miles in 364 min., the very length of the run is enough to make it a major proposition. I could not help recalling the early days of the first Stanier 'Pacifics' 6200 and 6201, and how frequently the Scots crew would hand over at Carlisle and say: 'She won't steam!' a pleasant piece of news to a fresh crew who had to take the up *Royal Scot,* 299 miles non-stop to Euston.

In discussing the Hurlford–Polquhap ascent made by the Pacific on the Ghost train I referred briefly to a run with the 'Converted Scot' No. 46133 *The Green Howards;* this was a trip recorded from the footplate by Mr Ronald Nelson, on the Thames–Clyde Express, when the art of driving on the reverser was practised almost to its limits. There are extraordinary variations between one engine class and another, no less than between the technique adopted by different drivers; but the Converted Royal Scots seem to lend themselves to what might be termed, short cut-offs *in excelsis.* It is, of course, very dangerous and misleading to compare engine performance by the cut-offs used on one class and another, as indicating relative degrees of efficiency in working. The reverser has more than once been called 'the biggest liar on the engine' but even if the actual percentage of cut-off indicated is correct, one cannot judge by the percentages alone. Much depends upon the port openings. On some engines the valve timings are such that '15 per cent cut-off' gives such a gulp of steam at each stroke as to produce a far better performance, even with a full opening of the regulator in each case than on another engine of similar tractive power using 25 per cent. Down to about 20 per cent cut-off, or even to 18 the Converted Scots seem to give what one would expect from a locomotive of their proportions. It is below 10 per cent that the privileged observer begins to open his eyes. I had ridden on the Converted Scots before I made my first footplate trips on the 'Duchess' class Pacifics, and from the affinity in design I was expecting to see similarly short cut-offs used on the bigger engines. But it is not the practice; with the 'Pacifics' the general tendency is to use longer cut-offs, with no more than partial openings of the regulator.

With this introduction we might mention the very detailed log of the work of No. 46133, which was recorded by Mr Nelson. The engine was not steaming too well, and pressure was hovering around the 200–210 mark, instead of where it ought to have been. Some $3\frac{3}{4}$ min. were lost between Kilmarnock and Sanquhar, and with a permanent-way slack at Carronbridge nothing was regained after-wards. Although the engine and crew were embarked upon a long through working, and might perhaps be excused for a tendency to nurse their engine, the section between Kilmarnock and Carlisle was the only one on which they were not assisted. A Class 2 4–4–0 had piloted them from St Enoch, and at that time it was always customary for the train to be double-headed south of Carlisle, with an unbalanced engine working home. With this reservation it was a very interesting performance. The speeds up to Mossgiel Tunnel were what one might expect in response to a cut-off of 26 per cent, but then shorter admissions began to come in. There was a spell in 8 per cent after Mauchline, and in 5 per cent after New Cumnock. But it was after the Carronbridge check that the most extraordinary demonstration took place, using no more than a nominal 3 per cent from Closeburn southwards.

I have added the word ' nominal ' to the reading taken off the reverser scale. I have no doubt that the latter was accurate, unlike some I have seen, and others I could name. On the basis of the cut-offs used on the majority of modern engines one might expect the ' Converted Scots ' to be exceptionally economical, and after my earlier experiences on their footplates I was rather surprised at their relatively high coal-and-water consumption. I should at once add that their consumptions were high only in relation to the nominal cut-offs shown on the reverser scales; in other respects they were economical enough. But shortly after my earliest trips Mr H. G. Ivatt was kind enough to send me copies of a number of indicator diagrams taken on trials with engine No. 6138, and from the power developed at very short cut-offs it is evident that the valve design permits of an unusually large volume of steam to enter the cylinders even though the cut-off is early. The following figures tell their own tale:

Cut-off per cent	Speed mph	Indicated horsepower
5	62	925
10	60	1,070
15	60	1,520

There seems to have been little difference in the power developed on 5 and 10 per cent cut-offs.

On another run with the up Thames–Clyde Express, recorded

from the footplate by Mr Nelson, the performance was immeasurably finer—in fact the average speed between Hurlford and the Polquhap cabin was no less than 49½ mph. Full details of the engine working are given in the accompanying table, and it will be seen that this driver used no more than a partial opening of the

THE THAMES–CLYDE EXPRESS

9.20 A M GLASGOW–LEEDS

Engine Converted Royal Scot class 4–6–0 No 46112 *Sherwood Forester*
Load 12 cars 379 tons tare 405 tons full
Driver G Dransfield, Fireman Malyon (Holbeck)

Mls		Sch	m	s	mph	BP	Reg	Cut-off
0·0	KILMARNOCK	0	0	00		245	1st valve	67
						240	½ main	30
						240	½ main	17
1·2	Milepost 35		2	57	44	235	½ main	17
1·7	Hurlford (Milepost 35½)		3	37	47½	240	½ main	17
2·2	Milepost 36		4	14½	46	240	½ main	19
3·2	Milepost 37		5	34½	43	240	½ main	21
3·7	Milepost 37½		6	18½	40½	230	½ main	23
4·7	Milepost 38½		7	50	38	240	½ main	25
5·7	Milepost 39½		9	27	36½	240	½ main	25
6·7	Milepost 40½		11	04½	38½	245	½ main	25
7·2	Milepost 41		11	52	41	240	½ main	17
9·4	Mauchline	16	14	29	58	240	½ main	15
					63½	235	½ main	15
11·2	*Brackenhill Jc* (Milepost 45)		16	26½	60	240	½ main	17
13·2	Milepost 47		18	28	57½	240	½ main	17
13·8	Auchinleck		19	01	59	235	½ main	17
15·2	Milepost 49		20	32	56½	245	½ main	17
15·8	Old Cumnock		21	07	59½	240	½ main	17
17·2	Milepost 51		22	37½	55	245	½ main	17
18·6	*Polquhap*		24	06	54	245	¼ main	15
21·1	New Cumnock	32	26	45	64	240	¼ main	13
					67	235	1st valve	13
24·7	*Upper Cairn* (Milepost 58½)		29	54	62	230	1st valve	13
28·6	Kirkconnel		33	37	70½	225	1st valve	11
					75½	220	Drifting	50
			p w s		15	225	1st valve	24
31·9	SANQUHAR	44	37	27	23½	230	1st valve	16
34·2	*Mennock* (Milepost 68)		40	19	55½	235	1st valve	13
36·7	*Ardoch* (Milepost 70½)		42	43	68½	230	1st valve	13
40·2	Milepost 74		46	12	53	230	1st valve	16
40·5	Carronbridge		46	31		230	Drifting	50
43·8	Thornhill	56	49	46	65½	225	Drifting	50
46·6	Closeburn		52	12	69	240	Drifting	50
					62	240	Drifting	50
50·4	Auldgirth		55	45	64	245	Drifting	50
					65½	230	Drifting	50
54·6	Holywood		59	48	58	220	Drifting	50
56·3	*Cairn Valley Jc*		61	31		220	Drifting	50
			sigs		20	215	1st valve	50
58·0	DUMFRIES	70	64	29				

main regulator for the uphill sections, and had things so well in hand that he could put the regulator into the drifting position for the final descent from Carronbridge to Dumfries.

Early in 1945 I had a run in the reverse direction with engine No. 6117 of the same class on which the driver used 15 per cent as far as Drumlanrig Tunnel, and then 10 per cent for the rest of the climb to New Cumnock. The 36·9 miles up from Dumfries were covered in 44¾ min., with a load of 325 tons behind the tender, and yet with apparently most economical working we were using 50 gallons of water per mile on the steeper part of the ascent, and 38 gallons per mile from Drumlanrig northwards. But despite the prowess of the ' Scots ' and the ' Pacifics ' over this route I always feel that engine performance had passed its zenith of achievement by the time those big modern locomotives had arrived on the scene. Casting around, one can usually light upon some period in the history of a line of railway when its engines and men are veritably touching the heights. On the Caledonian it was undoubtedly in the days of the first ' Dunalastairs,' while on the North Western, over Shap, the first years of the ' George the Fifth ' class 4–4–0s have probably never been equalled. On the G & SW line I always feel that it was with the Midland compounds that the Sou' West men excelled themselves. Day after day, month after month they produced running equivalent of the most vigorous days of the Settle and Carlisle trials in the middle twenties. I have had a number of good runs myself, but there was one that was outstanding. One need do no more than compare its baldest details with others to sense its quality:

Engine No Class Load t/full	913 Compound 375	45739 ' Jubilee ' 305	6117 ' Con. Scot ' 325	46222 ' Duchess ' 545
Times Dumfries to Carron- bridge 17·5 miles	m s 23 25	m s 22 30	m s 22 23	m s 22 00
Carronbridge to New Cumnock 19·4 miles	21 45	22 23	22 23	23 20
Average speed Holywood to New Cumnock 33·5 miles	51·3	51·1 *	51·4	50·8 †

* Inclusive of slight p.w. check   51·8 mph net

† Inclusive of p.w. slack   52·7 mph net

I will readily agree that the 'Jubilee' and the 'Scot' were being worked under easier steam on the ascent. The 'Jubilee' was in 20 per cent with full regulator throughout from Holywood till the check near Carronbridge, and again from Mennock Box to the summit; but on the other hand the 'Scot' despite the short cut-offs used had a very healthy thirst for water and appetite for coal. Yet the compound, with no more than two-thirds of the tractive effort of the 4-6-0s was making equivalent times with a load of 375 tons. No wonder she roared! But it was not so much the demonstration of engine capacity that I found so thrilling on that run as the readiness of the crew to go for it, and make the outstanding effort they did. The glory belongs primarily to the fireman, for the finest engine design, and the most resolute use of regulator and reverser can be of no avail on a run like this if the man with the shovel is not up to it. I must not dwell on the exploits of engine No. 913 on that memorable Saturday in August 1930, as the run has been described in detail several times before. It was made several years before my earliest footplating, so I cannot give any details as to how the engine was being worked, but a sustained minimum speed of $43\frac{1}{2}$ mph on the 1 in 150 between Thornhill and Carronbridge suggested and sounded (!) something very near to 'all-out.'

The 'Jubilee,' No. 45739 *Ulster*, had the same train under normal midweek loading conditions, when the schedule had been considerably accelerated. In 1930, the booked time from Dumfries to Kilmarnock was 69 min. whereas when Mr Nelson made his footplate trip in 1951 it was no more than 65 min. Curiously enough however there was only a difference of one minute in the passing time booked at New Cumnock—44 against 45 min.—*Ulster* had a second permanent-way check, and although coming down hard from Polquhap, with speeds of $77\frac{1}{2}$ mph before Ballochmyle, and 79 after Mossgiel Tunnel, dropped $1\frac{1}{2}$ min. to Kilmarnock, $62\frac{1}{2}$ min. net. The compound did not exceed 67 mph downhill, but would have had enough in hand to offset a permanent-way check at Hurlford had it not been for a signal check as well. Her actual time was $70\frac{1}{2}$ min. and net time $67\frac{1}{2}$ min. It is going beyond our territory to refer to what happened north of Kilmarnock, but I cannot refrain from telling how *Ulster* continued with a reduced load of 225 tons, and after climbing the formidable Stewarton Bank, with its 5 miles of 1 in 87–152–75 passed Lugton (10 miles) in

17 min. 29 sec. The minimum speed on the bank was 24¼ mph. The compound, much to my astonishment, was not provided with a pilot here, and continued with the 375-ton load. Believe it or not, her time to Lugton was 17 min. 50 sec., with an almost unbelievable minimum of 26 mph on the Bank!

And so we come finally to my most recent trip over the G & SWR line, of which the logging commenced in a sleeping car, and continued from the breakfast car of the *Night Scot*. The briefest details have already been given in the table on page 149, but the log, as between Dumfries and Kilmarnock is now given in detail.

SCOTTISH REGION   DUMFRIES–KILMARNOCK

THE DOWN NIGHT SCOT

Load 519 tons tare 545 tons full
Engine 46222 *Queen Mary*

Mls		m	s	mph
0·0	DUMFRIES	0	00	
1·7	*Cairn Valley Jc*	3	50	
3·4	Holywood	5	50	55/57
7·6	Auldgirth	10	17	52½
11·4	Closeburn	14	35	58
14·2	Thornhill	17	45	49½
17·5	Carronbridge	22	00	43
21·2	*Ardoch*	26	15	
		p w s		30
26·1	Sanquhar	33	10	
29·4	Kirkconnel	37	25	56
33·4	*Upper Cairn*	41	50	52
36·9	New Cumnock	45	20	63
42·2	Old Cumnock	50	45	easy
44·2	Auchinleck	52	45	66 (max)
48·6	Mauchline	57	10	
56·2	Hurlford	64	40	
58·0	KILMARNOCK	68	20	

It was a grand start to three very busy days in Scotland. With her big load of 545 tons the *Queen Mary* sailed up to Carronbridge with no more than a deep ' purr ' from her exhaust. My sleeper was in the second coach from the engine, and as we went up by Thornhill I could not fail to remember the continuous roar of old 913 on that now far-off journey on the 1 p.m. in 1930. Of course in relation to her tractive effort the Pacific was not loaded anything like so heavily as the compound, but even so she was doing no mean job. The check near the Mennock box was not a severe one, and speed was easily regained on the rising gradients above Sanquhar; and so, with nothing very much above 60 mph downhill we came into Kilmarnock in 68 min. 20 sec. from Dumfries.

For some little time before then I had been in the restaurant car towards the rear of the train, breakfasting with my signalling colleagues. There was then no time for anything but the present and the immediate future. Reflections came later, and it seems appropriate now to close this book with a journey behind a locomotive that probably represents the ultimate in express passenger steam-power on the railways crossing the Scottish Border. Such a remark will no doubt be set down as controversial, and the partisans of Darlington and Doncaster will probably seize pens and paper to remind me that such engines as the Gresley A4s and the Peppercorn A1s also cross the Border regularly. But if one wishes to start a controversy what better place to do it could there be than on the Border, that age-old scene of skirmish, raids, and forays galore. Besides, the time is fast approaching when the partisans of one route or another will have little tangible to fight about, when standard diesels haul the Scotch expresses on both sides of the country, and preserved examples of the ' Pacific ' of our own times appear only as museum pieces at times of anniversary and celebrations. And so, in imagination, out in the Debatable Land, I make no apology for seeming to kindle the century-old fires that set King's Cross against Euston, Doncaster against Crewe, St Rollox against Gateshead and Cowlairs. But it is time to end; the *Queen Mary* was wheeling her great train over the Clyde and round the long curve into St Enoch—on time.

54 The magnificent Ballochmyle viaduct near Mauchline, with the overnight sleeping car express from St Pancras to Glasgow crossing (April 1962): the locomotive is rebuilt 'Scot' No. 46157 *The Royal Artilleryman*.

55 Carronbridge viaduct, on the south approach to Drumlanrig Tunnel, July 1964: the morning Leeds-Glasgow express crossing is hauled by 'Peak' class diesel No. D15.

56 At Cumnock in April 1962 a short but well loaded northbound coal train passing, hauled by a standard Class 3 2-6-0 No. 77018.

57 The beautiful scenery of the Nith Valley, in July 1964 a relief to the up 'Thames-Clyde Express' entering the Drumlanrig Gorge, hauled by 'Peak' class diesel No. D134.

58 Animation at Auldgirth in April 1962: a Workington to Largs excursion train hauled by Class 6 4-6-2 No. 72007 *Clan Mackintosh* taking water, beside a standard 'BR5' 4-6-0 No. 73072. At that time Upper Cairn water troughs were out of action.

59 Glasgow, St Enoch: to complement the note in the text of *Queen Mary*'s arrival there is this impressive shot of her departure for the south, in September 1962, on the 17.30 express.

CHAPTER 15

NEWCASTLE TO EDINBURGH IN THE DIESEL AGE

TWENTY years ago when the first edition of this book was published it seemed very unlikely that the new power then beginning to come into use on the main lines across the Border would generate a fraction of the interest and enthusiasm lavished upon the old favourites of the steam age. Was a 'tin-box' on wheels, albeit containing a very powerful internal combustion engine, to be compared in the appeal it made to the emotions, to a Gresley Pacific roaring up the Cockburnspath bank with the up 'Flying Scotsman,' or to another of that breed sweeping north at 75 mph over Lucker troughs, and flinging the spray from the water scoop far and wide! Yet it is sometimes good to be a false prophet. Today, a generation of enthusiasts to whom the grandeur of the steam age, in those thrilling later years of the 1950s when so remarkable a 'come-back' had been made from the austerity of wartime and after, can be little more than hearsay, or the evocations of their elders, is expressing just as much affection and nostalgia over the superseding of the 'Deltics' by the HSTs, as the older ones amongst us did, on the Newcastle-Edinburgh run, when the Gresley 'Pacifics' began to oust the North Eastern 'Atlantics' from the premier duties.

I have titled this chapter 'diesel age', but really it should more correctly be the 'Deltic' age, from the way those splendid locomotives have stolen the show on the East Coast main line. They were introduced in 1961, and in the following year some spectacular cuts were made in the journey times between King's Cross and Edinburgh. These involved the maintenance of average speeds of 60 mph between Newcastle and Edinburgh. In one respect this was nothing new, because as long previously as 1937 the Gresley streamlined 'Coronation' express was allowed no more than the level two hours for the run of 124.4 miles, and as related in Chapter 8 of this book the time was closely approached on occasions in the 1950s by Pacifics working the lighter East Coast expresses, like the North Briton and the Talisman. But before the year 1962 was out the 'Deltics' were showing they had a very substantial margin in reserve on the accelerated timings, even when conveying maximum loads. In September 1962 in *The Railway Magazine*, I published details of a run on the down 'Flying Scotsman' when following a late start a 13-coach train having a gross trailing load of 485-tons was taken from Newcastle to Edinburgh in $103\frac{3}{4}$ min., despite two slight checks. It was a remarkable performance beside the very best standards of steam to which we were then accustomed; but I was amused to find that by way of commentary I then wrote:

'I cannot help feeling a little less exhilarated than I suppose one should be, because here, I think, we are getting very near to the ultimate in British locomotive running. Wherever the road was suitable this heavy train was run at, or near, 90 mph and it was evident that physical conditions rather than locomotive power were applying the limit. The day of 15- and 16-coach trains on the ordinary day East Coast expresses seem to have gone for the time being, and with the ordinary formations of "eleven" or even with one or two extras the "Deltics" can run up to the limit of the road. On this run speed was reduced by braking to observe engineering restrictions at no fewer than nine places, quite apart from the subsidence slack near Monktonhall Junction, and while these remain it would be difficult to improve very much upon a time of about 100 min. from Newcastle to Edinburgh.'

On that splendid run the net time was 101 min. representing a start to stop average speed of 74 mph and the schedule time was subsequently shortened to 111 min. instead of the initial 'Deltic' timing of 123 min. This quickening, which remained until the introduction of the HST service, in 1978, itself involved a fine average of 67.2 mph. At first the maximum speed permitted anywhere was 90 mph, though this was later relaxed to 100 mph on some of the straighter stretches such as that between Christon Bank and Smeafield, and again along the Lothian coast. But the outstanding feature of 'Deltic' performance was the very high availability of the 22 locomotives of the fleet. It is true that they had very preferential treatment in the way of maintenance. Not long after they had first been introduced I remember an occasion when I had to visit several installations of signalling in the North-East with not a great deal of time between them. I went down to Newcastle one evening from King's Cross on the 'Talisman,' 'Deltic' hauled, and spent the next morning out at the new hump marshalling yard at Lamesley. I then had to get on to Edinburgh for an evening appointment. When 'The Flying Scotsman' arrived from London it was hauled by the same 'Deltic' that had brought us down on the previous evening. It had gone on to Edinburgh, worked an up sleeping car express, and arrived at King's Cross in time to take the 10 a.m. down (!) — 785 miles in 18 hours.

The managements of the Eastern and Scottish Regions were anxious to inaugurate the new HST service on the East Coast Route in the early summer but a great amount of work on the permanent way was necessary, and on the inaugural run there were four temporary speed restrictions to 20 mph in operation between Newcastle and Edinburgh. The new schedule allowed $106\frac{1}{2}$ min. for the run of 124.4 miles, not very much faster than the ultimate 'Deltic' time. But north of Newcastle the maximum permitted was no more than 100 mph, and in addition there was a signal stop at Acklington that cost us four precious minutes. So, with all these delays the time from Newcastle to Edinburgh was $110\frac{3}{4}$ min. The shape of things to come, so far as the HSTs were concerned, was shown, on the return run that same day with the 'Talisman', when with only one slight check we ran the 124.4 miles to Newcastle in $95\frac{1}{4}$ min. or 93 min, net, an average speed of $80\frac{1}{2}$ mph without exceeding the stipulated maximum of 100 mph.

The new service had barely had time to settle down when tragedy struck this historic main line across the Border. When news came through in March 1979 of the collapse of part of the roof in Penmanshiel Tunnel, and the entombment of two men engaged on maintenance and repair work thoughts naturally went back to that incredible 12th of August 1948 when a cloudburst more severe than anything in living memory caused three large landslips and swept away seven bridges, between Reston Junction and Cockburnspath. As already related in Chapter 8 however, it was nothing short of a miracle that this convulsion of nature was accompanied by no personal injuries, let alone any loss of life. Unhappily the disaster in Penmansheil Tunnel, in March 1979, not only involved the deaths of two men, but emergency measures to circumvent the obstruction were less easy to organise. In 1948 there were several other lines in the Border country, that have since been closed, all within the former

192

LNER system. From Tweedmouth Junction the line following the river valley, through Coldstream and Kelso joined the famous Waverley route just south of St. Boswells, and although a rather drastic speed limit had to be imposed the main line Pacific engines were allowed to work through. On a number of occasions indeed the summer-service 'Capitals Limited', nominally non-stop between Kings Cross and Edinburgh was actually worked through non-stop. More usually however a stop was necessary to take water.

In 1979 all these railway by-ways of the Border, including the Waverley route itself had been closed, and the only alternative route was westwards from Newcastle to Carlisle, and then over the former Caledonian route to Edinburgh. The latter is of course a very busy route in itself, especially between Carlisle and Carstairs, and it was not possible to provide paths for all the East Coast Expresses. Some services were terminated at Berwick and through passengers were conveyed by bus to Dunbar, whence a connecting train completed the journey to Edinburgh. In the emergency conditions much interest was aroused by the working of certain of the HST services via the Newcastle and Carlisle line, and thence to Edinburgh via Carstairs, but that did not mean the making of new speed records over that pictures-que cross-country line. Over much of it the maximum permissible speed is less than 60 mph, though it was a pleasant experience to ride over it in the cab of an HST. By stretching a point this line could be included in those covered in this book; but because it was not in any way a *cross-border line,* and not one on which Eric Treacy and I had any joint associations, I have thought it best to leave it with no more than this passing mention.

The restoration of regular train services over the East Coast Main Line in such a relatively short time was the result of a magnificent combined operation. The decision was taken in April to close the tunnel altogether and to build a diversion line; and with modern machinery and an immense sense of urgency the contractors, Sir Robert McAlpine & Sons, enabled the new line to be opened to through traffic on 20th August 1979. I thought of that 100-minute 'bogey' that I once had fixed in my mind for the Newcastle-Edinburgh run when I enjoyed the privilege of a driver's cab pass for the down 'Flying Scotsman' on a blustering day in early March 1980 when the schedule time was $99\frac{1}{2}$ minutes, and when work on the line at several places was going to make a net time considerably less than that necessary if end-to-end time was to be kept. One severe restriction, at a place when we could have been really *going*, was at the automatic half-barrier crossing at Falloden. From this point onwards the line speed limit has now been raised to 125 mph until nearing Beal; but on this trip of mine a reduction to 20 mph over the crossing was required because of engineering work.

Passing Falloden thoughts always go back to the great statesman of my boyhood, Sir Edward Grey, afterwards Viscount Grey of Falloden; he who, as Foreign Secretary in 1914, delivered the ultimatum to Imperial Germany that preceded our declaration of war. In the present context however I like to think of his later years when it was traditional for guests at Falloden to be taken for an afternoon walk to the lineside to see the down 'Flying Scotsman' pass. In those days it would have been around 4.30 p.m. It was not yet two o'clock, when we passed on this recent run of mine. Grey had been a director of the North Eastern Railway from July 1898, and was Chairman in 1904-5. He resigned in January 1906, on taking cabinet office in the Liberal Government of Sir Henry Campbell-Bannerman. We crept over the crossing with the speedometer needle precisely on the '20.' It is only when one has ridden in the cab of the HSTs that appreciation comes of the artistry needed in handling such power. It is so easy to lose time simply by the over-emphasis of speed restrictions, and the power available was equally demonstrated by the way we dashed away once the termination sign was passed. In just over 2 miles we accelerated from 20 to 95 mph! Even so, the way ahead was not quite clear, and just north of Chathill there was a short length restricted to 80 mph to be negotiated. After that we were really away, to average exactly ninety over the next 60 miles.

It was a majestic way to cross the Border, not that even this stretch was free entirely from restrictions. As we sped down the slight gradient from Belford, with speed just topping 120 mph, with the Holy Isle of Lindisfarne riding out across a stormy sea, and a sight of the hills of Scotland ahead of us, memories of many other approaches to the Border might have come crowding if, in a time almost unprecedented in my experience we had not crossed the slight summit on the cliffs above Scremerston at 94 mph, and seen the whole panorama of Berwick and its bridges ahead of us. There is a limit of 70 mph over the Royal Border Bridge now, but having observed this precisely full power was on again. We were climbing at 1 in 190, under lowering skies, and rain sweeping across the track; but where Atlantics and Pacifics used to struggle, and in weather conditions like this to slip and find it difficult to hold 40 mph we accelerated quickly to 90(!), and had to ease briefly to 82 mph for the curve just beyond the Border sign. It is still the road, rather than tractive capacity that governs the speed on the mainly rising length to Grantshouse; generally however we were doing 85 to 89 mph until we neared the summit, and speed was eased to 75 prior to the more marked reduction round the Penmanshiel diversion. Although this is relatively short the curves have been skilfully laid in to permit of 60 mph and it was impressive to see what had been needed to circumvent that tragic tunnel.

So, down the Cockburnspath bank at 90 mph; a spell at the 'ton' to the outskirts of Dunbar, 85 round the curve there, and then 100 mph continuously through the Lothian country till we were slowed for permanent way work to 20 mph at Longniddry. But with all the numerous slight restrictions we had covered the 60.6 miles from Chathill to Drem in $40\frac{1}{4}$ min., a splendid average of 90.3 mph.; and although that check at Longniddry slowed our approach to Edinburgh we eventually stopped in Waverley in $99\frac{1}{4}$ min. from Newcastle. But the checks we had experienced, including even a brief signal stop before we had reached the crossing at Falloden, had cost us at least 11 min. in running, leaving a net time of $88\frac{1}{4}$ min., equal to an average speed of $84\frac{1}{2}$ mph. Excellent though this is one feels that, contrary to what I thought a few years ago, this is only a stepping stone to the time when the HSTs will bring Edinburgh within $4\frac{1}{2}$ hours from London.

60 Within sight of the sea: Kings Cross-Edinburgh express near Innerwick on the Lothian Coast in June 1971 hauled by a 'Deltic' No. D9006 *The Fife and Forfar Yeomanry*.

61 The down 'Flying Scotsman' passing through the dismantled station at East Linton, in June 1971, hauled by a 'Deltic' No. 9005 *The Prince of Wales's Own Regiment of Yorkshire*.

62 The Penmanshiel Diversions: a southbound East Coast High Speed Train, under the wires, on the West Coast main line in Upper Clydesdale.

63 A 'meet' at 200 mph — plus! An Edinburgh bound HST photographed from the driver's cab of a southbound HST near Scremerston, south of Berwick, Northumberland in August 1978.

197

64 Diversions in the Border Country July 1972: an Edinburgh-Kings Cross express, rounding the curve at Strawfrank Junction, Carstairs, on to the West Coast main line, to continue thus to Carlisle, hauled by 'Deltic' No. 9002 *The Kings Own Yorkshire Light Infantry*.

65 Edinburgh, Waverley: a panoramic view in June 1968 looking west, with an express from Aberdeen leaving for the south hauled by a Class 47 diesel No. 1958.

CHAPTER 16

SETTLE AND CARLISLE — ABIDING MEMORIES

IT is easy to wax lyrical over a railway including so many features of superb engineering, and set in a countryside of such grandeur, especially to one like myself whose vivid personal memories of it go back to the year 1916. But for Eric and me the district had other associations beside railways. As Lord Bishop of Wakefield he was principal guest on Speech Day at Giggleswick School. He preached in Chapel, and there was the ever memorable occasion of the Centenary of the line, on 1st May 1976, when he graced the banquet in the marquee at Settle station. At that time steam locomotives were still prohibited over the line, but he and his wife joined us on the special Centenary-Saloon train at Carnforth, which we had previously been advised would be hauled to Hellifield by two very appropriate Settle and Carlisle engines — Midland compound No. 1000 and a 'Black Five,' No. 44871. But when we arrived at Giggleswick on the Friday evening it was to learn that they had *both* failed! Frantic last minute efforts were being made to get two substitutes, and the shades of Guy Granet must surely have been stirred at the thought of a North Western, and a Great Northern engine having to step into the breach for the Midland! Nevertheless *Hardwicke* and *Flying Scotsman*, however incongruous a pair, did us proud, though it was a pity the special had to be diesel hauled over THE line.

The return trip had some diverting moments for some of us on the saloon train. There was to be some split-second timing between our arrival in Settle, and the reception before the banquet, and the organisers had done their preliminary work well. Eric and I, and our wives had been told there was no need to wear our 'party' clothes all day. We could dress casually for the railway journeys, which for my wife and me began with a DMU ride from Giggleswick to Carnforth, to pick up the saloon train. A lengthy stop on the return run from Carlisle had been scheduled at Ribblehead for photographs, and so on, and arrangements had been made for the four of us to change into our party clothes in the station house. How the special came to lose so much time on the round trip to Carlisle I cannot remember; but the upshot of it was that to make our target of arrival in Settle the stop at Ribblehead was of no more than 5 minutes. Panic stations in the saloon! We had little more than a quarter of an hour in which to change — but where? The ladies dashed one after the other into the lavatory at the end of the car. Eric and I, shielded from public gaze by friendly male screens, changed in the saloon itself, while the train rocketed down 'The Long Drag' so as not to be late in Settle. Eric was quicker than I was; as he explained: 'We shall be sitting down at the banquet. No one will see I've got the wrong trousers on!'

At the beginning of 1978 came the welcome news that the line had been added to the list of those over which charter steam specials were permitted. The Gresley 'V2' class 2-6-2 No. 4771 *Green Arrow* opened the ball on Saturday 25th March, Easter weekend, with a special organised by the Steam Locomotive Operators Association, and a very good time was had by all. For those who study the details of locomotive performance it was evident that the locomotive was not being extended in climbing 'The Long Drag.' Nor would it have been wise to do so. There is a world of difference between the regular running of a link of locomotives tuned up for the job, backed by well established servicing and maintenance facilities at the shed, and driven and fired by men who are in the pink of condition for the job, and taking out an engine that spends a good deal of its time as little more than a museum piece, with little or no shed back-up, other than what can be given at centres like York and Carnforth. There is every reason for treating these priceless examples of railway archaeology gently. The great thing is to run them at all — not to try and emulate the service performance of past years.

The running of these steam specials over the Settle and Carlisle line has given a great amount of pleasure to a vast number of people. Since those inaugural runs at Easter 1978, *Green Arrow* has been followed by *Flying Scotsman, Sir Nigel Gresley* and the rebuilt Bulleid Pacific *Clan Line*, and photographs have showed spectators in their hundreds at the linesides, and the trains themselves like nothing that has gone before with heads out of every window that could be opened, braving the roughest of weather to hear and record on tape the sounds of steam fighting the gradients. But of course a railway cannot live on the revenue derived from a few charter specials, and the daily passenger traffic is sparse. Fortunately the

200

Settle and Carlisle line carries a considerable amount of freight, and it is invaluable as a relief to the West Coast main line at weekends when engineering possessions are in operation.

The line is subject to an overall maximum speed limit of 60 mph and with the regular passenger trains loading to no more than 8 or 9 coaches the diesel locomotives, especially if Class '47s' are available, make speed almost up to the line maximum uphill as well as down. From the smooth riding of the coaches the track would appear to be in excellent shape, and there have been occasional instances of speeds rising briefly to 70 mph, to be quickly reduced by brakes. On the 13.22 up from Carlisle, for example, a Class '40' diesel with a very crowded 9-coach train of 340-tons ran the 40.8 miles from Appleby over Aisgill to Settle in $44\frac{1}{2}$ min. start to stop, making an average speed of 55 mph over this mountain section. The 15 miles from Ormside up to Aisgill took $18\frac{3}{4}$ min., and the subsequent $17\frac{1}{4}$ miles across the tableland to Blea Moor and down to Horton 16 min. — with a slight 'bending' of the rules. In this way 7 min. of a late start from Carlisle was recovered on arrival at Settle. At the present time Hellifield has little or no significance as a junction, and the stops of the regular trains at Settle instead have become a great convenience to me.

A sterling locomotive performance, with a closer adherence to the 60mph speed limit was provided one Sunday morning by the 11.34am train from Carlisle, the Glasgow-Birmingham express, when diverted via Hellifield. A Class '47' diesel was provided for a 12-coach train of 425-tons, and the running was so good as to justify tabulating. It shows how, with first class motive power and sound enginemanship, it is possible to maintain an overall average speed of 50 mph over this mountainous route with no more than momentary excesses over the line maximum speed limit. Furthermore, the train was checked by signal on leaving Carlisle and observance had to be made of the long-prevailing speed restriction to 30 mph between Newbiggin and Long Marton. These two checks accounted for $2\frac{1}{2}$ min. between them so leaving a net time of 89 min, and a net average speed of $51\frac{3}{4}$ mph. The uphill speeds were very good including an average of 49.6 mph Ormside to Aisgill, while the subsequent downhill average of 58 mph from Garsdale to Settle Junction showed appropriate restraint, and observance of the rules. After he retired, and went to live near Keswick Eric Treacy rarely missed an opportunity of visiting the line when there were some steam workings, and it was on Appleby station that he died on 13th May 1978. Just over four months later two special trains were run, one from London and one from Leeds for a deeply impressive memorial service at Appleby station, on Saturday 30th September at which no fewer than three Bishops, those of Carlisle, Sheffield and Wakefield took part, and his widow Mrs Mary Treacy unveiled a commemorative plaque to his memory on the station itself. Both special trains were steam hauled north of Hellifield. The 2-10-0 No. 92220 *Evening Star* hauled the first train, the 'Bishop

LMR 11.34 SuO CARLISLE-HELLIFIELD
Load 12 cars 403 tons tare 425-tons full
Loco: Class '47' diesel-electric No 47.441

Mls		m	s	mph
0.0	CARLISLE	0	00	
		sigs		
2.1	Milepost 306	6	15	
3.9	Cumwhinton	8	48	44/55½
8.1	Milepost 300	13	27	53
10.0	Armathwaite	15	15	68 (max)
—	Barons Wood	—		52½
15.2	Lazonby	20	52	66
18.3	Little Salkeld	23	46	58
19.7	Langwathby	25	23	52/61
23.4	Culgaith	29	10	49
24.7	Newbiggin	30	46	56
—		p.w. slack		30
27.9	Long Marton	35	47	45
30.8	APPLEBY	39	16	57
33.2	Ormside	41	37	64½
36.1	Griseburn Box	45	07	47
38.3	Crosby Garrett	47	40	53
—	Smardale Viaduct			58½
41.5	Kirkby Stephen	51	09	52
44.1	Milepost 264	54	18	47½
—	Mallerstang	—		50
47.1	Milepost 261	58	02	46½
48.3	Aisgill	59	45	39
51.4	Garsdale	62	48	64½
54.6	Dent	66	18	55
59.5	Blea Moor	71	34	60
60.8	Ribblehead	72	41	69
65.5	Horton	77	25	max on
71.6	SETTLE	83	39	descent
73.5	Settle Junc.	85	38	—
76.6	Milepost 231½ (HELLIFIELD)	91	35	—

Treacy,' throughout from Leeds, while the London train, 'The Lord Bishop' was diesel hauled over the former L & Y line, into Hellifield, and taken forward by the *Flying Scotsman*. It was a pleasing touch that the lady cleaners who do such a thorough job on the engines for the 'Cumbrian Coast Express' at Steamtown, Carnorth, should have travelled to Hellifield with *their* engine, to give 4472 a final polish before going north over 'The Long Drag.'

I was one of the guests on 'The Lord Bishop' that day, and I think one of its happiest recollections is of the delight of Mrs Treacy and her family friends at the well-nigh incredible numbers of people who had gathered at every conceivable vantage point between Hellifield and Aisgill to see and photograph the train, and then to speed on to Appleby in their cars to join in the deeply impressive memorial service at the lineside, with the engine *Evening Star*, as a backdrop to the platform from which the officiating clergy conducted the service, in which also the General Manager of the London Midland Region of British Railways, Mr David S. Binnie also took part. After the ceremony 'The Lord Bishop' train was taken forward to Armathwaite by *Evening Star*, where the Southern 4-6-2 No. 35028 *Clan Line* was waiting to work the train back to Hellifield, *Flying Scotsman* had in the meantime gone forward to Carlisle for turning, and worked the 'Bishop Treacy' train back as far as Hellifield. For me, who had known Eric for 50 years, the day's proceedings were a most moving experience.

It was of course inevitable that purely railway interests and enthusiasm would many times impinge upon the solemnity of the occasion; while the *Flying Scotsman* was hauling the heavy 485-ton special train up 'The Line Drag' several fellow travellers asked me how the engine performance compared with that on some of the heaviest trains I had previously logged over the route. 'The Lord Bishop' was actually the heaviest passenger train of which I have a personal record and I have had to go back to 1945 and 1931 in my notebooks to find loads of 450-tons and more. The comparison between the three brings out the different conditions in which the pre-served locomotives of today are operating, and need to be handled. The 'Claughton' which was one of several transferred to the Midland Division was of the original small-boiled type, and which became much appreciated engines at Leeds, Holbeck shed. The load limit for Class '5' engines over the Hellifield-Carlisle section, which also applied to the Stanier 'Black Five' 4-6-0s, when they came out in 1934, was 340-tons; but on this run of 1931, even with a pilot some hard work was needed with such a load as 470-tons. The division of that load would be about 170-tons to the pilot and 300 tons to the 'Claughton,'

CLIMBING THE "LONG DRAG"

Year		1931		1945		1978	
Engine No		5932*		6117		4472	
Engine Name		*Sir Thomas Williams*		*Welsh Guardsman*		*Flying Scotsman*	
Engine Class		ex-LNWR 'Claughton'		Converted 'Royal Scot'		LNER 'A3'-4-6-2	
Load tons, gross		470		450		485	
Mls		m	s	m	s	m	s
0.0	HELLIFIELD	0	00	0	00	0	00
3.3	Settle Jc	4	45	5	15	5	51
7.3	Milepost 238½	9	55	11	12	12	43
11.3	Horton	16	05	18	49	21	52
16.0	Ribblehead	23	45	26	53	33	34
17.3	Blea Moor (pass)	25	50	28	57	36	53
Average speed (mph)		37.1		32.8		25.5	
Post 238½-Blea Moor							
Actual dhp		1281		1065		864	
Equivalent dhp		1761		1332		1099	
Edhp per ton		94.6		89.2		67.8	

*Piloted by Class '2' ex MR 4-4-0 No 458

So far as the comparative times were concerned the schedule of the morning Leeds-Glasgow express in 1931 was much the fastest of the three trains, and in slightly improving upon booked times the work of the 'Claughton' and its pilot was considerably harder in relation to nominal tractive effort than either of the others. The 'Converted Scot' was on a wartime schedule, and working through from Leeds to Glasgow, while of course *Flying Scotsman* was being quite gently handled. On the return journey with 'The Lord Bishop' the ex-Southern 4-6-2 *Clan Line*, from start at Appleby, took the 485-ton train past Aisgill summit, 17.5 miles, in 35 min. 6 sec. averaging almost exactly 30 mph. On this side of the summit there are several breaks in the climbing and on the longer stretch of 1 in 100 the minimum speeds of the Southern engine were much the same as those of *Flying Scotsman* earlier in the day. Climbing the 'Long Drag' the minimum speed approaching Ribblehead was 23½ mph, and with the engine eased a little on the viaduct speed fell finally to 21 mph before entering Blea Moor tunnel, *Clan Line* had fallen to 25 mph at the South end of Birkett tunnel, and to $22\frac{1}{2}$ mph on the final stretch of 1 in 100 gradient up to Aisgill.

In January 1980 there was inaugurated the 'Cumbrian Mountain Express' providing a round trip from Preston to Carlisle and back. It has been run several times up to the time of writing, on some going north via the Settle and Carlisle line and back over Shap, with electric haulage, and on others the reverse way. In each case the Carnforth-Skipton, and Skipton-Carlisle sections have been steam hauled. The inaugural run, on 19th January, saw some impressive locomotive performance with a 10-coach train of 380-tons gross behind the tender. From Carnforth to Skipton the train was worked by a 'Black Five' 4-6-0 No. 5305 and the allowance of 57 min. for the run of 37.8 miles proved insufficient, despite some excellent hill-climbing; but at Skipton 4-6-2 No. 4498 *Sir Nigel Gresley*, came on and the running was excellent by any standards.

The train was leaving Skipton just over half an hour late, with an allowance of 46 min. to cover the $27\frac{1}{4}$ miles to Blea Moor. From the very outset the work was most vigorous, with speeds between 50 and 55 mph up the continuous rising gradients from Gargrave to the summit before Hellifield. Then the engine was severely restrained on the tempting downhill stretch to Settle Junction, not exceeding $57\frac{1}{2}$ mph, in contrast to the initial dash of the 'Claughton' and its pilot on the run of 1931, when 66 mph was attained in $3\frac{1}{4}$ miles from the dead start at Hellifield. Then *Sir Nigel Gresley* was driven hard up the bank. From Settle station, passed at 49 mph the average speed for the next $7\frac{1}{2}$ miles was 44.5 mph on 1 in 100, except for the brief interlude for $\frac{1}{4}$ miles level at Helwith Bridge. The engine slipped above Horton, and speed fell rapidly from 45 to $30\frac{1}{2}$ mph but there was no lack of steam and speed recovered to 37 mph over Ribblehead viaduct and was sustained at that figure into the Blea Moor tunnel. The average speed over the $14\frac{1}{2}$ miles of the 'Long Drag' was 41.3 mph. The remaining level miles to the photographic stop at Dent were covered easily to complete the 32.2 miles from Skipton in the excellent time of 44 min. 49 sec. — 43 mph without exceeding $57\frac{1}{2}$ mph on the favourable stretch from Hellifield down to Settle Junction. Similar restraint in speed was shown throughout the descent from Aisgill to Carlisle. It was an auspicious start to the 'Cumbrian Mountain Express'; the only regret is that Eric Treacy was not there to photograph it.

Two months later, at the invitation of the London Midland Region I was able to make a trip myself on this already celebrated train, in the reverse direction, and hauled by the positively glittering 'Black Five' 4-6-0 No. 5305, a gross load of about 385 tons. The astonishing success of this enterprise is evident from the train being fully booked each way, and followed by a swarm of lineside photographers, whatever the climatic conditions. In the bleak weather of March 1980 we ran through heavy snow on the electric run from Preston to Carlisle, and a blizzard between Carnforth and Tebay; but the snow was very local, and on passing Clifton and getting our first sight of the mountains east of the Eden Valley it looked as though they had hardly been affected by the storm. In Carlisle there was no snow at all. The run back to Skipton however proved to be one of the most memorable in all my experience of travel over the Settle and Carlisle Railway. This was not in respect of the locomotive performance, excellently though No. 5305 climbed and ran; but in the marvellous snow-bound mountain panorama, as we mounted above Kirkby Stephen.

The sunshine was brilliant for most of the way, and most of our full complement of passengers took full advantage of the photographic stops at Appleby and Garsdale to record the brilliance of No 5305's turn out. The majestic array of the mountains, dazzling in their fresh coating of snow was a sheer delight, while we listened to the crisp bark of the engine climbing the 1 in 100 gradients. At Appleby the passengers had been joined in the photographic quest by many who were following the train by car, and as we came up to Aisgill summit the nearby road was lined with cars of all kinds. So far as actual performance was concerned we bettered the time of *Clan Line* on the southbound 'Lord Bishop' special in September 1978, covering the 17.5 miles from Appleby start to Aisgill in $33\frac{1}{4}$ min. against 35 min., though of course the Southern 4-6-2 had a load of 100-tons the heavier. The high tableland from Garsdale to Blea Moor looked simply glorious in its winter garb, but I suppose I ought to have saved a few superlatives for the scene that burst upon as soon after leaving Blea Moor Tunnel, and the mountains grouped around glistened in the sun. In all my association with this district I have never seen Ingleborough looking more magnificent. Then came a brisk run down to Settle Junction and on to Skipton, where *Flying Scotsman* was waiting to take the train westwards to Carnforth.

206

66 Abiding Memories: Midland compounds, a shot in July 1951 when these were rarely seen on the 'Settle' and 'Carlisle' but were common enough across to Lancaster and Morecambe, Here engine No. 41157 is on a Leeds-Morecambe Train near Hellifield.

67 Midland memories: a Standard LMS Class '4' 0-6-0, No. 44570 on northbound express goods in June 1960 passing Bell Busk.

68 'The Border Venturer': one of numerous special trains run in later years: in May 1978, No. 92220 *Evening Star* at Garsdale during a photographic stop. It was while photographing this very train earlier, at Appleby, that Eric Treacy slipped on the old cattle bank, picked himself up with a characteristic remark about having a well-padded backside, and dropped dead a few minutes later. This train was the last he ever saw.

69 North end of the Settle and Carlisle: an enthusiasts' special for Leeds passing Durran Hill Junction in April 1967 hauled 'A4' 4-6-2 No. 4498 *Sir Nigel Gresley*.

CHAPTER 17

Electric Scots over Shap

IF I were asked which was my favourite among all British main lines, whether they were 'Over the Border' or not, I think I would find it difficult to decide whether it would be the Settle and Carlisle, or the West Coast over Shap. In Chapter 2 of this book I was hard put to restrain myself from allowing personal memories of the line between Oxenholme and Shap Summit from obtruding too much into the story; but now I do not think there is any stretch of line in the whole country where I have personally witnessed such tremendous changes, from my first boyhood glimpses of it to the heartrending first years of the transition from LNWR to LMS; to the majesty of the Stanier age, to the climax of steam traction, and then through the diesel era to the breathtaking Electric Scots. Even in the exciting days of the 1930s could we then have envisaged a time when going through from Carnforth to Carlisle, with the mid-point of that 62.8 miles so precisely marked by Shap Summit, that the uphill half of the journey would be made in quicker time than the downhill that followed!

By the time the first edition of this book was published the diesels were getting amongst us, and there was some gratification among steam enthusiasts that the new English Electric Type '4s', which we know so well nowadays as the Class '40s' could not do so well on the mountain sections as a 'Duchess,' when worked at normal full capacity. The two original LMS diesels, Nos. 10000 and 10001, were worked as a pair on the maximum Anglo-Scottish duties, which a 'Duchess' could work single-handed. Be that as it may, the speed-up in the 10 years that culminated in the start of the full electric service to Glasgow was truly astonishing. Apart from the brief period in 1936 when the down 'Midday Scot' had its very fast start-to-stop timing from Lancaster to Penrith and the allowance from Carnforth to Shap Summit was 37 min. the norm remained virtually unchanged from the 42 min. of LNWR days. True, there were times when, with less than 500-ton loads, the time was substantially cut; but that does not alter the standard of performance that the time table demanded — an average speed, pass to pass, of 44.8 mph. I have tabulated basic details of six runs to show how things changed over this famous route in a matter of no more than 10 years.

CARNFORTH-SHAP SUMMIT
TEN YEARS QUICKENING

		46241	D268	1861	443	417 & 427	87.015
Loco No		'Duchess'	'40'	'47'	'50'	2-'50s'	'87'
Class							
Load, tons, gross		415	430	465	435	455	420
Mls		m s	m s	m s	m s	m s	m s
0.0	Carnforth (pass)	0 00	0 00	0 00	0 00	0 00	0 00
12.8	Oxenholme	11 19	11 46	9 49	10 14	8 13	8 30
19.9	Grayrigg	19 06	21 30	16 32	17 56	13 21	13 22
25.9	Tebay	24 28	27 56	22 32	22 58	17 44	17 30
—			sigs	pws	—	—	—
31.4	Shap Summit (pass)	30 50	36 44	33 19	28 57	22 00	21 24
Average speed: mph							
Carnforth-Grayrigg		62.5	56.0	72.1	66.6	89.3	89.3

The first of these runs, with the Pacific engine *City of Edinburgh*, was the fastest I ever logged personally with steam. It was made on the morning Glasgow and Edinburgh express from Birmingham, after a string of delays had been experienced south of Preston. But it was no more than marginally the fastest, because on another occasion when I was riding on the footplate of the *City of Bristol* we came within a few seconds of the same time between Carnforth and Tebay, but were checked thereafter. The Class '40' diesel put up a characteristic performance, but the first evidence of a real advance in standards was in the third run, with a '47' class diesel, when the minimum speed at Grayrigg summit was 58 mph and the average from Carnforth up to this point 72.1 mph. The times on the first run with a Class '50,' locomotive No. 443 in the original numbering, are a little misleading because the effort was eased down considerably on the upper part of Grayrigg bank and speed was allowed to fall to 48 mph at the summit. Then followed a tremendous spurt through the Lune valley, and a charge on Shap that took the train over Summit at 42 mph.

In the years 1968-9 there seemed every likelihood that finance for the extension of the electrified system from Weaver Junction northward to Glasgow would not be forthcoming; yet it was felt to be essential to offer some substantial quickening of the service north of Crewe to match what was being operated between Crewe and Euston.

It was then, in the summer of 1970, that a greatly accelerated time-table between Crewe and Glasgow was put into operation, using Class '50' diesels in pairs. Schedule time between Carnforth and Shap Summit then became 24 min., demanding an average speed throughout of 78.5 mph. This was, of course, achieved only by piling on the power, 5,400 engine horsepower; but it was not double-heading in the ordinary sense, as the two locomotives were coupled in mulitple and were operated by a single crew. When electrification did come, in 1974, the schedule time came down to $22\frac{1}{2}$ min., an average of 83.7 mph that would have been considered sensationally impractic-able only a few years previously. I must not, however, allow the 'Duchesses' and the diesels to monopolise the stage at this time; and apart from the Stanier 4-6-0s, and the British standard Pacifics of the 'Briannia' and 'Clan' classes there were two interesting 'one-offs' that must be mentioned, though both seem to have eluded the cameras of most of the regular lineside habitues between Oxenholme and Penrith. These were the gas-turbine locomotive 'GT3' and the one and only BR Class '8P' Pacific, the *Duke of Gloucester.*

The last mentioned was a locomotive that was never fully developed. While taken all-round poppet valve gears did not prove generally successful in Great Britain there was no doubt that No. 71000 showed definite potentialities. In the full dress trials on the stationary testing plant at Swindon, and in dynamometer car trials on the road much excellent work was done; but those trials were con-cluded without establishing the cause of the inordinately high coal consumption, or of the limitation in ultimate performance, which placed the engine in a class below the Great Western 'Kings,' and far below the 'Duchess' class Pacifics'. Consequently the engine, stationed at Crewe North, never took its place in the important double-home links, Crewe-Glasgow, and Crewe-Perth. The testing section at Swindon, who carried out the full-dress trials, having regard to the intended use of the engine on the West Coast main line, worked out the predicted maximum performance under various conditions of loading. With a 400-ton train the predicted time from Carnforth to Shap Summit was $32\frac{3}{4}$ min., and with a 460-ton train $34\frac{1}{2}$ min. This it will be seen, by comparison with the table of my own runs, puts the engine definitely below the standard of performance by the Duchesses'.

The gas-turbine locomotive 'GT3' was an experimental project of the English Electric Company, and built at the Rugby works of that company. It was oil-fired and had mechanical transmission. To all outward appearances it was a 4-6-0, and by courtesy of the designer, J. O. P. Hughes, I was able to ride on it during a test run from Crewe to Carlisle. It was unfortunate that on the day I travelled there was a very long slowing for permanent way work just north of Milnthorpe. The 'path' for the test train allowed the classic 42 min., of LNWR days from Carnforth to Shap Summit; but despite the check 'GT3' took a load of 385-tons over this length in $37\frac{1}{2}$ min. While time was lost between Carnforth and Oxenholme speed had increased from the 20 mph of the check to $49\frac{1}{2}$ mph on passing the latter station, and from there no less than 7 min., was gained on the allowance of 27 min., thence to Shap Summit. Speed increased to 52 mph on Grayrigg bank, touched 77 mph at Tebay and came down to a minimum of $40\frac{1}{2}$ mph on Shap itself.

My most vivid recollections of working over this line before the diesels completely displaced steam are of an afternoon in February 1964, when I had an engine-pass to ride the 'Midday Scot' through from Euston to Carlisle, with a diesel. We made a sound, though uneventful run down from London, until we were stopped by signal in the approach to Crewe station. Then, when the inspector who was riding with me climbed down to telephone the signal box he saw that we had a considerable leak from the water tank, and immediately realised we must have a replacement locomotive, especially as it was a through working to Glasgow. The platform locomotive inspector, faced with this sudden demand for a fresh engine gave us the first immediately available — not a diesel, but a Pacific No. 46228 *Duchess of Rutland.* Knowing of the poor condition in which many locomotives were at that late stage in steam locomotive history the crew were not amused. I, too, was anything but prepared to ride steam. Diesels were a 'white-collar' job; but an overall 'slop' was produced for me, and I climbed up on to No. 46228.

The engine however proved to be a real lady — and the crew, despite their early apprehensions, did a splendid job. We were certainly fortunate in getting an absolutely clear road. We were inside 'even time' by Warrington, and by Preston all sense of an emergency had receded, so far as I was concerned and I realised I was logging my fastest run yet over this route. We entered the mountain section in great style, passing Carnforth, 78.3 miles from Crewe, in $76\frac{3}{4}$ min., at

77 mph but the skies were lowering, and in February one never knows what kind of weather to expect in these regions. The fireman who had come on duty expecting to have nothing more energetic to do than the job of 'second man' had stoked like a Trojan and a master, and the engine was steaming very freely; nevertheless, as I knew all too well from several previous footplate experiences a slippery rail can prove a greater handicap than an ailing engine. Already however $4\frac{1}{4}$ min., of our late start had been recovered, and on that celebrated 31.4 miles of ascent we regained another $3\frac{3}{4}$ min., by climbing this steeply adverse stretch in $35\frac{1}{4}$ min. This was not quite so fast as expected of the *Duke of Gloucester* when worked all out, but on this memorable trip with the *Duchess of Rutland* the weather conditions were not good, with mist and drizzling rain as we got up to the higher contours, and on the Shap incline in particular the engine was inclined to slip. The minimum speed on the Grayrigg bank was 40 mph, and after a rapid recovery to 71 mph at Tebay, the speed at Shap Summit was 30 mph. But the 109.7 miles from Crewe to this point had taken no more than 112 min., and a fast run down to Carlisle brought us into the Citadel station, 141.1 miles, in $141\frac{1}{2}$ min., from Crewe, a truly splendid gain of $9\frac{1}{2}$ min., on schedule.

It was the last time I ever rode steam over Shap, and the memory of it all is as fresh as ever: the consternation at Crewe, when, at a moment's notice we needed a fresh engine; the fireman, discarding his nice clean uniform jacket and cap, substituting a knotted handkerchief, and beginning at once to 'dig'; and when I donned that overall 'slop' on Crewe platform if anyone had told me then I was about to log the fastest run I had ever experienced from Crewe to Carlisle I am afraid I should have told him not to be silly! Yet so it turned out.

Since then I have gathered many more abiding memories of the line over Shap. While riding in the driver's cab of an 'Electric Scot' one can be thrilled by the way the mountain section has been mastered, but I always think back to the men who had to grapple with it in the past: the locomotive engineers who had to provide the power, Webb Bowen Cooke, Stanier, the men who had to drive and fire, right back to the man who engineered and built it, Joseph Locke. What would they think of going from Carnforth to Summit in less than 22 min? Yet among my own more recent experiences I think my night ride on the Garston-Glasgow freight liner was among the most impressive:

213

twenty fully loaded flat cars, 1,067-tons, and *two* '87' class electric locomotives — *ten thousand* horse power. We were stopped at Carnforth to let the West Coast Postal special go ahead, and from the restart we climbed the 31.4 miles to Shap Summit in 28 min. 16 sec. As compared to the speeds of the 'Electric Scots,' and of the postal train, to which we had to give way, these great freight trains are limited to a maximum speed of 75 mph and it was this, rather than any lack of engine power that prevented us making an even faster time than we did. All the way up Grayrigg bank we were doing $73\frac{1}{2}$ to 75 mph. Some day one of the great railway artists of our time must capture the thrill of one of the night 'heavy weights' thundering up into the mountains!

Yet to one like myself, of whose professional life so much was spent on the design of equipment for power signalling, the panel signal box at Carlisle is equally a never-ending place of the utmost interest. For it covers the line as far south as the former wayside station of Burton and Holme, and it is there that northbound trains check-in, as it were, into the domain of the Carlisle Regulator. There they are automatically reported on the print-out record, but in addition the speed at which they are travelling is also reported. From the time they enter the Carlisle control area one can watch their progress by the indication lights on the illuminated diagram. One snowy November night when I was in the box I watched the running of 13 trains that came on to the panel between 11..12 pm and 2.03 am an average of only 13 min. apart, and these consisted of six freight-liners, one newspaper, two parcels, three express passenger, and the West Coast Postal special. This latter passed Burton and Holme at 101 mph while at the other end of the scale the Dover-Dundee freight-liner was doing no more than 60 mph. The remaining 11 trains entered the Carlisle area at between 74 and 89 mph.

But this was nothing to the intensity of working that developed from 02.06 onwards when eight trains entered the area in 31 min. — an average interval between each of barely $4\frac{1}{2}$ min. It was an amazing sight to see the indication light of those trains on the illuminated diagram. There was not quite such a variety as in the earlier period, because five out of the eight were express passenger trains. But even so, they were all running at much the same speed, with a 750-ton freight liner amongst then. It was a thrilling experience to log the running of eight trains at once, from the movement of their indication

214

lights, to see that they were all making excellent time, covering the 7 miles between Oxenholme and Grayrigg in $5\frac{1}{2}$ to 6 min., and that all this was happening in the depths of a snowy winter's night when rail conditions were not exactly favourable.

The eerie thought occurred to me that apart from the very few men that would be on duty at Oxenholme and Penrith there would not be a soul out on the line to watch their progress — such is the situation created by modern signalling technology.

That snowy northbound run of the 'Cumbrian Mountain Express' in March 1980 referred to in Chapter 16 gave me yet another excellent example of the way the one time spectre of Shap has been completely mastered with modern equipment. The train was hauled by one of the earlier of the electrics, No 81.001, and from a stop to pick up passengers at Lancaster we were slightly checked at first following a DMU for Barrow, which soon cleared out of our way at Carnforth. Then, in semi-blizzard conditions we climbed the 31.4 miles to Shap Summit in 3 seconds under the standard 'Electric Scot' allowance of 22 minutes. We averaged 93 mph up the full 13.6 miles of the Grayrigg bank, from Milnthorpe, did the last $5\frac{1}{2}$ miles up to Shap Summit in 4 min. 7 sec. The 26.5 miles downhill to Wreay, took $17\frac{1}{2}$ min., but we were stopped by signal outside Carlisle.

Main lines across the Border — ! It is surely significant of the honour in which Eric Treacy was held, not only in his own profession, and by countless railway enthusiasts, but also by professional railwaymen, that the London Midland Region should have chosen to name one of their electric locomotives after him. On 3rd April 1979 at a pleasing ceremony at Penrith station his widow, Mrs Mary Treacy named locomotive No. 86.240 *Bishop Eric Treacy*. The ceremony was attended by a number of high officers of British Railways, and musicians from the band of the Border Regiment blew a fanfare as Mrs. Treacy unveiled the nameplate on the locomotive. As on the occasion at Appleby in September 1978 I found it all very moving. In my travels up and down the West Coast main line I have not yet encountered locomotive No. 86.240 since it was named but I have no doubt it is amassing the high monthly mileage happily characteristic of the class.

The choice fell upon No. 86.240 because it was used to haul the 'Lord Bishop' train in both directions between Euston and Farington Junction (Preston) on 30th September 1978. On the outward journey

I had joined the special at Hellifield, but after the ceremony I returned to Euston, and although it is straying a little from 'Main Lines Across the Border,' in view of the special associations of the locomotive it is good to set on record the splendid run made up from Crewe. Despite two severe permanent checks the heavy train of 485-tons was taken over the 140.6 miles from Crewe to Watford Junction in 99 min., or 92 min., net, an average speed of 96.1 mph. We finished up with a smart run from Watford to Euston, 17.5 miles in $15\frac{1}{2}$ min — an average of 68 mph over this short distance.

70 The passing of steam: 'Britannias' relegated to goods trains. A scene at Grayrigg in September 1966, with the morning Birmingham-Glasgow Express hauled by a Class 47 diesel, No. D.1847, passing a side-tracked freight hauled by No. 70053, once named *Moray Firth*.

216

71 A remarkable experimental locomotive, GT3, the Gas Turbine locomotive built by English Electric passing Shap summit on a Crewe-Carlisle test run in October 1962. GT3 was described by enginemen as 'equal to a good "Scot" '.

72 Electric Scots: the morning Birmingham-Glasgow express passing Harrison's Sidings, north of Shap, hauled by locomotive No. 87.022 in June 1974.

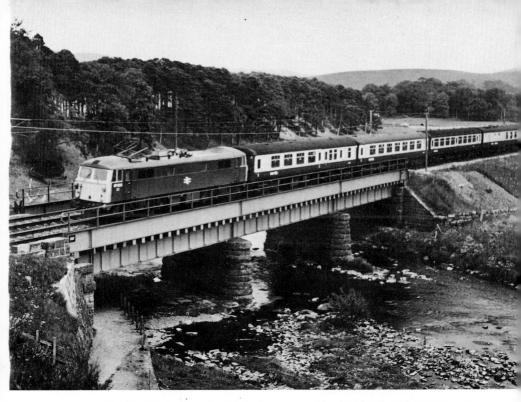

73 'Electric Scots' on the Caledonian: Bristol-Glasgow express crossing the Clyde at Crawford, hauled by locomotive No. 87.025, in June 1974.

74 Crossing the M6 motorway near Penrith; the morning Birmingham-Glasgow 'Electric Scot' hauled by locomotive No. 86.232 in June 1974.

75 Southbound near Plumpton in June 1974: Glasgow-Euston 'Electric Scot' hauled by locomotive No. 87.008.

INDEX